Better Homes and Gardens®

GlutenFree
COOKBOOK

250+ DELICIOUS RECIPES FOR EVERY DAY OF THE WEEK

MEREDITH CORPORATION
DES MOINES, 2015

Better Homes and Gardens
GlutenFree
COOKBOOK

MEREDITH CONSUMER MARKETING
Consumer Marketing Product Director: Heather Sorensen
Consumer Marketing Product Manager: Wendy Merical
Consumer Marketing Billing/Renewal Manager: Tami Beachem
Business Director: Ron Clingman
Senior Production Manager: Al Rodruck

WATERBURY PUBLICATIONS, INC.
Editorial Director: Lisa Kingsley
Associate Editors: Tricia Bergman, Annie Peterson
Creative Director: Ken Carlson
Associate Design Director: Doug Samuelson
Contributing Art Director: Mindy Samuelson
Contributing Writer: Lisa Kingsley
Contributing Copy Editors: Gretchen Kauffman, Peg Smith
Contributing Indexer: Mary Williams

BETTER HOMES AND GARDENS® MAGAZINE
Editor in Chief: Stephen Orr
Deputy Editor, Food and Entertaining: Nancy Wall Hopkins

MEREDITH NATIONAL MEDIA GROUP
President: Tom Harty

MEREDITH CORPORATION
Chairman and Chief Executive Officer: Stephen M. Lacy

In Memoriam: E.T. Meredith III (1933–2003)

Copyright© 2015 by Meredith Corporation.
Des Moines, Iowa.
First Edition. All rights reserved.
Printed in the U.S.A.
ISBN: 978-0696-30222-0

Our seal assures you that every recipe in *Gluten-Free Cookbook* has been tested in the Better Homes and Gardens® Test Kitchen. This means that each recipe is practical and reliable and meets our high standards of taste appeal. We guarantee your satisfaction with this book for as long as you own it.

All of us at Meredith Consumer Marketing are dedicated to providing you with information and ideas to enhance your home. We welcome your comments and suggestions. Write to us at: Meredith Consumer Marketing, 1716 Locust St., Des Moines, IA 50309-3023.

Pictured on front cover:
Easy Peanut Butter Cookies, page 313

Contents

Gluten-Free—Deliciously

Navigating the world of gluten-free eating can be overwhelming, especially if you're just getting started. Gluten is found in many different types of food—far beyond bread and pasta. Salad dressings, condiments, seasonings, processed meats, and many more commonly used products can contain gluten.

The key to avoiding hidden gluten sources is to know exactly what goes into your food. That's why learning to cook at home is so important. By preparing most of your meals yourself, you can be sure that the ingredients that go into each dish are completely free from gluten. So many tasty, nutritious foods available are naturally gluten-free. Let this cookbook teach you how to use those foods to embrace the art of gluten-free cooking.

Packed with more than 250 enticing recipes, this cookbook will make a no-gluten lifestyle more enjoyable than ever. The best part: You won't feel like you're on a restricted diet when you prepare these recipes. They're designed to be incredibly tasty for everyone, not just those who are on a gluten-free diet. Plus, there's something for every occasion—whether you're looking for an easy weeknight supper, a company-special dinner, or just a quick snack. With so many choices at your fingertips, you'll never get bored or feel limited. This book even covers your basics. Check out the "DIY Pantry" chapter, where you'll find an assortment of make-at-home staples you can keep on hand, including pasta sauces, salad dressings, spice mixes, and more.

As you embark on the world of gluten-free eating, realize how delicious living without gluten can be. When you focus more on what you can eat—rather than what you need to avoid—you'll take on your new lifestyle with enthusiasm and enjoyment. Let this book become your go-to source for gluten-free living.

The Basics of Gluten-Free Eating

What is gluten?

Found in wheat, barley, and triticale (a cross between rye and wheat), gluten is a protein created when two subproteins (glutenin and gliadin) combine with water. Gluten development contributes to several characteristics in food, including structure, texture, and kneadability.

Why go gluten-free?

Originally, gluten-free diets were designated only for those who suffer from celiac disease, an autoimmune disease that causes the body to attack and damage the lining of the small intestine in response to gluten consumption. This symptom leads to improper nutrient absorption and the potential for other health complications. Some people may experience some or all of the symptoms associated with celiac disease but, when tested for celiac disease, receive a negative diagnosis. Many of them find relief by eliminating gluten from their diets. Some people decide to follow a gluten-free diet simply because they feel healthier doing so. By eating more whole foods, such as vegetables, nuts and seeds, gluten-free whole grains, and lean proteins—and cutting back on processed foods—you can adopt a healthier diet.

The Gluten-Free Pantry

What does a "gluten-free?" label mean?

To be labeled gluten-free by the U.S. Food and Drug Administration (FDA), food products must either contain no gluten or contain gluten at such a minimal level that it does not cause a reaction. The maximum limit for a food to receive a gluten-free label is 20 parts per million (PPM). (Many products contain less than 20 parts per million.)

Natural Gluten-Free Foods

A gluten-free diet can seem rather limiting, but plenty of foods naturally do not contain gluten. Focus your diet around foods in this list, which are naturally gluten-free.

Fruits, vegetables, and beans	Milk and butter
Honey, maple syrup, and sugar	Nuts and seeds
Meat, poultry, fish, and eggs	Vegetable and nut oils

Know Your Whole Grains

Whole wheat may be off-limits, but plenty of other whole grains are naturally gluten-free. Each of these grains pairs stellar nutrition profiles with delicious tastes and textures:

Note: Check labels carefully to avoid purchasing grains that may have been cross-contaminated with gluten-containing grains.

Amaranth	Oats
Brown rice	Quinoa
Buckwheat or kasha	Teff
Millet	Wild rice

Shop Smart

Read nutrition information and ingredients lists carefully.

- Check the ingredients list when purchasing a new brand—one brand's product may be gluten-free, and another brand's product may contain gluten.
- Keep in mind that "wheat-free" is not the same thing as "gluten-free."
- Note that other gluten-containing grains, such as barley and rye, are not required to be labeled.

- Check product labels to determine whether foods were processed or packaged in a facility with potential gluten cross-contamination.
- As a general rule, avoid products with ingredient lists that include wheat, durum, germ, barley, and bleached flour.

Ingredient Know-How

This book calls only for ingredients that are not likely to contain gluten. However, it cannot guarantee that every brand available does not contain gluten. Therefore, be sure to check all food labels for gluten-containing ingredients, and pay particular attention to these products:

Canned beans	Mayonnaise
Canned coconut milk	Nonstick cooking spray
Corn chips, tortillas, and tostada shells	Packaged precooked meats
Cornmeal, polenta, and grits	Packaged shredded, crumbled, and grated cheeses
Cornstarch	Pasta sauces
Cottage cheese	Quick-cooking and rolled oats
Cream cheese	
Extracts and flavorings	Ricotta cheese
Hot sauces, chili pastes, and chili sauces	Seasoned nuts
	Sour cream
Jams, jellies, and spreadable fruit	Spice mixes and seasonings
	Yogurt

Stock Up

These commonly used products often contain small to moderate amounts of gluten. We recommend filling your pantry with gluten-free versions of these items:

All-purpose flour	Peanut butter
Baking powder	Sausage, bacon, and other cured meats
Chicken, beef, and vegetable broths	
Mustard	Soy sauce and tamari
Pasta sauces	Worcestershire sauce

Appetizers & Snacks

When you're on a gluten-restricted diet, little bites of this and that can be essential to satisfy between-meal hunger. Whether you need a quick snack to take on the go or an irresistible party food, these finger foods are sure to hit the spot.

Crispy Greens Chips

PREP: 20 minutes   BAKE: 20 minutes at 300°F   MAKES: 6 servings

10 to 12 ounces fresh green curly kale, Swiss chard, mustard greens, or collard greens
1 tablespoon olive oil
¼ teaspoon salt
¼ teaspoon smoked paprika or ground chipotle chile pepper

1. Preheat oven to 300°F. Thoroughly wash and drain greens; pat dry with paper towels. Remove and discard the tough center stalks from leaves. Tear leaves into 2- to 3-inch pieces (you should have about 8 cups kale or collard green pieces, 6 cups Swiss chard pieces, or 10 cups mustard green pieces). In an extra-large bowl combine oil, salt, and smoked paprika. Add greens; toss to coat.

2. Place a wire rack on each of four baking sheets. Arrange greens in a single layer on the wire racks. Bake on separate oven racks about 20 minutes or until greens are crisp, rearranging baking sheets halfway through baking (if all four baking sheets won't fit in oven, bake in two batches). (For a dehydrator, place leaves in a single layer on mesh-lined dehydrator trays. Dehydrate at 135°F for 2½ to 3 hours or until dry and brittle.)

3. Cool greens on wire racks. Transfer to an airtight storage container. Cover and seal. Store at room temperature for 5 to 7 days.

PER SERVING: 34 cal., 3 g fat (0 g sat. fat), 0 mg chol., 108 mg sodium, 3 g carb., 1 g fiber, 1 g pro.

Spicy Asiago Greens Chips: Prepare as directed, except substitute 2 tablespoons freshly grated Asiago cheese and ½ teaspoon crushed red pepper for the smoked paprika or ground chipotle chile pepper. Store in the refrigerator.

Tip: If the greens chips begin to lose crispness, place on a baking sheet and bake in a 325°F oven for 2 to 3 minutes.

Root Veggie Chips with Sea Salt

PREP: 20 minutes
DEHYDRATE: 8 hours at 135°F
MAKES: 6 servings

3 to 4 cups peeled (if desired) and thinly sliced sweet potatoes, blue potatoes, beets, parsnips, carrots, rutabagas, and/or celery root*

½ teaspoon fine sea salt

1. Bring a large pot of salted water to boiling over high heat. Add the vegetable slices;** cook for 30 seconds. Drain vegetable slices in a colander set in a sink. Rinse with cold water and drain again. Pat vegetable slices dry with paper towels.

2. In a large bowl combine vegetable slices and the ½ teaspoon sea salt; toss to coat. Arrange in a single layer on mesh-lined dehydrator trays.

3. Dehydrate at 135°F for 8 to 10 hours or until dry and crisp,*** shifting trays as necessary to dry chips evenly. (Timing may vary depending on air humidity and the amount of moisture in the vegetables.) If desired, sprinkle with additional sea salt.

PER SERVING: 50 cal., 0 g fat, 1 mg chol., 223 mg sodium, 12 g carb., 2 g fiber, 1 g pro.

*Tip: Use a mandoline to slice vegetables evenly.

**Tip: If using beets, precook beet slices separately to prevent the red color of the beets from "bleeding" onto the other vegetables.

***Tip: When done, the chips will look evenly dry, the edges will have curled, and the chips will be crisp. Remove a chip or two during dehydrating and let cool a few minutes. Taste for crispness. Continue drying if chips are not yet crisp.

Sweet-and-Savory Potato Chips

PREP: 25 minutes
SOAK: 10 minutes
FRY: 3 minutes per batch at 350°F
MAKES: 12 servings

3 **medium sweet potatoes (1 pound)**
3 **medium baking potatoes (1 pound)**
  Peanut oil or other vegetable oil
  Coarse salt

1. Peel potatoes; cut into very thin slices (about 1/16 inch thick).* Place potato slices in a large bowl of ice water; soak for 10 minutes. Drain potato slices; pat dry with paper towels.

2. Preheat oven to 300°F. In a deep, heavy 3-quart saucepan or deep-fat fryer heat oil to 350°F. Fry half of the potato slices in hot oil for 3 to 5 minutes or until golden and crisp.** Remove with a slotted spoon and drain on wire racks.

3. Transfer chips to a shallow baking pan. Sprinkle with salt. Keep chips warm in the oven while frying the remaining potato slices. If desired, store in an airtight container at room temperature for up to 2 days.

PER SERVING: 101 cal., 5 g fat (1 g sat. fat), 0 mg chol., 103 mg sodium, 14 g carb., 2 g fiber, 1 g pro.

*Tip: Use a mandoline slicer to make quick work of slicing thin, even potato slices.

**Tip: Be cautious of spattering oil and avoid overcrowding the fryer, which will lower the oil temperature.

Rosemary Roasted Nuts

PREP: 15 minutes **BAKE:** 12 minutes at 375°F **MAKES:** 30 servings

3 **cups whole unblanched almonds**
1½ **cups walnut halves**
1 **cup raw pumpkin seeds (pepitas)**
2 **tablespoons finely snipped fresh rosemary**
2 **teaspoons packed brown sugar**
1 **teaspoon sea salt**
½ **teaspoon cayenne pepper**
2 **tablespoons butter, melted**

1. Preheat oven to 375°F. In a 15×10×1-inch baking pan combine almonds, walnuts, and pumpkin seeds. Bake about 12 minutes or until toasted, stirring once.

2. In a small bowl combine rosemary, brown sugar, salt, and cayenne pepper. Stir in melted butter. Drizzle butter mixture over warm nuts; toss to coat. Serve warm or at room temperature. Store in an airtight container for up to 3 days.

PER SERVING: 177 cal., 15 g fat (2 g sat. fat), 2 mg chol., 60 mg sodium, 5 g carb., 2 g fiber, 6 g pro.

Sweet and Spicy Apple Crisps

PREP: 15 minutes
BAKE: 2 hours at 200°F
MAKES: 4 servings

2 large apples, such as Braeburn, Jazz, Pink Lady, or Gala, cored
¼ cup granulated sugar
¼ teaspoon ground chipotle chile pepper

1. Preheat oven to 200°F. Line two or three baking sheets with parchment paper; set aside.

2. Using a mandoline or a serrated knife, cut apples crosswise into ⅛-inch slices. Arrange slices in a single layer on baking sheets. In a small bowl combine sugar and chipotle pepper. Sprinkle apple slices with half of the sugar mixture. Use a pastry brush to brush sugar mixture over apple slices to cover evenly. (Or place the sugar mixture in a small sieve. Hold the sieve over the apple slices and stir sugar mixture with a spoon to evenly coat the apples.) Turn apple slices and repeat with remaining sugar mixture.

3. Bake for 2 to 2½ hours or until crisp, turning apple slices and rotating pans every 30 minutes. Cool completely on wire racks before serving.

PER SERVING: 112 cal., 0 g fat, 0 mg chol., 1 mg sodium, 29 g carb., 3 g fiber, 0 g pro.

To Make Ahead: Place cooled apple crisps in an airtight container; cover. Store at room temperature for up to 1 week.

Barbecue Spiced Roasted Chickpeas

PREP: 5 minutes
ROAST: 30 minutes at 450°F
MAKES: 12 servings

2 15-ounce cans no-salt-added garbanzo beans (chickpeas), rinsed and drained*
¼ cup olive oil
1 teaspoon barbecue spice*
1 teaspoon paprika
1 teaspoon chili powder*
¼ teaspoon garlic salt*
¼ teaspoon celery salt*
¼ teaspoon onion powder

1. Preheat oven to 450°F. In a medium bowl combine garbanzo beans, oil, barbecue spice, paprika, chili powder, garlic salt, celery salt, and onion powder. Spread in an even layer in a 15×10×1-inch baking pan. Roast about 30 minutes or until browned and crisp, stirring once halfway through roasting. Cool completely before serving.

PER SERVING: 101 cal., 5 g fat (1 g sat. fat), 0 mg chol., 122 mg sodium, 10 g carb., 3 g fiber, 4 g pro.

To Make Ahead: Place cooled chickpeas in an airtight container; cover. Store at room temperature for up to 1 week.

*Tip: Check the labels of these products carefully to be sure they do not contain added gluten.

Marinated Mozzarella with Basil

PREP: 15 minutes
CHILL: 1 hour
MAKES: 14 servings

¼ cup fresh basil leaves
¼ cup olive oil
1 teaspoon coarsely ground black pepper
1 to 2 teaspoons balsamic vinegar
1 pound bocconcini or fresh mozzarella cheese, cut into 1-inch cubes
Red and/or yellow grape or cherry tomatoes, halved (optional)
Fresh basil leaves
Gluten-free pita chips or gluten-free baguette slices

1. Using a sharp knife, chop the ¼ cup basil leaves. In a medium bowl combine chopped basil, oil, pepper, and vinegar. Add cheese, tossing gently until well coated. Cover and chill for at least 1 hour or up to 5 days.

2. Transfer cheese to a serving bowl. If desired, stir in tomatoes. Garnish with whole basil leaves and serve with gluten-free pita chips or baguette slices.

PER SERVING: 100 cal., 7 g fat (4 g sat. fat), 18 mg chol., 120 mg sodium, 1 g carb., 0 g fiber, 8 g pro.

Avocado-and-Pesto-Stuffed Tomatoes

START TO FINISH: 45 minutes
MAKES: 30 servings

30 **cherry tomatoes (about 2½ cups)**
½ **of a medium avocado, seeded, peeled, and cut up**
2 **ounces cream cheese,* softened**
2 **tablespoons Homemade Pesto (recipe, page 282) or purchased gluten-free pesto**
1 **teaspoon lemon juice**
 Snipped fresh basil (optional)

1. Cut a thin slice from the top of each tomato. (If desired, cut a thin slice from the bottom of each tomato so it stands upright.) Using a small spoon or small melon baller, carefully hollow out tomatoes. Line a baking sheet with paper towels. Invert tomatoes onto paper towels. Let stand about 30 minutes to drain excess moisture.

2. Meanwhile, for filling, in a food processor combine avocado, cream cheese, pesto, and lemon juice. Cover and process until smooth. If desired, spoon filling into a pastry bag fitted with a large round tip or open star tip.

3. Place tomatoes, open sides up, on a platter. Pipe or spoon filling into tomatoes. Serve immediately or cover loosely with plastic wrap and chill for up to 4 hours. If desired, sprinkle with basil before serving.

PER SERVING: 18 cal., 1 g fat (1 g sat. fat), 2 mg chol., 16 mg sodium, 1 g carb., 0 g fiber, 0 g pro.

*Tip: Check the label of this product carefully to be sure it does not contain added gluten.

Nacho Chicken Drummettes

PREP: 15 minutes
BAKE: 30 minutes at 400°F
MAKES: 6 servings

1½ cups gluten-free mild taco sauce

4 cups crushed corn tortilla chips*

3 pounds chicken drummettes or 12 chicken drumsticks
Shredded Mexican cheese blend* (optional)
Gluten-free dipping sauce(s), such as ranch salad dressing, salsa, taco sauce, and/or barbecue sauce (optional)

1. Preheat oven to 400°F. Line a 15×10×1-inch baking pan with foil. Grease foil; set pan aside. Pour the 1½ cups taco sauce into a shallow dish. Place tortilla chips in another shallow dish. Dip chicken into taco sauce, then into tortilla chips, turning to coat. Place chicken in the prepared baking pan.

2. Bake for 30 to 40 minutes or until chicken is no longer pink (180°F). (Do not turn chicken while baking.) If desired, sprinkle with cheese and serve with dipping sauce(s).

PER SERVING: 603 cal., 40 g fat (10 g sat. fat), 112 mg chol., 609 mg sodium, 29 g carb., 2 g fiber, 31 g pro.

*Tip: Check the labels of these products carefully to be sure they do not contain added gluten.

Tequila Shrimp Nachos

PREP: 35 minutes
MARINATE: 15 minutes
GRILL: 5 minutes
MAKES: 4 servings

2 pounds fresh or frozen medium shrimp, peeled and deveined
½ cup orange juice
1 teaspoon cumin seeds, crushed
4 tablespoons tequila
½ teaspoon ground ancho chile pepper or hot chili powder
2 to 3 medium heirloom tomatoes, cut into wedges
1½ cups red and/or yellow grape and/or cherry tomatoes, halved
5 tablespoons canola oil, avocado oil, and/or olive oil
2 tablespoons lime juice
1 large clove garlic, minced
¼ teaspoon salt
4 to 6 roma tomatoes
1 fresh jalapeño chile pepper, halved and seeded*
2 tablespoons snipped fresh cilantro
1 ounce queso fresco or feta cheese, crumbled (optional)

1. Thaw shrimp, if frozen. Rinse shrimp; pat dry. For marinade, in a large bowl whisk together orange juice, cumin, 2 tablespoons of the tequila, and the ground ancho chile pepper. Add shrimp; toss with marinade to coat. Let stand to marinate for 15 minutes, stirring twice.

2. On a large platter arrange tomato wedges and grape tomatoes; set aside. For vinaigrette, in a screw-top jar combine 4 tablespoons of the oil, the remaining 2 tablespoons tequila, the lime juice, garlic, and salt. Cover and shake well; set aside.

3. Drain shrimp; discard marinade. Place shrimp in a grill basket. Halve the roma tomatoes; brush tomatoes and the jalapeño pepper halves with the remaining 1 tablespoon oil. For a charcoal or gas grill, place grill basket with shrimp, halved roma tomatoes, and jalapeño pepper

halves on the rack of a covered grill directly over medium heat for 5 to 7 minutes or until shrimp are opaque and tomatoes and jalapeño halves are slightly soft and lightly browned, stirring shrimp occasionally and turning tomatoes and pepper halves halfway through grilling time. When cool enough to handle, finely chop the jalapeño pepper and stir into the shrimp.

4. Add shrimp and grilled tomatoes to the tomatoes on the platter. Drizzle with vinaigrette. Top with cilantro and, if desired, feta. Serve immediately or cover and chill for up to 4 hours.

PER SERVING: 160 cal., 8 g fat (1 g sat), 114 mg chol., 580 mg sodium, 6 g carb., 1 g fiber, 13 g pro.

*Tip: Chile peppers contain oils that can irritate your skin and eyes. Wear plastic or rubber gloves when handling them.

Shrimp Spring Rolls with Chimichurri Sauce

PREP: 30 minutes   STAND: 15 minutes   MAKES: 10 servings

1 recipe Chimichurri Sauce
4 ounces cooked shrimp, peeled, deveined, and chopped
1 cup shredded romaine lettuce
¾ cup packaged coarsely shredded carrots
½ cup fresh cilantro leaves
½ cup fresh mint leaves
2 green onions, cut into thin bite-size strips
1 ounce dried rice vermicelli noodles
10 8-inch gluten-free rice papers
10 to 20 sprigs fresh Italian parsley and/or cilantro
  Gluten-Free soy sauce or gluten-free tamari (optional)
  Sesame seeds (optional)

1. Prepare Chimichurri Sauce. For shrimp filling, in a medium bowl combine the sauce, shrimp, lettuce, carrots, cilantro, mint, and green onions. Let stand for 15 to 30 minutes to allow shrimp and vegetables to soften slightly and absorb flavor from the sauce, stirring occasionally.

2. Meanwhile, in a medium saucepan cook the vermicelli in lightly salted boiling water for 3 minutes or just until tender; drain. Rinse under cold water; drain well. Use kitchen shears to snip the noodles into small pieces; set aside.

3. To assemble, pour warm water into a shallow pot or pie plate. Carefully dip a rice paper into the water; transfer to a clean round dinner plate. Let stand for several seconds to soften. For each roll, place a parsley or cilantro sprig just below the center of the paper. Spoon about ⅓ cup of the shrimp filling onto sprig. Arrange some of the vermicelli noodles on filling. Tightly roll up rice paper from the bottom, tucking in sides as you roll. If desired, add another parsley sprig

to rice paper as you roll. If desired, serve spring rolls with soy sauce sprinkled with sesame seeds.

Chimichurri Sauce: In a blender or food processor combine 1½ cups lightly packed fresh Italian parsley; ¼ cup olive oil; ¼ cup rice vinegar; 4 to 6 cloves garlic, minced; ¼ teaspoon salt; ¼ teaspoon black pepper; and ¼ teaspoon crushed red pepper. Cover and blend or process with several on/off pulses until chopped but not pureed.

PER SERVING: 128 cal., 6 g fat (1 g sat), 22 mg chol., 312 mg sodium, 15 g carb., 2 g fiber, 4 g pro.

To Make Ahead: Prepare as directed. Layer spring rolls between damp paper towels in an airtight container. Store in the refrigerator for up to 4 hours.

Vegetarian Spring Rolls: Prepare as directed, except omit shrimp and substitute ¾ cup diced gluten-free firm tofu (fresh bean curd).

Mediterranean Salmon Spread

PREP: 15 minutes
CHILL: 2 hours
MAKES: 4 servings

3 tablespoons light sour cream*
2 teaspoons snipped fresh mint
⅛ teaspoon garlic powder
1 6-ounce pouch skinless, boneless pink salmon
⅓ cup bottled roasted red sweet pepper, drained and chopped
16 1-inch-thick diagonal slices zucchini, with centers hollowed out slightly
8 Belgian endive leaves
Snipped fresh mint (optional)

1. For spread, in a small bowl combine sour cream, the 2 teaspoons mint, and the garlic powder. Stir in salmon and roasted sweet pepper. Cover and chill for 2 to 24 hours.

2. Stir spread. Spoon evenly onto zucchini slices and endive leaves. If desired, garnish with additional snipped mint.

PER SERVING: 78 cal., 3 g fat (1 g sat), 18 mg chol., 227 mg sodium, 5 g carb., 1 g fiber, 9 g pro.

*Tip: Check the label of this product carefully to be sure it does not contain added gluten.

Baked Santa Fe Dip

PREP: 20 minutes
BAKE: 25 minutes at 350°F
MAKES: 28 servings

- 8 ounces cheddar cheese, shredded (2 cups)
- 4 ounces shredded Monterey Jack or mozzarella cheese (1 cup)
- ½ cup light mayonnaise*
- 1 8-ounce can whole kernel corn, drained (¾ cup)
- 1 4-ounce can chopped green chile peppers, drained
- 2 teaspoons finely chopped gluten-free canned chipotle chile peppers in adobo sauce
- ¼ teaspoon garlic powder
- 1 medium tomato, seeded and chopped (¾ cup)
- ¼ cup sliced green onions
- 2 tablespoons snipped fresh cilantro
  Vegetables, such as sweet pepper wedges and sliced jicama
  Lightly salted corn tortilla chips*

1. Preheat oven to 350°F. In a large bowl stir together cheeses, mayonnaise, corn, green chile peppers, chipotle peppers, and garlic powder. Spread mixture into a shallow 1-quart casserole or 9-inch pie plate.

2. In a small bowl combine tomato, green onions, and cilantro; set aside.

3. Bake dip for 25 minutes or until heated through. Spoon tomato mixture in the center. Serve warm with vegetables and tortilla chips.

PER SERVING: 69 cal., 5 g fat (3 g sat. fat), 12 mg chol., 137 mg sodium, 2 g carb., 0 g fiber, 3 g pro.

*Tip: Check the labels of these products carefully to be sure they do not contain added gluten.

Supreme Pizza Fondue

PREP: 20 minutes
SLOW COOK: 3 hours 15 minutes (low)
MAKES: 22 servings

- 8 **ounces gluten-free bulk Italian turkey sausage**
- ½ **cup finely chopped onion**
- 2 **cloves garlic, minced**
- 2 **26- to 30-ounce jars gluten-free meatless spaghetti sauce**
- 3 **cups sliced fresh mushrooms (8 ounces)**
- 2 **teaspoons dried basil or oregano, crushed**
- ½ **cup chopped green or yellow sweet pepper (optional) Vegetable dippers, cheese, and/or gluten-free bread slices or cubes**

1. In a large skillet cook sausage, onion, and garlic over medium-high heat until sausage is browned, using a wooden spoon to break up sausage as it cooks. Drain off fat.

2. In a 3½- or 4-quart slow cooker combine spaghetti sauce, mushrooms, and basil. Stir in sausage mixture. Cover and cook on low-heat setting for 3 hours. If desired, stir in sweet pepper. Cover and cook on low-heat setting for 15 minutes more.

3. To serve, spear vegetable dippers and/or bread with fondue forks and dip into the fondue, swirling to coat.

PER SERVING: 48 cal., 1 g fat (0 g sat. fat), 8 mg chol., 300 mg sodium, 6 g carb., 1 g fiber, 3 g pro.

Hummus

START TO FINISH: 15 minutes
MAKES: 14 servings

- 1 **15-ounce can garbanzo beans (chickpeas), rinsed and drained***
- 1 **clove garlic, minced**
- ¼ **cup gluten-free tahini**
- ¼ **cup lemon juice**
- ¼ **cup olive oil**
- ½ **teaspoon salt**
- ¼ **teaspoon paprika**
  Stir-ins (such as ¼ cup sliced green onions, ⅓ cup chopped olives, and/or 1 tablespoon snipped fresh dill or basil) (optional)
- 1 **tablespoon snipped fresh parsley**
- 2 **teaspoons olive oil (optional)**
- 2 **tablespoons pine nuts, toasted (optional)**
  Toasted gluten-free pita wedges and/or assorted vegetable dippers

1. In a blender or food processor combine garbanzo beans, garlic, tahini, lemon juice, ¼ cup oil, salt, and paprika. Cover and blend or process about 1 minute or until very smooth, scraping sides as necessary.

2. If desired, add one or more of the optional stir-ins. Spoon the hummus onto a platter or into a serving bowl. Sprinkle with parsley. If desired, drizzle with additional oil and sprinkle with pine nuts. Serve at room temperature with pita wedges and/or vegetable dippers.

PER SERVING: 97 cal., 6 g fat (1 g sat. fat), 0 mg chol., 176 mg sodium, 8 g carb., 2 g fiber, 2 g pro.

Roasted Red Pepper Hummus: Preheat oven to 425°F. Cut 2 red sweet peppers in half lengthwise; remove stems, seeds, and membranes. Place pepper halves, cut sides down, on a foil-lined baking sheet. Arrange 4 unpeeled garlic cloves around peppers. Roast for 20 to 25 minutes or until peppers are charred and very tender. Bring the foil up around peppers and garlic and fold edges together to enclose. Let stand about 15 minutes or until cool enough to handle. Use a sharp knife to loosen edges of the pepper skins; gently pull off the skins in strips then discard. Peel garlic. In a blender or food processor combine roasted peppers and garlic; one 15-ounce can garbanzo beans (chickpeas),* rinsed and drained; ¼ cup sliced green onions; ¼ cup tahini; 2 tablespoons lemon juice; ½ teaspoon salt; ¼ teaspoon paprika; and, if desired, a dash crushed red pepper. Cover and blend or process until smooth, scraping down sides as needed. With the machine running, add ⅓ cup olive oil in a slow steady stream until combined. Serve with gluten-free pita wedges and/or assorted vegetable dippers.

***Tip:** Check the label of this product carefully to be sure it does not contain added gluten.

Breakfasts

A nutritious and energizing morning meal is such an important beginning for the day—and that's not always easy when eating gluten-free. Take your breakfasts beyond the basics with homemade muffins, granola, quinoa, frittatas, and more.

Quinoa-Pumpkin Seed Granola

PREP: 20 minutes
BAKE: 20 minutes at 350°F
COOL: 15 minutes
MAKES: 13 servings

¾ cup uncooked quinoa, rinsed and well drained
½ cup raw pumpkin seeds (pepitas)
½ cup whole and/or slivered almonds
¼ cup flaxseeds
¼ cup honey
2 tablespoons canola oil
1 teaspoon ground cinnamon
½ teaspoon coarse salt
¾ cup dried cherries, cranberries, golden raisins, and/or snipped dried apricots*

1. Preheat oven to 350°F. In a large bowl combine quinoa, pumpkin seeds, almonds, and flaxseeds. Place honey in a small microwave-safe bowl; microwave for 20 seconds. Add oil, cinnamon, and salt to honey, whisking to combine. Pour honey mixture over quinoa mixture; toss to coat. Spread in a 15×10×1-inch baking pan.

2. Bake, uncovered, about 20 minutes or until golden brown, stirring twice. Stir in dried fruit. Cool in pan for 15 minutes. Spread out on a large sheet of foil. Cool completely, breaking up any large pieces. Transfer to an airtight container to store. Seal and store up to 2 weeks in the refrigerator.

PER SERVING: 191 cal., 11 g fat (1 g sat. fat), 0 mg chol., 94 mg sodium, 22 g carb., 3 g fiber, 6 g pro.

*Tip: Choose your favorite dried fruit for this granola. For extra color and flavor, use a combination of dried fruits.

Banana Bread

PREP: 25 minutes
BAKE: 70 minutes at 350°F
COOL: 10 minutes
STAND: overnight
MAKES: 16 servings

5 unpeeled bananas
2 cups Gluten-Free Flour Mix (recipe, page 162) or purchased gluten-free all-purpose flour
1½ teaspoons gluten-free baking powder
½ teaspoon baking soda
½ teaspoon ground cinnamon
¼ teaspoon salt
¼ teaspoon ground nutmeg
⅛ teaspoon ground ginger
2 eggs, lightly beaten
1 cup sugar
½ cup vegetable oil or melted butter
¼ cup chopped walnuts

1. Preheat oven to 350°F. Grease the bottom(s) and ½ inch up the sides of one 9×5×3-inch or two 7½×3½×2-inch loaf pan(s); set aside. Line a 15×10×1-inch baking pan with foil. Arrange bananas in the foil-lined pan. Prick banana peels with the tines of a fork at 1-inch intervals. Bake for 15 minutes (peels will turn dark brown). Cool bananas in pan.

2. In a large bowl combine Gluten-Free Flour Mix, baking powder, baking soda, cinnamon, salt, nutmeg, and ginger. Make a well in the center of flour mixture; set aside.

3. In a medium bowl combine eggs, sugar, and oil; set aside. Split banana peels with a small sharp knife; remove and discard peels. Measure 1½ cups roasted bananas by gently pressing the pulp into measuring cups; stir the roasted bananas into egg mixture. Add egg mixture all at once to flour mixture. Stir just until moistened (batter should be lumpy). Fold in walnuts. Spoon batter into the prepared loaf pan(s).

4. Bake for 55 to 60 minutes for the 9-inch pan, 45 to 55 minutes for the 7½-inch pans, or until a wooden toothpick inserted near the center(s) comes out clean.* If necessary to prevent overbrowning, cover loosely with foil for the last 15 minutes of baking.

5. Cool in pan(s) on a wire rack for 10 minutes. Remove from pan(s). Cool completely on wire rack. Wrap and store overnight before slicing. (The texture of the bread will be more evenly moist and less crumbly after standing overnight.)

PER SERVING: 234 cal., 9 g fat (1 g sat. fat), 23 mg chol., 136 mg sodium, 38 g carb., 2 g fiber, 2 g pro.

*Tip: When you remove the toothpick, a few crumbs may cling to it, but there should be no unbaked batter on the toothpick.

Pumpkin-Walnut Streusel Muffins

PREP: 25 minutes
BAKE: 15 minutes at 375°F
COOL: 5 minutes
MAKES: 12 servings

Nonstick cooking spray*
1¼ cups brown rice flour
⅓ cup gluten-free quick-cooking rolled oats
¼ cup flaxseed meal
2 teaspoons pumpkin pie spice*
1½ teaspoons gluten-free baking powder
½ teaspoon salt
2 eggs, lightly beaten
¾ cup canned pumpkin
½ cup packed brown sugar
½ cup milk
3 tablespoons canola oil
1 teaspoon vanilla extract*
¼ cup chopped walnuts
2 tablespoons gluten-free quick-cooking rolled oats
1 tablespoon packed brown sugar
1 tablespoon canola oil
1 ounce reduced-fat cream cheese (Neufchâtel),* softened (optional)
2 tablespoons powdered sugar (optional)
1 to 2 tablespoons milk (optional)

1. Preheat oven to 375°F. Coat twelve 2½-inch muffin cups with cooking spray (do not use paper bake cups); set aside. In a medium bowl stir together flour, the ⅓ cup oats, the flaxseed meal, pumpkin pie spice, baking powder, and salt. Make a well in the center of flour mixture; set aside.

2. In a medium bowl combine eggs, pumpkin, the ½ cup brown sugar, the ½ cup milk, the 3 tablespoons oil, and the vanilla. Add pumpkin mixture all at once to flour mixture. Stir just until moistened (batter should be lumpy). Spoon batter evenly into the prepared muffin cups.

3. For walnut streusel, in a small bowl combine walnuts, the 2 tablespoons oats, the 1 tablespoon brown sugar, and the 1 tablespoon oil. Sprinkle evenly on top of batter in muffin cups.

4. Bake about 15 minutes or until a wooden toothpick inserted in the centers comes out clean. Cool in muffin cups on a wire rack for 5 minutes. Remove muffins from muffin cups. Cool slightly on wire rack.

5. If desired, for cream cheese icing, in a small bowl stir together cream cheese and powdered sugar until smooth. Gradually stir in enough of the 1 to 2 tablespoons milk to reach drizzling consistency. Drizzle icing over warm muffins.

PER SERVING: 216 cal., 9 g fat (1 g sat. fat), 34 mg chol., 188 mg sodium, 30 g carb., 2 g fiber, 4 g pro.

*Tip: Check the labels of these products carefully to be sure they do not contain added gluten.

Zucchini Muffins with Greek Yogurt Frosting

PREP: 25 minutes
BAKE: 25 minutes at 350°F
COOL: 5 minutes
MAKES: 12 servings

Nonstick cooking spray*
1 cup Gluten-Free Flour Mix (recipe, page 162) or purchased gluten-free all-purpose flour
¼ cup granulated sugar
¼ cup packed brown sugar
1 teaspoon ground cinnamon
½ teaspoon gluten-free baking powder
½ teaspoon salt
¼ teaspoon baking soda
2 eggs, lightly beaten
¼ cup fat-free milk
1 cup cooked quinoa**
1 cup coarsely shredded zucchini
½ cup unsweetened applesauce
¼ cup canola oil
1 teaspoon vanilla extract*
1 recipe Greek Yogurt Frosting
½ to 1 teaspoon finely shredded lemon peel

1. Preheat oven to 350°F. Lightly coat twelve 2½-inch muffin cups with cooking spray; set aside.

2. In a large bowl stir together flour, granulated sugar, brown sugar, cinnamon, baking powder, salt, and baking soda. Make a well in the center of flour mixture; set aside.

3. In a medium bowl combine eggs and milk. Stir in quinoa, zucchini, applesauce, oil, and vanilla. Add quinoa mixture all at once to flour mixture, stirring gently to combine. Spoon batter into the prepared muffin cups, filling each three-fourths full.

4. Bake about 25 minutes or until a wooden toothpick inserted in the centers comes out clean. Cool in muffin cups on a wire rack for 5 minutes. Remove muffins from muffin cups. Cool completely on wire rack. Before serving, spread Greek Yogurt Frosting over muffins and sprinkle with lemon peel.

Greek Yogurt Frosting: In a small bowl stir together one 5.3- to 6-ounce carton plain fat-free Greek yogurt, 3 tablespoons powdered sugar, and 1 teaspoon gluten-free vanilla. Makes about ¾ cup.

PER SERVING: 164 cal., 6 g fat (1 g sat. fat), 31 mg chol., 166 mg sodium, 24 g carb., 2 g fiber, 4 g pro.

*Tip: Check the labels of these products carefully to be sure they do not contain added gluten.

**Tip: For 1 cup cooked quinoa, rinse and drain ⅓ cup uncooked quinoa. In a small saucepan combine the quinoa and ⅔ cup water. Cook according to package directions; cool.

To Store: Place unfrosted muffins in a single layer in an airtight container. Store at room temperature up to 24 hours or freeze up to 2 months. To serve, thaw muffins if frozen. If desired, frost as directed.

Lemon–Strawberry Cornmeal Scones

PREP: 20 minutes BAKE: 12 minutes at 400°F MAKES: 12 servings

1⅔ cups brown rice flour
½ cup gluten-free finely ground
  yellow cornmeal
¼ cup granulated sugar
1 tablespoon gluten-free
  baking powder
2 teaspoons finely shredded
  lemon peel
¼ teaspoon salt
⅓ cup butter
1 egg, lightly beaten
½ cup milk
1 cup chopped fresh
  strawberries
  Powdered sugar (optional)

1. Preheat oven to 400°F. Lightly grease a large baking sheet or line with parchment paper; set aside. In a large bowl stir together flour, cornmeal, granulated sugar, baking powder, lemon peel, and salt. Using a pastry blender, cut in butter until mixture resembles coarse crumbs. Make a well in the center of flour mixture; set aside.

2. In a small bowl combine egg and milk. Add egg mixture all at once to flour mixture; stir just until moistened. Gently stir in strawberries (dough will not completely come together in a ball).

3. Turn dough out onto a well-floured surface (use brown rice flour). Using floured hands, knead dough by folding and gently pressing 10 to 12 strokes or until nearly smooth (dough will be wet and sticky). Divide dough in half. Transfer dough portions to the prepared baking sheet. Pat or lightly roll each portion into a 5-inch circle. Cut each circle into six wedges; separate wedges about 1 inch apart.

4. Bake for 12 to 15 minutes or until golden brown. Transfer to a wire rack; cool slightly. If desired, sprinkle lightly with powdered sugar. Serve warm.

PER SERVING: 173 cal., 6 g fat (3 g sat. fat), 14 mg chol., 232 mg sodium, 27 g carb., 2 g fiber, 3 g pro.

Peanut Butter and Jelly Breakfast Quinoa

START TO FINISH: 20 minutes
MAKES: 4 servings

1 cup quinoa
2 cups water
¼ cup apple juice or apple cider
3 tablespoons gluten-free, reduced-fat peanut butter spread
1 small banana, chopped
2 tablespoons raspberry or strawberry spreadable fruit*
4 teaspoons unsalted blanched peanuts
Sliced apple (optional)

1. Rinse quinoa in a fine-mesh strainer. In a medium saucepan combine the quinoa and water. Bring to boiling; reduce heat to medium-low. Cook, covered, for 10 to 15 minutes or until water is absorbed. Remove from heat.

2. Add apple juice and the peanut butter spread to quinoa, stirring until combined. If necessary, stir in additional apple juice to desired consistency. Stir in banana.

3. Divide quinoa mixture among four bowls. Top with spreadable fruit, peanuts, and, if desired, sliced apple.

PER SERVING: 289 cal., 9 g fat (1 g sat. fat), 0 mg chol., 81 mg sodium, 44 g carb., 4 g fiber, 10 g pro.

Chocolate-Almond-Blackberry Breakfast Quinoa: Prepare as directed, except substitute water for the apple juice and almond butter for the peanut butter. Omit banana, spreadable fruit, peanuts, and apple. Stir about 2 tablespoons unsweetened cocoa powder, 1 tablespoon honey, and ⅛ teaspoon salt into cooked quinoa. If necessary, stir in additional water to desired consistency. Top servings with fresh blackberries, toasted sliced almonds, and, if desired, miniature semisweet chocolate pieces. Drizzle with honey.

*Tip: Check the label of this product carefully to be sure it does not contain added gluten.

Strawberries and Cream Quinoa

PREP: 30 minutes
COOK: 10 minutes
MAKES: 4 servings

¾ **cup quinoa**
1½ **cups water**
1¾ **cups strawberries, quartered**
2 **tablespoons sugar**
⅛ **teaspoon ground cardamom or ground cinnamon**
Dash salt
¼ **cup fat-free half-and-half**
½ **teaspoon vanilla extract***
¼ **cup sliced strawberries**

1. Rinse quinoa in a fine-mesh strainer. In a medium saucepan combine the quinoa and water. Bring to boiling; reduce heat to medium-low. Cook, covered, for 10 to 15 minutes or until water is absorbed. Drain well and keep warm.

2. Meanwhile, in a large saucepan combine the 1¾ cups strawberries, the sugar, cardamom, and salt. Heat over medium-low heat just until berries are warm. Stir in the half-and-half; heat through. Stir in the reserved quinoa and the vanilla.

3. Divide quinoa mixture evenly among four bowls. Top each serving with 1 tablespoon sliced strawberries.

PER SERVING: 175 cal., 2 g fat (0 g sat. fat), 1 mg chol., 54 mg sodium, 34 g carb., 4 g fiber, 5 g pro.

***Tip:** Check the label of this product carefully to be sure it does not contain added gluten.

Almond Breakfast Risotto with Dried Fruit

PREP: 15 minutes   COOK: 20 minutes   MAKES: 4 servings

 1 **cup water**
 ⅔ **cup Arborio rice**
 ¼ **teaspoon salt**
 ⅓ **cup dried cherries**
 ¼ **cup coarsely chopped dried apricots**
 3 **cups fat-free milk**
 ½ **teaspoon ground cinnamon**
 ½ **teaspoon almond extract***
 ¼ **cup sliced almonds, toasted**

1. In a medium saucepan bring the water to boiling over medium-high heat. Stir in rice and salt. Cook, uncovered, for 5 to 6 minutes or until water is absorbed, stirring occasionally. Stir in dried cherries and apricots.

2. Meanwhile, pour milk into a 4-cup microwave-safe liquid measuring cup or medium bowl; microwave for 2 minutes or until hot. Stir in cinnamon.

3. Add the hot milk mixture, ½ cup at a time, to the rice mixture, stirring until liquid is absorbed (this should take 20 to 25 minutes total). Remove from heat. Stir in almond extract. Just before serving, sprinkle with toasted almonds.

PER SERVING: 258 cal., 3 g fat (0 g sat. fat), 4 mg chol., 227 mg sodium, 50 g carb., 2 g fiber, 10 g pro.

*Tip: Check the label of this product carefully to be sure it does not contain added gluten.

Caramelized Onion and Potato Breakfast Casserole

PREP: 45 minutes
bake: 45 minutes 350°F
STAND: 15 minutes
MAKES: 8 servings

4 **cups sliced golden potatoes, cut ⅛ to ¼ inch thick (about 1½ pounds)**
1 **tablespoon olive oil**
2 **ounces gluten-free pancetta, chopped**
3 **cups thinly sliced sweet onions, such as Vidalia or Maui**
6 **eggs, lightly beaten**
½ **cup milk**
4 **ounces Gruyère or Swiss cheese, shredded (1 cup)**
1 **teaspoon salt**
1 **teaspoon snipped fresh rosemary**
½ **teaspoon black pepper**

1. Preheat oven to 350°F. In a large saucepan cook potatoes, covered, in lightly salted boiling water about 5 minutes or until slightly tender but still firm. Drain; set aside. In a large skillet heat olive oil over medium-high heat. Add pancetta; cook until lightly browned. Using a slotted spoon, remove pancetta, reserving drippings in skillet. Set pancetta aside. Add onions to skillet. Cook and stir over medium-low heat about 20 minutes or until lightly browned and very tender. Remove from heat. Carefully stir potatoes and pancetta into onions in skillet.

2. Lightly butter a 2-quart rectangular baking dish. Spread potato mixture in the prepared dish. In a medium bowl whisk together eggs and milk. Stir in cheese, salt, rosemary, and pepper. Pour evenly over potato mixture in baking dish.

3. Bake, uncovered, for 45 to 50 minutes or until golden and a knife inserted in the center comes out clean. Let stand for 15 minutes before serving.

PER SERVING: 250 cal., 13 g fat (5 g sat. fat), 180 mg chol., 535 mg sodium, 22 g carb., 3 g fiber, 13 g pro.

To Make Ahead: Prepare as directed through Step 2. Cover and chill for 4 to 24 hours. Bake as directed.

Squash, Bacon, and Feta Breakfast Bake

PREP: 35 minutes
BAKE: 1 hour at 375°F +
25 minutes at 350°F
MAKES: 6 servings

- 1 3-pound spaghetti squash
- 2 eggs, lightly beaten
- ⅓ cup finely shredded Parmesan cheese*
- 3 tablespoons Gluten-Free Flour Mix (recipe, page 162) or purchased gluten-free all-purpose flour
- 2 tablespoons snipped fresh sage
- 6 slices gluten-free, lower sodium, less fat bacon, coarsely chopped Nonstick cooking spray*
- 3 cups coarsely chopped, trimmed Swiss chard
- 2 ounces reduced-fat feta cheese, crumbled (about ⅓ cup)
- 6 eggs
- ¼ teaspoon salt
- ¼ teaspoon black pepper

1. Preheat oven to 375°F. Line a baking pan with parchment paper. Cut spaghetti squash in half; scoop out and discard seeds and strings. Place squash halves, cut sides down, on prepared baking pan. Bake about 1 hour or until tender when pierced with a sharp knife. Cool on a wire rack. Reduce oven to 350°F.

2. For crust, in a large bowl combine the lightly beaten eggs, Parmesan cheese, flour, and sage. Scrape squash pulp into the bowl with the egg mixture. Stir until well combined. Spread evenly in a greased 2-quart rectangular baking dish. Bake, uncovered, about 20 minutes or until crust is set and edges are brown.

3. Meanwhile, in a large skillet cook bacon just until browned but not crisp. Using a slotted spoon, transfer bacon to a small bowl. Discard bacon drippings. Spray skillet with cooking spray. Add chard to skillet; cook and stir for 1 minute.

4. Top squash crust with chard, feta cheese, and bacon. Bake, uncovered, about 5 minutes more or until heated through.

5. Coat the same skillet with cooking spray; heat over medium heat. Break three eggs into skillet. Sprinkle with half of the salt and half of the pepper. Reduce heat to low; cook eggs for 3 to 4 minutes or until whites are set and yolks start to thicken. Remove from heat for sunny-side-up eggs. For over-easy or over-hard eggs, turn the eggs and cook for 30 seconds more (for over-easy) or 1 minute more (for over-hard). Remove eggs from skillet; keep warm. Repeat with remaining three eggs and remaining salt and pepper.

6. To serve, cut casserole into six equal portions. Serve each portion with an egg.

PER SERVING: 225 cal., 11 g fat (4 g sat), 257 mg chol., 534 mg sodium, 16 g carb., 3 g fiber, 16 g pro.

*Tip: Check the labels of these products carefully to be sure they do not contain added gluten.

Farmer's Casserole

PREP: 25 minutes BAKE: 40 minutes at 350°F STAND: 5 minutes MAKES: 6 servings

Nonstick cooking spray*
3 **cups frozen shredded hash brown potatoes**
1 **cup diced gluten-free cooked ham or gluten-free cooked breakfast sausage**
3 **ounces Monterey Jack cheese with jalapeño peppers or cheddar cheese, shredded (¾ cup)**
¼ **cup sliced green onions**
4 **eggs, lightly beaten**
1½ **cups milk**
⅛ **teaspoon salt**
⅛ **teaspoon black pepper**

1. Preheat oven to 350°F. Coat a 2-quart square baking dish with cooking spray. Spread potatoes evenly in the prepared baking dish. Sprinkle with ham, cheese, and green onions.

2. In a medium bowl combine eggs, milk, salt, and pepper. Pour egg mixture over potato mixture in dish.

3. Bake, uncovered, for 40 to 45 minutes or until a knife inserted near the center comes out clean. Let stand for 5 minutes before serving.

PER SERVING: 265 cal., 12 g fat (6 g sat. fat), 175 mg chol., 590 mg sodium, 23 g carb., 2 g fiber, 17 g pro.

Farmer's Casserole for 12: Prepare as directed, except double all of the ingredients and use a 3-quart rectangular baking dish. Bake, uncovered, for 45 to 55 minutes or until a knife inserted near the center comes out clean. Let stand for 5 minutes before serving.

To Make Ahead: Prepare as directed through Step 2. Cover and chill for 2 to 24 hours. To serve, preheat oven to 350°F. Bake, uncovered, for 50 to 55 minutes or until a knife inserted near the center comes out clean. Let stand for 5 minutes before serving.

***Tip:** Check the label of this product carefully to be sure it does not contain added gluten.

Potato Frittata

PREP: 25 minutes
COOK: 10 minutes
BAKE: 15 minutes at 375°F
STAND: 5 minutes
MAKES: 6 servings

1 pound Yukon gold or russet potatoes, scrubbed and thinly sliced
2 tablespoons olive oil
1½ cups thinly sliced carrots
12 eggs, lightly beaten
½ cup chopped green onions
½ teaspoon salt
¼ teaspoon black pepper
½ cup halved yellow cherry tomatoes
1 tablespoon snipped fresh parsley and/or cilantro
1 clove garlic, minced

1. Preheat oven to 375°F. In a large ovenproof nonstick skillet cook potatoes in hot oil over medium heat for 5 minutes. Add carrots; cook about 5 minutes more or until potatoes and carrots are tender and lightly browned, turning occasionally.

2. In a medium bowl whisk together the eggs, half of the green onions, the salt, and pepper. Pour egg mixture over potato mixture in skillet. Place skillet in oven. Bake, uncovered, for 15 to 18 minutes or until frittata appears dry on top. Remove from oven. Let stand on a wire rack for 5 minutes.

3. Meanwhile, for topping, in a small bowl gently toss together the remaining ¼ cup green onions, the cherry tomatoes, parsley, and garlic. Set aside.

4. With a spatula, loosen edges of frittata from skillet. Place a large platter over the skillet. Using both hands, carefully invert platter and skillet to release frittata onto platter. Cut frittata into wedges. Serve with green onion and cherry tomato topping.

PER SERVING: 259 cal., 14 g fat (4 g sat. fat), 372 mg chol., 362 mg sodium, 18 g carb., 3 g fiber, 15 g pro.

Bacon, Potato, and Kale Frittata

START TO FINISH: 30 minutes
MAKES: 6 servings

12 ounces tiny red-skin new potatoes, quartered
6 slices gluten-free, lower sodium, less-fat bacon, coarsely chopped
2 cups chopped fresh kale
½ cup coarsely chopped onion
8 eggs, lightly beaten
¼ teaspoon salt
¼ teaspoon black pepper

1. In a covered medium saucepan cook potatoes in enough boiling lightly salted water to cover for about 10 minutes or just until tender. Drain; set aside.

2. Meanwhile, preheat broiler. In a large broilerproof skillet with flared sides cook bacon over medium-high heat until starting to crisp. Add kale and onion; cook about 5 minutes or until onion is tender. Stir in the cooked potatoes.

3. In a medium bowl whisk together eggs, salt, and pepper. Pour eggs over potato mixture. Cook over medium-low heat. As eggs set, run a spatula around edge of skillet, lifting eggs so uncooked portion flows underneath. Continue cooking and lifting edges until eggs are almost set (surface will be moist).

4. Place skillet under the broiler, 4 to 5 inches from heat. Broil for 1 to 2 minutes or until top is set and no longer wet. (Or preheat oven to 400°F and bake about 5 minutes or until top is set and no longer wet.) Let stand for 5 minutes. Slide frittata out onto a platter. Cut into six wedges.

PER SERVING: 175 cal., 8 g fat (3 g sat. fat), 251 mg chol., 281 mg sodium, 13 g carb., 2 g fiber, 13 g pro.

Savory Egg and Sweet Potato Scramble

START TO FINISH: 35 minutes   MAKES: 4 servings

8 **eggs**
⅓ **cup milk**
½ **teaspoon ground cumin**
¼ **teaspoon salt**
¼ **teaspoon black pepper**
1 **tablespoon butter**
2 **medium sweet potatoes (about 1 pound), peeled, quartered lengthwise, and thinly sliced**
2 **tablespoons sliced green onion**
2 **cups fresh baby spinach**
Fresh Italian parsley
Hot pepper sauce* (optional)

1. In a medium bowl whisk together eggs, milk, cumin, salt, and pepper; set aside.

2. In a large skillet melt butter over medium heat. Add sweet potatoes and green onion. Cook about 8 minutes or just until potatoes are tender and lightly browned, stirring occasionally. Add spinach. Cook and stir about 1 minute or until spinach is slightly wilted.

3. Pour egg mixture over potato mixture in skillet. Cook over medium heat, without stirring, until egg mixture begins to set on the bottom and around the edges. Using a spatula or large spoon, lift and fold the partially cooked egg mixture so the uncooked portion flows underneath. Continue cooking for 2 to 3 minutes or until egg mixture is cooked through but is still glossy and moist. Remove from heat.

4. Sprinkle with parsley. If desired, serve with hot pepper sauce.

PER SERVING: 258 cal., 13 g fat (5 g sat. fat), 381 mg chol., 390 mg sodium, 20 g carb., 3 g fiber, 15 g pro.

***Tip:** Check the label of this product carefully to be sure it does not contain added gluten.

Sweet Potato and Turkey Sausage Hash

PREP: 25 minutes
ROAST: 20 minutes at 400°F
MAKES: 4 servings

2 medium russet potatoes, peeled, if desired, and diced
1 medium sweet potato, peeled, if desired, and diced
Nonstick cooking spray*
½ of a 14-ounce ring gluten-free smoked turkey sausage, halved lengthwise and sliced ½ inch thick
½ cup chopped green sweet pepper
½ cup chopped onion
1 tablespoon snipped fresh sage or 1 teaspoon dried sage, crushed
¼ teaspoon black pepper

1. Preheat oven to 400°F. Place russet and sweet potatoes on a 15×10×1-inch baking sheet. Lightly coat with cooking spray and toss to coat.

2. Roast about 20 minutes or until tender and lightly browned, turning once with spatula.

3. Meanwhile, in a large nonstick skillet cook sausage, sweet pepper, and onion for 8 to 10 minutes or until tender. Stir in roasted potatoes, sage, and pepper.

PER SERVING: 170 cal., 5 g fat (1 g sat. fat), 33 mg chol., 493 mg sodium, 22 g carb., 3 g fiber, 10 g pro.

***Tip:** Check the label of this product carefully to be sure it does not contain added gluten.

Breakfast Migas

START TO FINISH: 35 minutes
MAKES: 4 servings

8 **ounces gluten-free bulk pork sausage**
3 **6-inch corn tortillas,* cut into ¾-inch pieces**
⅓ **cup chopped red sweet pepper**
⅓ **cup chopped onion**
2 **tablespoons canned diced green chile peppers**
6 **eggs, lightly beaten**
2 **ounces queso Oaxaca, queso Chihuahua, or cheddar cheese, shredded (½ cup)**
½ **cup Fire-Roasted Tomato Salsa (recipe, page 288) or purchased gluten-free salsa**
1 **avocado, peeled, seeded, and chopped**
½ **cup sour cream**
  Fire-Roasted Tomato Salsa (recipe, page 288) or purchased gluten-free salsa

1. In a large nonstick skillet cook sausage over medium heat about 5 minutes or until browned, using a wooden spoon to break up meat as it cooks. Drain off fat. Add tortillas, red sweet pepper, onion, and green chile peppers; cook about 5 minutes or until onion is tender.

2. Add eggs and cook, without stirring, until eggs begin to set on bottom and around edges. With a spatula or large spoon, lift and fold the partially cooked eggs so the uncooked portion flows underneath. Cook for 2 to 3 minutes or until eggs are cooked through but still glossy and moist. Fold in cheese and ½ cup salsa. Immediately remove from heat.

3. Serve migas with avocado, sour cream, and additional salsa.

PER SERVING: 489 cal., 36 g fat (11 g sat. fat), 345 mg chol., 807 mg sodium, 18 g carb., 5 g fiber, 25 g pro.

*Tip: Check the label of this product carefully to be sure it does not contain added gluten.

Huevos Oaxaqueños

START TO FINISH: 30 minutes
MAKES: 4 servings

½ cup chopped onion
1 small fresh Anaheim chile pepper, stemmed, seeded, and chopped (see tip, page 21)
1 clove garlic, minced
1 tablespoon olive oil
4 large tomatoes, chopped
1 small zucchini, halved lengthwise and thinly sliced
1 teaspoon dried savory or cilantro, crushed
½ teaspoon salt
4 eggs
Queso fresco, crumbled
Fresh snipped cilantro (optional)
Corn tortillas,* warmed (optional)

1. In a large skillet cook onion, chile pepper, and garlic in hot oil over medium heat about 5 minutes or until tender. Add tomatoes, zucchini, savory, and salt; cook for 5 minutes or until tomatoes release their liquid and zucchini is tender.

2. Break one of the eggs into a measuring cup. Carefully slide egg into the tomato mixture in skillet. Repeat with the remaining three eggs, allowing each egg equal space in the tomato mixture. Cover and simmer over medium-low heat for 3 to 5 minutes or until egg whites are completely set and yolks begin to thicken but are not hard. Sprinkle with queso fresco. If desired, sprinkle with fresh cilantro and serve with corn tortillas.

PER SERVING: 176 cal., 10 g fat (3 g sat. fat), 191 mg chol., 395 mg sodium, 13 g carb., 3 g fiber, 11 g pro.

*Tip: Check the label of this product carefully to be sure it does not contain added gluten.

Hearty Breakfast Tacos

PREP: 20 minutes
BAKE: 7 minutes at 375°F
MAKES: 4 servings

- 8 **6-inch corn tortillas***
- 1 **teaspoon canola oil**
- ¼ **teaspoon salt**
  Nonstick cooking spray*
- 1 **cup frozen shredded hash brown potatoes**
- 2 **tablespoons chopped green sweet pepper**
- 4 **eggs, lightly beaten**
- 2 **egg whites**
- 5 **tablespoons Fire-Roasted Tomato Salsa (recipe, page 288) or purchased gluten-free salsa**
- ½ **cup canned reduced-sodium black beans, rinsed and drained***
- 1 **ounce reduced-fat cheddar cheese, shredded (¼ cup) Lime wedges (optional) Fire-Roasted Tomato Salsa (recipe, page 288) or purchased gluten-free salsa (optional)**

1. Position oven rack in center of oven. Preheat oven to 375°F. Stack tortillas and wrap in damp paper towels. Microwave about 40 seconds or until warm and softened. Lightly brush both sides of tortillas with oil; sprinkle with salt. Slide oven rack out slightly. Carefully drape each tortilla over two bars of oven rack, forming shells with flat bottoms (sides will drape farther as they bake). Bake about 7 minutes or until crisp. Using tongs, transfer warm shells to a plate.

2. Meanwhile, lightly coat a large nonstick skillet with cooking spray; heat skillet over medium-high heat. Add hash brown potatoes and sweet pepper to skillet; cook for 2 to 3 minutes or until potatoes are lightly browned, stirring occasionally. Reduce heat to medium. In a small bowl combine eggs, egg whites, and 1 tablespoon of the salsa. Pour egg mixture over potato mixture in skillet. Cook, without stirring, until egg mixture begins to set on the bottom and around edges. Using a spatula or large spoon, lift and fold partially cooked egg mixture so the uncooked portion flows underneath. Continue cooking over medium heat for 2 to 3 minutes or until egg mixture is cooked through but still glossy and moist. Immediately remove from heat.

3. Spoon egg mixture into tortilla shells. Top with beans and the remaining 4 tablespoons salsa; sprinkle with cheese. If desired, serve with lime wedges and additional salsa.

PER SERVING: 238 cal., 8 g fat (3 g sat. fat), 191 mg chol., 498 mg sodium, 28 g carb., 3 g fiber, 14 g pro.

*Tip: Check the labels of these products carefully to be sure they do not contain added gluten.

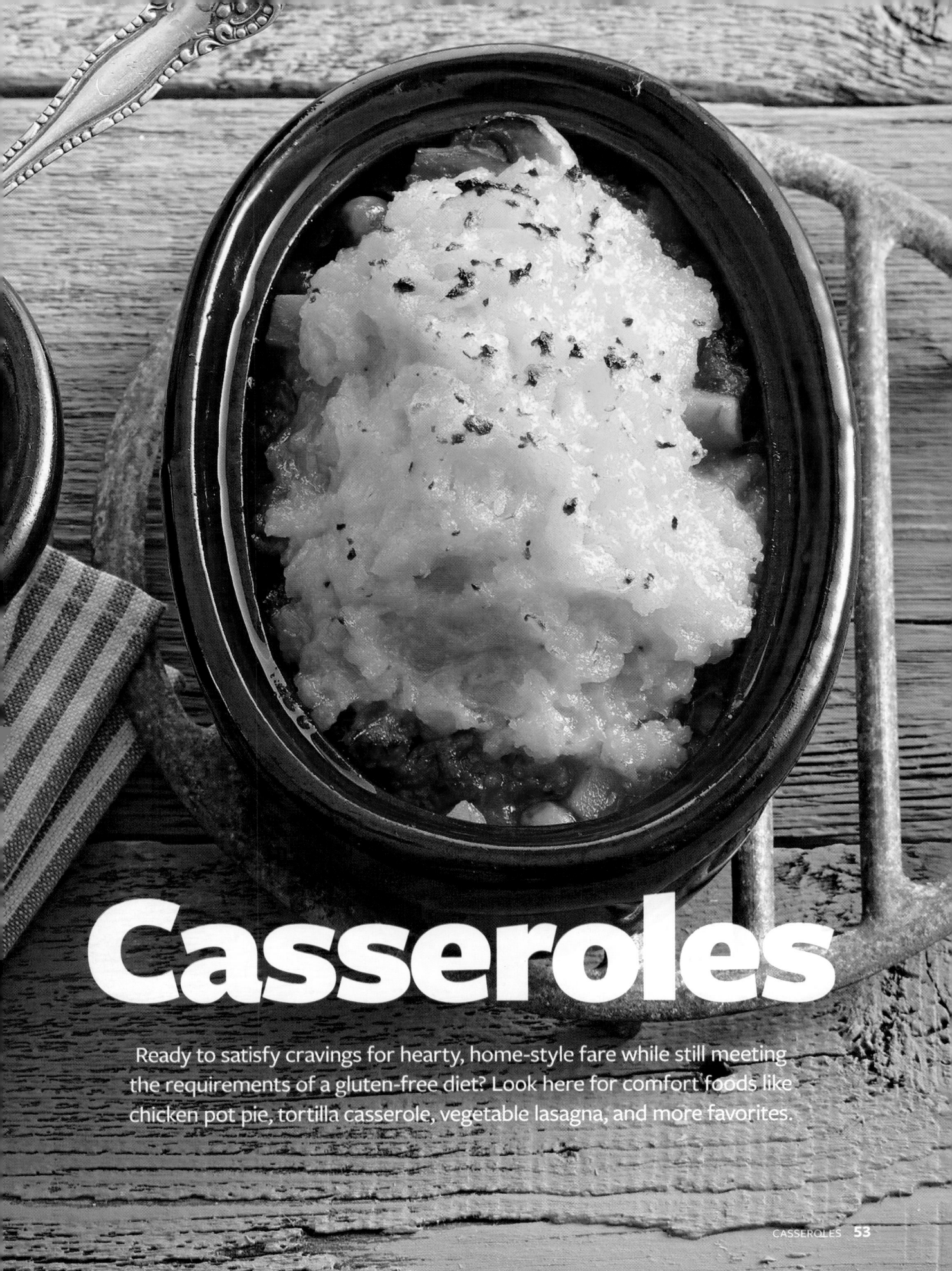

Casseroles

Ready to satisfy cravings for hearty, home-style fare while still meeting the requirements of a gluten-free diet? Look here for comfort foods like chicken pot pie, tortilla casserole, vegetable lasagna, and more favorites.

Tandoori-Spiced Chicken and Rice Bake

PREP: 20 minutes   **COOK:** 15 minutes   **BAKE:** 20 minutes at 350°F   **MAKES:** 4 servings

Nonstick cooking spray*
4½ teaspoons Tandoori Spice Mixture or gluten-free tandoori spice blend
4 4- to 5-ounce skinless, boneless chicken breast halves
2 tablespoons vegetable oil
½ cup coarsely chopped onion
½ cup coarsely shredded carrot
½ cup chopped red sweet pepper
½ of a fresh Anaheim chile pepper, seeded and chopped (see tip, page 21)
1 small zucchini, halved lengthwise and sliced ¼ inch thick
2 cloves garlic, thinly sliced
1 14.5-ounce can gluten-free, reduced-sodium chicken broth
1 cup unsweetened light coconut milk*
⅔ cup uncooked long grain rice
½ cup water
¼ cup no-salt-added tomato paste
Snipped fresh cilantro (optional)

1. Preheat oven to 350°F. Lightly coat a shallow 2-quart baking dish with cooking spray; set aside.

2. Sprinkle 1½ teaspoons of the Tandoori Spice Mixture evenly over chicken; rub in with your fingers. In a large skillet heat 1 tablespoon of the oil over medium-high heat. Add chicken; cook about 8 minutes or until chicken is done (170°F), turning once. Remove from skillet.

3. In the same skillet heat the remaining 1 tablespoon oil over medium heat. Add onion, carrot, sweet pepper, and Anaheim pepper; cook for 2 minutes, stirring occasionally. Add zucchini and garlic; cook and stir for 2 minutes more.

4. Stir in broth, coconut milk, rice, the water, tomato paste, and the remaining 3 teaspoons Tandoori Spice Mixture. Bring to boiling; reduce heat. Simmer for 15 to 20 minutes. Slice chicken; stir into vegetable mixture.

5. Transfer chicken mixture to the prepared baking dish. Bake, covered, about 20 minutes or until heated through and rice is tender. If desired, sprinkle with cilantro before serving.

PER SERVING: 438 cal., 15 g fat (5 g sat. fat), 91 mg chol., 586 mg sodium, 38 g carb., 3 g fiber, 37 g pro.

Tandoori Spice Mixture: In a small bowl combine 1 teaspoon mild yellow curry powder,* 1 teaspoon garam masala,* ½ teaspoon ground ginger, ½ teaspoon ground cumin, ½ teaspoon ground coriander, ½ teaspoon ground cardamom, ¼ teaspoon salt, ⅛ teaspoon ground cinnamon, and ⅛ teaspoon black pepper. Makes 4½ teaspoons.

***Tip:** Check the labels of these products carefully to be sure they do not contain added gluten.

Chicken Pot Pie

PREP: 45 minutes
BAKE: 40 minutes at 400°F
STAND: 10 minutes
MAKES: 8 servings

½ cup butter
3⅓ cups Gluten-Free Flour Mix (recipe, page 162) or purchased gluten-free all-purpose flour
1 14.5-ounce can gluten-free, reduced-sodium chicken broth
2¾ cups milk
3 cups chopped cooked chicken
1 16-ounce package frozen mixed vegetables
1½ cups frozen small whole onions
1½ teaspoons salt
1 teaspoon poultry seasoning*
⅛ teaspoon black pepper
1 tablespoon sugar
1 tablespoon gluten-free baking powder
¾ teaspoon cream of tartar
¾ cup butter
1 tablespoon milk
1 ounce Parmesan cheese, grated (¼ cup)

1. Preheat oven to 400°F. In a large saucepan heat the ½ cup butter over medium heat until melted. Stir in ⅓ cup of the flour; cook and stir for 1 minute. Gradually stir in broth and 1½ cups of the milk. Cook and stir until thickened and bubbly. Stir in chicken, frozen vegetables, frozen onions, ½ teaspoon of the salt, the poultry seasoning, and pepper. Cook until heated through, stirring frequently. Keep warm.

2. For biscuits, in a large bowl stir together the remaining 3 cups flour, the remaining 1 teaspoon salt, the sugar, baking powder, and cream of tartar. Using a pastry blender, cut in the ¾ cup butter until mixture resembles coarse crumbs. Make a well in the center of flour mixture. Add the remaining 1¼ cups milk all at once. Using a fork, stir just until moistened. Turn dough out onto a work surface and pat into a ¾-inch-thick rectangle. Cut into 12 squares.

3. Transfer hot chicken mixture to a 3-quart oval or rectangular baking dish. Arrange biscuits on top. Brush biscuits with the 1 tablespoon milk; sprinkle with cheese.

4. Place baking dish on middle oven rack. Place a large baking sheet on bottom rack to catch any drips. Bake about 40 minutes or until edges are bubbly and biscuits are lightly browned. Let stand for 10 minutes before serving.

PER SERVING: 703 cal., 36 g fat (21 g sat. fat), 132 mg chol., 1,163 mg sodium, 71 g carb., 4 g fiber, 24 g pro.

*Tip: Check the label of this product carefully to be sure it does not contain added gluten.

Green Chile Chicken Tortilla Casserole

PREP: 45 minutes
BROIL: 6 minutes
BAKE: 1 hour at 375°F
STAND: 10 minutes
MAKES: 9 servings

Nonstick cooking spray*
1 pound tomatillos, outer husks removed and rinsed
1 teaspoon vegetable oil
½ cup chopped onion
1 fresh poblano chile pepper, seeded and chopped (see tip, page 21)
¼ cup snipped fresh cilantro
1 teaspoon sugar
½ teaspoon ground cumin
¼ teaspoon salt
12 6-inch corn tortillas,* halved
3 cups shredded cooked chicken breast
1¾ cups shredded reduced-fat Mexican-style four-cheese blend* (7 ounces)
1 16-ounce jar salsa*
Chopped tomato, sliced fresh jalapeño chile peppers (see tip, page 21), and/or sliced green onions (optional)

1. Preheat broiler. Lightly coat a 2-quart square baking dish with cooking spray; set aside. Place tomatillos in a large foil-lined baking pan. Broil 4 to 5 inches from heat for 6 to 8 minutes or until softened and charred, turning occasionally. Set aside to cool.

2. Preheat oven to 375°F. In a large skillet heat oil over medium heat. Add onion and poblano chile pepper; cook and stir for 4 to 5 minutes or until tender and onion starts to brown.

3. In a blender or food processor combine tomatillos, onion mixture, the cilantro, sugar, cumin, and salt. Blend or process until smooth.

4. Spread ¾ cup of tomatillo sauce in the prepared baking dish. Arrange six of the tortilla halves over tomatillo sauce, overlapping tortillas slightly. Top with 1 cup of the chicken, ½ cup of the cheese, and half of the salsa, spreading evenly.

Layer six more tortilla halves, 1 cup chicken, ½ cup cheese, and half of the remaining tomatillo sauce, spreading evenly. Add six more tortilla halves, the remaining 1 cup chicken, and the remaining tomatillo sauce. Top with the remaining six tortilla halves and the remaining salsa, spreading to cover evenly.

5. Cover dish with foil. Bake for 40 minutes. Remove foil. Sprinkle with the remaining ¾ cup cheese. Bake about 20 minutes more or until heated through. Let stand for 10 minutes before serving. If desired, top with chopped tomatoes, sliced jalapeños, and/or sliced green onions.

PER SERVING: 240 cal., 10 g fat (4 g sat. fat), 53 mg chol., 591 mg sodium, 17 g carb., 2 g fiber, 21 g pro.

*Tip: Check the labels of these products carefully to be sure they do not contain added gluten.

Pumpkin, Bean, and Chicken Enchiladas

PREP: 35 minutes
BAKE: 25 minutes at 400°F
MAKES: 4 servings

Nonstick cooking spray*
2 teaspoons olive oil
½ cup chopped onion
1 fresh jalapeño chile pepper, seeded and finely chopped (see tip, page 21)
1 15-ounce can pumpkin
1½ to 1¾ cups water
1 teaspoon chili powder*
½ teaspoon salt
½ teaspoon ground cumin
1 cup canned no-salt-added red kidney beans, rinsed and drained*
1½ cups shredded cooked chicken breast
2 ounces part-skim mozzarella cheese, shredded (½ cup)
8 6-inch white corn tortillas, softened*
Pico de gallo or gluten-free salsa (optional)
Lime wedges (optional)

1. Preheat oven to 400°F. Lightly coat a 2-quart rectangular baking dish with cooking spray; set aside. In a medium saucepan heat oil over medium-high heat. Add onion and jalapeño pepper; cook about 5 minutes or until onion is tender, stirring occasionally. Stir in pumpkin, 1½ cups of the water, the chili powder, salt, and cumin. Cook and stir until heated through. If necessary, stir in enough of the remaining ¼ cup water to reach desired consistency.

2. Place beans in a large bowl; mash slightly with a fork. Stir in half of the pumpkin mixture, the chicken, and ¼ cup of the cheese.

3. To soften tortillas, place them between paper towels. Microwave for 30 to 40 seconds. Spoon a generous ⅓ cup of the bean mixture onto each tortilla. Roll up tortillas; place, seam sides down, in the prepared baking dish. Pour the remaining pumpkin mixture over enchiladas.

4. Bake, covered, for 15 minutes. Sprinkle with the remaining ¼ cup cheese. Bake, uncovered, about 10 minutes more or until heated through. If desired, serve with pico de gallo and lime wedges.

PER SERVING: 357 cal., 8 g fat (3 g sat. fat), 54 mg chol., 465 mg sodium, 44 g carb., 12 g fiber, 28 g pro.

*Tip: Check the labels of these products carefully to be sure they do not contain added gluten.

Cheesy Pesto-Meatball Lasagna Rolls

PREP: 35 minutes
BAKE: 55 minutes at 350°F
MAKES: 6 servings

12 dried gluten-free lasagna noodles
1 egg, lightly beaten
8 ounces mozzarella cheese, shredded (2 cups)
4 ounces Parmesan cheese, finely shredded (1 cup)
½ cup finely chopped onion
½ cup finely chopped green sweet pepper
2 tablespoons Homemade Pesto (recipe, page 282) or purchased gluten-free pesto
1 pound lean ground beef
3 cups 20-Minute Marinara Sauce (recipe, page 287) or purchased gluten-free marinara sauce
  Fresh snipped basil (optional)

1. Cook lasagna noodles according to package directions, except cook for 2 minutes less than the suggested time on package; drain. Place noodles in a single layer on a sheet of greased foil.

2. Meanwhile, preheat oven to 350°F. For meatball filling, in a large bowl combine egg, 1 cup of the mozzarella cheese, ½ cup of the Parmesan cheese, the onion, sweet pepper, and pesto. Add ground beef; mix well. Divide into 12 portions. Mound each portion at one end of each noodle, then roll up. Arrange filled noodles in a 3-quart rectangular baking dish. Pour the marinara sauce over the lasagna rolls.

3. Bake, covered, for 45 minutes. Sprinkle with the remaining 1 cup mozzarella cheese and the remaining ½ cup Parmesan cheese. Bake, uncovered, about 10 minutes more or until cheeses are melted. If desired, garnish with basil.

PER SERVING: 585 cal., 28 g fat (12 g sat. fat), 124 mg chol., 1,009 mg sodium, 47 g carb., 3 g fiber, 38 g pro.

Roasted Butternut Squash and Chorizo Enchiladas with Avocado-Chard Slaw

PREP: 45 minutes **BAKE:** 30 minutes at 425°F **MAKES:** 4 servings

1 recipe Red Chile Sauce
Nonstick cooking spray*

4 ounces gluten-free uncooked chorizo sausage, casing removed

1 pound butternut squash, peeled, seeded, and cut into ½-inch cubes

2½ cups shredded cabbage

2½ cups Swiss chard, thick stems removed and leaves sliced into thin ribbons

2 teaspoons olive oil

1 avocado, halved, seeded, peeled, and diced

½ cup chopped yellow sweet pepper

½ cup chopped red onion

2 tablespoons lime juice

12 6-inch corn tortillas*

3 ounces Monterey Jack cheese or sharp cheddar cheese, shredded (¾ cup)
Snipped fresh cilantro
Mexican crema* or sour cream*

1. Prepare Red Chile Sauce. Preheat oven to 425°F. Lightly coat a 13×9×2-inch baking dish with cooking spray; set aside.

2. In a medium skillet cook chorizo over medium heat until browned; drain off fat. Combine chorizo and squash in prepared baking dish. Bake about 25 minutes or until squash is tender. Remove from baking dish and set aside.

3. Meanwhile, for slaw, in a large bowl combine cabbage, Swiss chard, and olive oil; toss to coat. Stir in avocado, sweet pepper, onion, and lime juice. Season to taste with salt; set aside.

4. Reduce oven temperature to 350°F. Prepare Red Chile Sauce. Dip a tortilla into the warm sauce until slightly softened. Fill dipped tortilla with 1 tablespoon of cheese and about 2 tablespoons of squash mixture. Roll up and place in the baking dish, seam side down. Repeat with remaining tortillas and filling. Pour any remaining warm sauce over the enchiladas.

5. Bake enchiladas, covered, about 30 minutes or until heated through. Place enchiladas on a plate and garnish with cilantro and Mexican crema. Serve chard slaw on the side.

Red Chile Sauce: In a 4-quart Dutch oven combine 7½ cups gluten-free, reduced-sodium chicken broth, 1½ onions (quartered), and 5 cloves garlic. Bring to boiling; reduce heat. Simmer, uncovered, for 15 minutes. Stir in 18 dried New Mexico chile peppers (4.5 ounces total) that are stemmed, seeded, and cut into pieces (see tip, page 21) and three 6-inch corn tortillas,* torn into pieces; remove from heat. Cover and let stand for 30 minutes. Working in batches, transfer mixture to a food processor or blender. Cover and process until smooth. Strain mixture through a fine-mesh sieve; discard solids. Return chile sauce to Dutch oven. Bring to boiling; reduce heat. Simmer sauce, uncovered, about 15 minutes or until slightly thickened. Season to taste with salt and hot pepper sauce.*

*Tip: Check the labels of these products carefully to be sure they do not contain added gluten.

PER SERVING: 782 cal., 41 g fat (17 g sat. fat), 91 mg chol., 2,108 mg sodium, 77 g carb., 18 g fiber, 34 g pro.

Sausage, Mushroom, and Polenta Bake

PREP: 50 minutes
BAKE: 25 minutes at 370°F
MAKES: 8 servings

1 pound gluten-free bulk Italian sausage
1 medium fresh jalapeño chile pepper, seeded and finely chopped (see tip, page 21) (optional)
4 cloves garlic, minced
1 24-ounce jar gluten-free marinara sauce
1 tablespoon olive oil
4 cups chopped fresh mushrooms
¾ cup thinly sliced green onions
1 teaspoon snipped fresh rosemary
½ cup whipping cream
¼ cup dry white wine or gluten-free chicken broth
½ teaspoon salt
4 cups gluten-free chicken broth
½ cup water
2 teaspoons dried Italian seasoning,* crushed
1½ cups gluten-free cornmeal
8 ounces smoked provolone cheese, shredded (2 cups)

1. In a large skillet cook sausage, jalapeño (if desired), and 2 cloves garlic over medium-high heat until sausage is browned, breaking up meat as it cooks. Drain off fat. Stir in marinara sauce. Bring to boiling; reduce heat. Simmer, uncovered, for 15 minutes, stirring frequently.

2. In another large skillet heat oil over medium heat. Add mushrooms, green onions, 2 cloves garlic, and the rosemary. Cook about 5 minutes or until mushrooms are tender and liquid is evaporated, stirring occasionally. Stir in whipping cream, wine, and salt. Cook over low heat about 10 minutes or until thickened.

3. Preheat oven to 375°F. Grease a 3-quart oval or rectangular baking dish. Spread half of the sausage mixture in the prepared baking dish. Set aside.

4. For polenta, in a large saucepan bring chicken broth, the water, and the Italian seasoning to boiling. Add cornmeal in a slow, steady stream, stirring constantly; reduce heat. Simmer, uncovered, about 1 minute or until polenta is thickened, stirring constantly.

5. Spread half of the cooked polenta over the sausage in the baking dish. Top with the mushroom mixture and half of the provolone cheese. Spoon the remaining polenta evenly over top. Top polenta with the remaining sausage mixture and remaining cheese. Cover with a sheet of greased foil. Bake for 25 to 30 minutes or until heated through.

PER SERVING: 495 cal., 30 g fat (14 g sat. fat), 83 mg chol., 1,504 mg sodium, 32 g carb., 3 g fiber, 21 g pro.

*Tip: Check the label of this product carefully to be sure it does not contain added gluten.

Squash and Sausage Shepherd's Pie

PREP: 40 minutes
BAKE: 15 minutes at 425°F
MAKES: 6 servings

Nonstick cooking spray*
2½ **pounds butternut squash, peeled, seeded, and cut into chunks**
¼ **cup light butter with canola oil**
1 **ounce Parmesan cheese, grated (¼ cup)**
¼ **teaspoon salt**
½ **teaspoon black pepper**
8 **ounces gluten-free sweet Italian sausage or lean ground beef**
½ **cup chopped onion**
1 **8-ounce package sliced fresh mushrooms**
1 **tablespoon olive oil**
3 **cloves garlic, minced**
1 **cup gluten-free, reduced-sodium beef broth**
½ **28-ounce can crushed tomatoes (about 1½ cups)**
1 **tablespoon snipped fresh rosemary or 1 teaspoon dried rosemary, crushed**
1 **teaspoon gluten-free Worcestershire sauce**
1 **cup frozen peas and carrots**

1. Preheat oven to 425°F. Lightly coat six 10- to 12-ounce individual casseroles with cooking spray.

2. In a 6-quart Dutch oven cook squash in lightly salted boiling water, covered, for 15 to 17 minutes or until tender. Drain; return to Dutch oven. Using a potato masher, mash squash with butter, Parmesan, salt, and ¼ teaspoon of the pepper; set aside.

3. In a large skillet cook sausage over medium-high heat until browned, using a wooden spoon to break up meat as it cooks. Transfer sausage to a colander; drain well. Wipe out skillet.

4. In the same skillet cook onion and mushrooms in hot oil over medium-high heat for 4 to 5 minutes or until tender, stirring occasionally. Add garlic; cook for 2 minutes more. Stir in broth, crushed tomatoes, rosemary, and Worcestershire sauce. Bring to boiling; reduce heat.

Simmer, uncovered, about 5 minutes or until thickened. Stir in sausage, peas and carrots, and the remaining ¼ teaspoon pepper; cook for 2 minutes. Spoon sausage mixture evenly into prepared casseroles. Spread mashed squash mixture on tops. Place casseroles on a large baking sheet.

5. Bake, uncovered, for 15 to 20 minutes or until tops are lightly browned.

PER SERVING: 303 cal., 16 g fat (6 g sat. fat), 32 mg chol., 606 mg sodium, 30 g carb., 6 g fiber, 12 g pro.

*Tip: Check the label of this product carefully to be sure it does not contain added gluten.

Italian Polenta Casserole

PREP: 40 minutes   **BAKE:** 20 minutes at 400°F   **MAKES:** 8 servings

2½ **cups gluten-free chicken broth**
3 **tablespoons butter**
2 **cups milk**
1½ **cups gluten-free quick-cooking polenta mix**
3 **ounces cream cheese,* cut up**
4 **ounces mozzarella cheese or provolone cheese, shredded (1 cup)**
2 **ounces Parmesan cheese, finely shredded or grated (½ cup)**
12 **ounces gluten-free sweet or spicy bulk Italian sausage**
1 **cup quartered fresh mushrooms**
1 **medium onion, cut into thin wedges**
2 **cloves garlic, minced**
2 **cups 20-Minute Marinara Sauce (recipe, page 287) or purchased gluten-free tomato-base pasta sauce**
Fresh basil leaves (optional)

1. Preheat oven to 400°F. Lightly grease a 3-quart rectangular baking dish; set aside.

2. In a large saucepan bring broth and butter to boiling. Meanwhile, in a medium bowl stir together milk and polenta mix. Stir polenta into boiling broth. Cook and stir until bubbly; cook and stir for 3 to 5 minutes more or until very thick. Remove from heat. Add cream cheese, ¾ cup of the mozzarella cheese, and ¼ cup of the Parmesan cheese, stirring until well mixed. Spread two-thirds of the polenta in the prepared baking dish; set aside.

3. In a large skillet cook sausage, mushrooms, onion, and garlic over medium heat until meat is browned and onion is tender, using a wooden spoon to break up meat as it cooks. Drain off fat. Stir pasta sauce into meat mixture; heat through. Spoon meat mixture over polenta in baking dish, spreading evenly. Spoon the remaining polenta over meat-sauce mixture; sprinkle with the remaining ¼ cup mozzarella cheese and the remaining ¼ cup Parmesan cheese.

4. Bake, uncovered, about 20 minutes or until heated through and top is lightly golden brown. If desired, sprinkle with basil.

PER SERVING: 584 cal., 34 g fat (18 g sat. fat), 93 mg chol., 1,879 mg sodium, 36 g carb., 4 g fiber, 31 g pro.

*Tip: Check the label of this product carefully to be sure it does not contain added gluten.

Mexican Rice and Black Bean Casserole

PREP: 20 minutes
BAKE: 40 minutes at 350°F
STAND: 5 minutes
MAKES: 8 servings

1 pound gluten-free bulk pork sausage

2 14.5-ounce cans gluten-free Mexican-style stewed tomatoes, undrained

2 cups cooked white rice

1 15-ounce can black beans, rinsed and drained*

¾ cup coarsely chopped green sweet pepper

2 ounces cheddar cheese, shredded (½ cup)
Sour cream, sliced fresh jalapeño chile pepper (see tip, page 21), and/or corn tortilla chips* (optional)

1. Preheat oven to 350°F. In an extra-large skillet cook sausage over medium-high heat until browned, using a wooden spoon to break up meat as it cooks. Drain off fat. Stir in tomatoes, cooked rice, black beans, and sweet pepper. Transfer to an ungreased 3-quart rectangular baking dish.

2. Bake, covered, for 40 to 45 minutes or until heated through. Sprinkle with cheese. Let stand for 5 minutes before serving. If desired, serve with sour cream, chile pepper, and/or tortilla chips.

PER SERVING: 343 cal., 19 g fat (8 g sat. fat), 40 mg chol., 811 mg sodium, 27 g carb., 3 g fiber, 14 g pro.

For 4 Servings: Prepare as directed, except halve the ingredients, cook sausage in a large skillet, and transfer mixture to a 2-quart square baking dish. Bake, covered, for 30 to 35 minutes or until heated through.

*Tip: Check the labels of these products carefully to be sure they do not contain added gluten.

Asparagus–Tuna Casserole

PREP: 40 minutes
BAKE: 25 minutes at 375°F
MAKES: 6 servings

- 1 cup gluten-free dried penne pasta
- 1 pound tiny new potatoes, cut into ½-inch pieces
- 3 tablespoons butter
- ¼ cup chopped onion
- 2 tablespoons Gluten-Free Flour Mix (recipe, page 162) or purchased gluten-free all-purpose flour
- ⅛ teaspoon salt
- ⅛ teaspoon black pepper
- 2¼ cups milk
- 2 teaspoons finely shredded lemon peel
- 4 ounces provolone cheese, shredded (1 cup)
- 1½ pounds fresh green, white, and/or purple asparagus spears, trimmed and cut into 1-inch pieces
- 3 4.5-ounce cans tuna packed in roasted garlic olive oil, undrained*
- ½ cup pitted Kalamata olives, halved
- ¼ cup gluten-free soft bread crumbs
- 1 ounce Parmesan cheese, finely shredded (¼ cup)

1. Preheat oven to 375°F. In a large saucepan cook pasta according to package directions, adding potatoes for the last 4 minutes of cooking; drain well.

2. Meanwhile, in a large Dutch oven heat 2 tablespoons of the butter over medium heat. Add onion; cook about 3 minutes or until tender, stirring occasionally. Stir in flour, salt, and pepper; cook and stir for 2 minutes. Gradually stir in milk; add lemon peel. Cook and stir until thickened and bubbly. Gradually add provolone cheese, stirring until melted. Gently fold in cooked pasta and potatoes, asparagus, tuna, and olives. Transfer to a 3-quart baking dish.

3. For topping, in a small saucepan melt the remaining 1 tablespoon butter over low heat. Stir in bread crumbs and Parmesan cheese. Sprinkle on casserole. Bake for 25 to 30 minutes or until heated through and topping is golden.

PER SERVING: 518 cal., 28 g fat (11 g sat. fat), 65 mg chol., 728 mg sodium, 38 g carb., 5 g fiber, 28 g pro.

***Tip:** If tuna packed in garlic olive oil is not available, substitute tuna packed in oil and add 2 cloves of garlic, minced, when cooking the onion.

Zucchini-Noodle Lasagna

PREP: 30 minutes **BROIL:** 12 minutes **BAKE:** 30 minutes at 375°F **STAND:** 10 minutes **MAKES:** 12 servings

2 **pounds medium or large zucchini**
   Nonstick cooking spray*
1 **pound 95% lean ground beef**
2 **cups chopped fresh portobello mushrooms**
2 **cloves garlic, minced**
1 **24- to 26-ounce jar gluten-free chunky-style pasta sauce**
1 **8-ounce can gluten-free tomato sauce**
1 **teaspoon dried basil, crushed**
1 **teaspoon dried oregano, crushed**
1 **teaspoon fennel seeds, crushed**
1 **egg, lightly beaten**
1 **15-ounce container fat-free ricotta cheese***
8 **ounces part-skim mozzarella cheese, shredded (2 cups)**

1. Preheat broiler. Trim ends off zucchini. Cut zucchini lengthwise into ¼-inch slices. Lightly coat both sides of zucchini slices with cooking spray; place half of the slices in a single layer on a wire rack set on a large baking sheet. Broil about 6 inches from the heat for 12 to 14 minutes or until lightly browned, turning once halfway through broiling. Repeat with remaining zucchini slices. Reduce oven temperature to 375°F.

2. For meat sauce, in a large skillet cook ground beef, mushrooms, and garlic over medium heat until meat is browned, using a wooden spoon to break up meat as it cooks. Remove from heat; drain if necessary. Stir pasta sauce, tomato sauce, basil, oregano, and fennel seeds into meat mixture in skillet. In a small bowl combine egg and ricotta cheese.

3. To assemble lasagna, spread 1 cup of the meat sauce into a 3-quart rectangular baking dish or 13×9×2-inch baking pan. Top with enough of the zucchini slices to cover the sauce. Spread half of the ricotta mixture on top of the zucchini. Sprinkle ¾ cup of the mozzarella cheese on top. Top with half of the remaining meat sauce. Repeat layers, ending with meat sauce.

4. Bake for 20 minutes. Sprinkle with the remaining ½ cup mozzarella cheese. Bake for 10 to 15 minutes more or until cheese is melted. Let stand for 10 minutes before serving.

PER SERVING: 209 cal., 8 g fat (3 g sat. fat), 58 mg chol., 565 mg sodium, 15 g carb., 3 g fiber, 20 g pro.

***Tip:** Check the labels of these products carefully to be sure they do not contain added gluten.

Quinoa Caprese Casserole

PREP: 35 minutes
STAND: 5 minutes
BAKE: 30 minutes at 350°F
MAKES: 5 servings

Nonstick cooking spray*
2 cups water
1 cup quinoa, rinsed and drained
½ teaspoon salt
1½ cups 20-Minute Marinara Sauce (recipe, page 287) or purchased gluten-free marinara sauce
2 tablespoons tomato paste
⅔ cup finely shredded Parmesan cheese*
⅓ cup whipping cream
½ teaspoon crushed red pepper
¼ teaspoon black pepper
1½ cups grape tomatoes or cherry tomatoes, halved
4 ounces part-skim mozzarella cheese, shredded (1 cup)
¾ cup shredded fresh basil
6 ounces fresh mozzarella, cut into ½-inch cubes

1. Preheat oven to 350°F. Lightly coat a 2-quart square baking dish with cooking spray; set aside. In a medium saucepan combine the water, the quinoa, and salt. Bring to boiling; reduce heat. Simmer, covered, about 15 minutes or until water is absorbed. Let stand for 5 minutes; uncover and fluff quinoa with a fork. Set aside.

2. In a large saucepan combine marinara sauce and tomato paste. Stir over low heat until smooth. Stir in Parmesan cheese, cream, crushed red pepper, and black pepper. Bring to boiling; remove from heat. Add cooked quinoa; mix gently. Using a rubber spatula, fold in ¾ cup of the grape tomatoes, the shredded mozzarella cheese, and ¼ cup of the basil. Spoon mixture into the prepared baking dish, spreading evenly.

3. Top with fresh mozzarella. Bake, uncovered, about 30 minutes or until heated through. Top with the remaining ¾ cup grape tomatoes and the remaining ½ cup basil.

PER SERVING: 433 cal., 23 g fat (13 g sat. fat), 70 mg chol., 1,040 mg sodium, 33 g carb., 5 g fiber, 23 g pro.

***Tip:** Check the labels of these products carefully to be sure they do not contain added gluten.

Roasted Vegetable Lasagna

PREP: 35 minutes
BROIL: 12 minutes
BAKE: 1 hour at 375°F
MAKES: 12 servings

- 4 cups bite-size pieces zucchini
- 2½ cups thinly sliced carrots
- 2 cups fresh cremini or button mushrooms, halved
- 1½ cups coarsely chopped red or green sweet peppers
- ¼ cup olive oil
- 1 tablespoon dried Italian seasoning,* crushed
- ½ teaspoon salt
- ½ teaspoon black pepper
- 9 dried brown rice lasagna noodles (such as Tinkyada brand)**
- 1 egg, lightly beaten
- 1 12-ounce container cottage cheese*
- 2 ounces Parmesan cheese, grated (½ cup)
- 1 24-ounce jar gluten-free marinara sauce or 3 cups 20-Minute Marinara Sauce (recipe, page 287)
- 12 ounces mozzarella cheese, shredded (3 cups)

1. Preheat broiler. In a large bowl combine zucchini, carrots, mushrooms, and sweet peppers. Drizzle vegetables with oil; sprinkle with Italian seasoning, salt, and black pepper. Toss to combine; place in a roasting pan.

2. Broil vegetables 5 to 6 inches from the heat for 6 minutes. Stir vegetables. Broil for 6 to 8 minutes more or until lightly browned and tender. Set vegetables aside.

3. Meanwhile, in a large pot cook lasagna noodles according to package directions; drain. Rinse with cold water; drain again. Lay noodles in a single layer on a sheet of foil.

4. In a medium bowl combine egg, cottage cheese, and ¼ cup of the Parmesan cheese; set aside.

5. Preheat oven to 375°F. Grease a 3-quart rectangular baking dish. Place one-third of the marinara sauce in the prepared baking dish.

Layer three of the cooked noodles on the sauce. Top with half of the roasted vegetables, one-third of the sauce, and one-third of the mozzarella cheese. Add three more noodles, all of the cottage cheese mixture, and one-third of the mozzarella cheese. Add the remaining three noodles, the remaining vegetables, the remaining sauce, and the remaining mozzarella cheese. Sprinkle with the remaining ¼ cup Parmesan cheese.

6. Cover with foil. Bake for 45 minutes Uncover; bake for 15 to 20 minutes more or until heated through.

PER SERVING: 294 cal., 15 g fat (6 g sat. fat), 45 mg chol., 724 mg sodium, 26 g carb., 3 g fiber, 16 g pro.

*Tip: Check the labels of these products carefully to be sure they do not contain added gluten.

**Tip: Do not use no-boil rice lasagna noodles.

Vegetable–Polenta Lasagna

PREP: 20 minutes   COOK: 10 minutes   CHILL: 30 minutes   BAKE: 40 minutes at 350°F   MAKES: 8 servings

2½ cups water
1½ cups gluten-free yellow cornmeal
1½ cups water
1   teaspoon salt
1   tablespoon olive oil
1   small onion, thinly sliced
4   cups fresh mushrooms, halved
¼   teaspoon salt
¼   teaspoon black pepper
2   12-ounce jars roasted red sweet peppers, drained and cut into pieces
1¼ cups 20-Minute Marinara Sauce (recipe, page 287) or purchased gluten-free marinara sauce
4   ounces mozzarella or Gouda cheese, shredded (1 cup)
    Snipped fresh Italian parsley

1. For polenta, in a medium saucepan bring the 2½ cups water to boiling. Meanwhile, in a small bowl combine cornmeal, the 1½ cups water, and the 1 teaspoon salt. Slowly add cornmeal mixture to the boiling water, stirring constantly. Cook and stir until mixture returns to boiling; reduce heat to low. Cook, uncovered, for 10 to 15 minutes or until very thick, stirring frequently. Spread evenly in an ungreased 2½- or 3-quart rectangular baking dish; cool. Cover and chill about 30 minutes or until firm.

2. Preheat oven to 350°F. In a large nonstick skillet heat oil over medium heat. Add onion; cook for 3 to 4 minutes or until tender. Add mushrooms, the ¼ teaspoon salt, and the black pepper. Cook and stir about 5 minutes or until mushrooms are tender. Remove from heat. Stir in roasted red peppers.

3. Spread marinara over chilled polenta. Top with vegetable mixture and cheese.

4. Bake, covered, for 30 minutes. Uncover and bake for 10 to 15 minutes more or until edges are bubbly. Sprinkle with parsley.

PER SERVING: 188 cal., 7 g fat (2 g sat. fat), 8 mg chol., 649 mg sodium, 27 g carb., 4 g fiber, 8 g pro.

Mashed Potato–Veggie Strata

PREP: 30 minutes
COOK: 25 minutes
BAKE: 30 minutes at 350°F
STAND: 20 minutes
MAKES: 10 servings

Nonstick cooking spray*
2¼ **pounds russet potatoes, peeled and cut up**
½ **cup roasted red sweet peppers**
1 **8-ounce container sour cream***
1 **tablespoon Homemade Pesto (recipe, page 282) or purchased gluten-free pesto**
¼ **teaspoon salt**
1 **tablespoon olive oil**
2 **medium zucchini, halved lengthwise and sliced**
1 **medium yellow summer squash, halved lengthwise and sliced**
¾ **cup chopped red sweet pepper**
¾ **cup chopped yellow sweet pepper**
¾ **cup chopped green sweet pepper**
½ **cup chopped onion**
½ **teaspoon salt**
8 **ounces cheddar cheese, shredded (2 cups)**

1. Preheat oven to 350°F. Lightly coat a 3-quart rectangular baking dish with cooking spray; set aside. In a large saucepan cook potatoes, covered, in a large amount of lightly salted boiling water for 20 to 25 minutes or until tender. Drain potatoes. Return to the hot saucepan; mash with potato masher, ricer, or mixer. Evenly spread mashed potatoes in prepared baking dish.

2. Place roasted red peppers in a blender or small food processor; blend or process until smooth. Transfer to a medium bowl. Whisk in sour cream, pesto, and the ¼ teaspoon salt until smooth. Spread over potatoes.

3. In an extra-large skillet heat oil over medium-high heat. Add zucchini, summer squash, chopped sweet peppers, and onion; cook until crisp-tender. Sprinkle with the ½ teaspoon salt. Spoon vegetables over roasted pepper layer. Sprinkle with cheese.

4. Bake, uncovered, about 30 minutes or until heated through. Let casserole stand for 20 minutes before serving.

PER SERVING: 269 cal., 14 g fat (8 g sat. fat), 36 mg chol., 598 mg sodium, 27 g carb., 4 g fiber, 9 g pro.

***Tip:** Check the labels of these products carefully to be sure they do not contain added gluten.

Vegetable-Pesto Risotto Casserole

PREP: 25 minutes
COOK: 10 minutes
BAKE: 35 minutes at 350°F
MAKES: 10 servings

- 2 tablespoons olive oil
- ½ cup finely chopped onion
- 2 cloves garlic, minced
- 1½ cups uncooked Arborio rice
- 3½ cups gluten-free chicken or vegetable broth
- ½ cup dry white wine
- 1 medium zucchini, halved lengthwise and sliced into ½-inch pieces
- 1 medium yellow summer squash, halved lengthwise and sliced into ½-inch pieces
- 1 cup fresh or frozen corn kernels
- ½ teaspoon salt
- ¼ teaspoon freshly ground black pepper
- 1 medium Japanese eggplant (about 1 pound), coarsely chopped
- 1 cup chopped roma tomatoes
- ¾ cup Homemade Pesto (recipe, page 282) or purchased gluten-free pesto
- 2 ounces Parmesan cheese, finely shredded (½ cup)

1. Preheat oven to 350°F. In a 4- to 5-quart Dutch oven heat oil over medium heat. Add onion and garlic; cook for 5 to 6 minutes or until onion is tender, stirring occasionally. Add rice. Cook and stir for 3 minutes more. Add broth and wine.

2. Bring to boiling; reduce heat. Simmer, covered, for 10 minutes. Remove from heat. Stir in zucchini, yellow squash, corn, salt, and pepper. Transfer to a shallow ungreased 3-quart baking dish.

3. Bake, covered, for 20 minutes. Stir in eggplant and tomatoes. Bake, covered, about 15 minutes more or until rice is tender but still firm. Quickly stir in pesto. Before serving, sprinkle with cheese.

PER SERVING: 284 cal., 13 g fat (3 g sat. fat), 12 mg chol., 682 mg sodium, 32 g carb., 3 g fiber, 8 g pro.

Caponata Casserole

PREP: 40 minutes
BAKE: 40 minutes at 350°F
STAND: 5 minutes
MAKES: 8 servings

Nonstick cooking spray*
2 tablespoons olive oil
1 small eggplant (about
1 pound), peeled and cut into
¾-inch pieces (2 to 3 cups)
2½ cups coarsely chopped yellow
and/or red sweet peppers
2 cups fresh button
mushrooms, coarsely
chopped
1 large onion, cut into thin
wedges
1 cup sliced celery
½ cup chopped pitted green
olives
1½ cups 20-Minute Marinara
Sauce (recipe, page 287)
or purchased gluten-free
tomato-basil pasta sauce
1 egg, lightly beaten
½ of a 15-ounce container
ricotta cheese*
5 ounces Asiago cheese, finely
shredded (1¼ cups)
¼ cup snipped fresh parsley
1 tablespoon dried Italian
seasoning, crushed*

½ teaspoon garlic powder
4 ounces sliced provolone
cheese
¼ cup pine nuts, toasted
(optional)
Snipped fresh parsley
(optional)

1. Preheat oven to 350°F. Lightly coat a 2-quart rectangular baking dish with cooking spray; set aside.

2. In an extra-large skillet heat 1 tablespoon of the oil over medium-high heat. Add eggplant; cook for 5 to 6 minutes or until tender and lightly browned, stirring occasionally. Transfer to a large bowl. Add the remaining 1 tablespoon oil to skillet. Add sweet peppers, mushrooms, onion, celery, and olives. Cook about 10 minutes or until onion is tender and liquid is evaporated, stirring occasionally. Transfer to bowl with eggplant; toss to mix. Drain off any liquid.

3. Transfer cooked vegetables to the prepared baking dish. Top with half of the marinara sauce. In a medium bowl combine egg, ricotta cheese, Asiago cheese, the ¼ cup parsley, the Italian seasoning, and garlic powder. Spoon ricotta mixture in mounds on top of marinara sauce in dish. Top with the remaining marinara sauce.

4. Bake, uncovered, for 30 minutes. Top with provolone cheese. Bake, uncovered, for 10 to 15 minutes more or until bubbly and cheese is melted. If desired, sprinkle with pine nuts and additional parsley. Let stand for 5 minutes before serving (casserole will be saucy).

PER SERVING: 274 cal., 18 g fat (9 g sat. fat), 59 mg chol., 754 mg sodium, 12 g carb., 3 g fiber, 17 g pro.

*Tip: Check the labels of these products carefully to be sure they do not contain added gluten.

Triple-Decker Tortilla Bake

PREP: 20 minutes
BAKE: 15 minutes at 450°F
MAKES: 4 servings

Nonstick cooking spray*
1 cup canned pinto beans,* rinsed and drained
1 cup gluten-free chunky salsa
4 6-inch corn tortillas*
¾ cup frozen whole kernel corn
½ cup shredded reduced-fat Mexican-style four cheese blend* (2 ounces)
½ of an avocado, halved, seeded, peeled, and chopped
1 tablespoon fresh cilantro leaves
Sour cream* (optional)

1. Preheat oven to 450°F. Lightly coat a 9-inch pie plate with cooking spray; set aside. Place beans in a small bowl; use a fork to slightly mash the beans. In a small saucepan or skillet cook and stir beans over medium heat for 2 to 3 minutes or until heated through; set aside.

2. Spoon ¼ cup of the salsa into prepared pie plate. Layer ingredients in the following order: one of the tortillas, half of the mashed beans, a second tortilla, all of the corn, ¼ cup of the cheese, ¼ cup of the salsa, a third tortilla, the remaining mashed beans, the remaining tortilla, and the remaining ½ cup salsa.

3. Cover with foil and bake about 12 minutes or until heated through. Remove foil. Sprinkle with the remaining ¼ cup cheese.

4. Bake, uncovered, about 3 minutes more or until cheese is melted. Top with avocado and cilantro. If desired, serve with sour cream.

PER SERVING: 217 cal., 7 g fat (2 g sat. fat), 9 mg chol., 734 mg sodium, 32 g carb., 7 g fiber, 10 g pro.

*Tip: Check the labels of these products carefully to be sure they do not contain added gluten.

Grilling

When you use the heat of a grill to infuse meat and veggies with smoky, flame-kissed flavor, you won't miss gluten one bit. From company-special main dishes to quick weeknight dinners, elevate grill-outs to the next level with these creative recipes.

Chicken Grillers Stuffed with Spinach and Smoked Gouda

PREP: 30 minutes   **GRILL:** 12 minutes   **MAKES:** 4 servings

⅓ cup finely chopped onion
2 cloves garlic, minced
1 tablespoon olive oil
1 cup chopped fresh mushrooms
4 ounces smoked Gouda cheese, shredded (1 cup)
½ 10-ounce package frozen chopped spinach, thawed and squeezed dry
¼ teaspoon ground nutmeg
4 skinless, boneless chicken breast halves

1. For filling, in a large skillet cook onion and garlic in hot oil over medium heat about 5 minutes or until onion is tender. Add mushrooms. Cook and stir about 5 minutes more or until mushrooms are tender. Remove from heat. Stir in cheese, spinach, and nutmeg. Set aside.

2. Using a sharp knife, cut a 2-inch pocket in the thickest part of each chicken breast half by cutting horizontally toward, but not through, the opposite side. Divide filling evenly among pockets in chicken. If necessary, secure openings with wooden toothpicks.

3. For a charcoal or gas grill, place chicken on the rack of a covered grill directly over medium heat. Grill for 12 to 15 minutes or until chicken is no longer pink (170°F), turning once halfway through grilling. Remove and discard toothpicks before serving.

PER SERVING: 328 cal., 13 g fat (6 g sat. fat), 121 mg chol., 578 mg sodium, 6 g carb., 2 g fiber, 47 g pro.

Ginger-Lemongrass Chicken with Cilantro Rice Noodles

PREP: 30 minutes
GRILL: 12 minutes
MAKES: 4 servings

¼ cup sliced green onions
¼ cup sliced fresh lemongrass
  or 1 teaspoon finely shredded
  lemon peel
2 tablespoons lime juice
2 tablespoons vegetable oil
1 tablespoon grated fresh
  ginger
6 cloves garlic
4 skinless, boneless chicken
  breast halves
1 recipe Cilantro Rice Noodles
  Lime wedges (optional)

1. For rub, in a food processor or blender combine green onions, lemongrass, lime juice, oil, ginger, and garlic. Cover and process until a thin paste forms. Spoon rub evenly over chicken; rub in with your fingers.

2. For a charcoal or gas grill, place chicken on the rack of a covered grill directly over medium heat. Grill for 12 to 15 minutes or until chicken is no longer pink (170°F), turning once halfway through grilling.

3. Slice chicken; serve over Cilantro Rice Noodles. If desired, serve with lime wedges.

PER SERVING: 541 cal., 13 g fat (2 g sat. fat), 82 mg chol., 1,670 mg sodium, 65 g carb., 2 g fiber, 39 g pro.

Cilantro Rice Noodles: In a large saucepan cook 8 ounces dried rice noodles (rice sticks) in a large amount of boiling water for 3 to 4 minutes or just until tender; drain. Meanwhile, in a large bowl combine ¼ cup fish sauce, 3 tablespoons lime juice, 2 tablespoons packed brown sugar, and 1 or 2 cloves garlic, minced, stirring until brown sugar is dissolved. Add cooked noodles, 1 cup shredded carrots, ¼ cup coarsely snipped fresh cilantro, and ¼ cup peanuts; toss gently to coat.

Jerk Chicken with Avocado-Orange Salsa

PREP: 30 minutes
GRILL: 12 minutes
MAKES: 4 servings

½ cup uncooked long grain white or brown rice
½ teaspoon cumin seeds (optional)
1 cup canned black beans, rinsed and drained*
½ cup snipped fresh cilantro
Salt
Black pepper
4 teaspoons packed brown sugar
2 teaspoons ground coffee
1½ teaspoons garlic powder
1½ teaspoons dried thyme, crushed
1½ teaspoons ground allspice
1½ teaspoons paprika
½ teaspoon cayenne pepper
8 skinless, boneless chicken thighs
1 avocado, seeded, peeled, and chopped
1 cup canned mandarin orange sections, drained
¼ cup finely chopped red onion
3 tablespoons lime juice
1 teaspoon olive oil

1. Cook rice according to package directions, adding cumin seeds (if desired) to cooking liquid. Remove from heat. Fluff rice with a fork. Stir in beans and cilantro. Season to taste with salt and black pepper; keep warm.

2. In a small bowl stir together brown sugar, ground coffee, garlic powder, thyme, allspice, paprika, and cayenne pepper. Sprinkle evenly over chicken; rub in with your fingers. Sprinkle chicken with additional salt.

3. For a charcoal or gas grill, place chicken on the rack of a covered grill directly over medium heat. Grill for 12 to 15 minutes or until no longer pink (180°F), turning once halfway through grilling.

4. For salsa, in a small bowl stir together avocado, mandarin oranges, onion, lime juice, and oil. Season to taste with additional salt and black pepper.

5. Serve chicken on rice. Spoon salsa over chicken.

PER SERVING: 409 cal., 12 g fat (2 g sat. fat), 115 mg chol., 616 mg sodium, 45 g carb., 7 g fiber, 33 g pro.

*Tip: Check the label of this product carefully to be sure it does not contain added gluten.

Mushroom, Plum, and Chicken Kabobs

PREP: 20 minutes   **GRILL:** 12 minutes   **MAKES:** 8 servings

1   **pound skinless, boneless chicken breast halves, cut into 1-inch pieces**

16   **fresh button mushrooms**

8   **green onions, cut into 2-inch pieces**

4   **firm, ripe plums or 3 peaches, cut into wedges**

¼   **cup balsamic vinegar**

2   **tablespoons canola oil**

¼   **teaspoon salt**

¼   **teaspoon freshly ground black pepper**

1. On eight 12-inch skewers* alternately thread chicken, mushrooms, green onions, and plums, leaving ¼ inch between pieces.

2. In a small bowl stir together vinegar and oil; brush onto kabobs.

3. For a charcoal or gas grill, place kabobs on the rack of a covered grill directly over medium heat. Grill, uncovered, for 12 to 15 minutes or until chicken is no longer pink (170°F), turning once. Sprinkle kabobs with salt and freshly ground black pepper.

PER SERVING: 244 cal., 8 g fat (0g sat. fat), 66 mg chol., 228 mg sodium, 14 g carb., 2 g fiber, 28 g pro.

*Tip: If using wooden skewers, soak them in enough water to cover at least 30 minutes before using.

Grilled Chicken and New Potato Salad

PREP: 25 minutes
GRILL: 12 minutes
COOK: 12 minutes
MAKES: 4 servings

12	ounces skinless, boneless chicken breast halves
¼	teaspoon salt
1	pound 2-inch round red potatoes, quartered
1	pound fresh asparagus, trimmed and cut into 2-inch pieces
1	tablespoon butter
½	cup chopped onion
½	cup thinly sliced celery
⅓	cup water
¼	cup white wine vinegar
2	tablespoons snipped fresh chives
1	tablespoon sugar
1	tablespoon gluten-free coarse ground mustard
¾	teaspoon cornstarch*
2	cups fresh baby spinach
4	slices gluten-free bacon, crisp-cooked, drained, and crumbled

1. Sprinkle chicken with ⅛ teaspoon of the salt. For a charcoal or gas grill, place chicken on the grill rack directly over medium heat. Cover and grill for 12 to 15 minutes or until no longer pink (170°F), turning once halfway through grilling. Thinly slice chicken.

2. In a covered large saucepan cook potatoes in enough gently boiling water to cover for 12 to 15 minutes or until tender, adding asparagus for the last 2 minutes of cooking. Drain well.

3. Meanwhile, for dressing, in a large skillet melt butter over medium heat. Add onion and celery; cook about 5 minutes or just until tender, stirring occasionally. In a small bowl stir together the water, vinegar, chives, sugar, mustard, cornstarch, and the remaining ⅛ teaspoon salt. Add to dressing. Cook and stir until thickened and bubbly.

4. Gently stir the chicken, potatoes, and asparagus into dressing in skillet. Cook, stirring gently, for 1 to 2 minutes more or until heated through. Stir in spinach and bacon before serving.

PER SERVING: 293 cal., 6 g fat (2 g sat. fat), 64 mg chol., 608 mg sodium, 30 g carb., 6 g fiber, 29 g pro.

***Tip:** Check the label of this product carefully to be sure it does not contain added gluten.

Chicken Kabobs and Grilled Pineapple

PREP: 30 minutes
GRILL: 10 minutes
MAKES: 4 servings

- ⅔ **cup gluten-free sweet-and-sour sauce***
- 2 **tablespoons snipped fresh Thai basil or basil**
- 1 **teaspoon Thai seasoning** or Chinese five-spice powder****
- 1 **clove garlic, minced**
- 1 **tablespoon packed brown sugar (optional)**
- 1 **tablespoon butter, melted**
- 1 **small fresh pineapple Vegetable oil**
- 1 **pound skinless, boneless chicken breast halves, cut into 1-inch pieces**
- 2 **cups hot cooked rice (optional)**

1. For Thai sauce, in a small bowl combine sweet-and-sour sauce, snipped basil, Thai seasoning, and garlic. Reserve ¼ cup of the sauce to use for basting. Stir brown sugar (if desired) and melted butter into the remaining sauce; cover and set aside.

2. Cut ends off pineapple. Cut pineapple in half lengthwise; cut each half crosswise into four slices. Brush pineapple with oil. Set aside.

3. Thread chicken onto four 10- to 12-inch skewers,*** leaving ¼ inch between pieces.

4. For a charcoal or gas grill, place kabobs on the rack of a covered grill directly over medium heat. Grill for 10 to 12 minutes or until chicken is no longer pink (170°F), turning occasionally and brushing with the ¼ cup reserved sauce during the first half of grilling. Discard any remaining basting sauce. Grill pineapple slices alongside kabobs for 6 to 8 minutes or until warm and grill marks appear, turning once halfway through grilling.

5. Serve chicken and pineapple with the reserved Thai sauce and, if desired, hot cooked rice.

PER SERVING: 269 cal., 5 g fat (2 g sat. fat), 73 mg chol., 333 mg sodium, 29 g carb., 1 g fiber, 27 g pro.

***Tip:** Bottled sweet-and-sour sauces vary in sweetness and thickness. With less sweet sauce, add the brown sugar. With thick sweet-and-sour sauce, adjust the consistency of the Thai sauce by adding a little water.

****Tip:** Check the labels of these products carefully to be sure they do not contain added gluten.

*****Tip:** If using wooden skewers, soak them in enough water to cover for at least 30 minutes before using.

Beef and Asparagus with Caramelized Onion Aïoli

PREP: 30 minutes   MARINATE: 1 hour   GRILL: 12 minutes   MAKES: 4 servings

1 pound beef flank steak
1 recipe Tare Sauce
1 tablespoon olive oil
½ cup chopped onion
⅓ cup mayonnaise*
2 tablespoons lime juice
1 tablespoon snipped fresh parsley
1 tablespoon grated Parmesan cheese*
¼ teaspoon black pepper
1 pound fresh asparagus spears, trimmed
1 tablespoon vegetable oil
  Snipped fresh parsley
  Toasted sesame seeds

1. Thinly slice meat across the grain into long strips. Place meat in a resealable plastic bag set in a shallow dish. Add ½ cup of the Tare Sauce. Seal bag; turn to coat meat. Marinate in the refrigerator for 1 to 12 hours, turning bag occasionally. Cover and chill the remaining Tare Sauce until needed.

2. Meanwhile, for aïoli, in a medium skillet heat olive oil over medium-low heat. Add onion. Cook, covered, for 13 to 15 minutes or until onion is tender, stirring occasionally. Cook, uncovered, over medium-high heat for 3 to 5 minutes or until onion is golden, stirring frequently. Transfer to a small bowl; cool. Stir in mayonnaise, lime juice, 1 tablespoon parsley, Parmesan cheese, and pepper. Cover and chill until ready to serve.

3. For kabobs, drain meat, discarding marinade. On eight 10- to 12-inch skewers** thread meat accordion-style, leaving ¼ inch between each piece.

4. Place asparagus in a shallow dish. Drizzle with 1 tablespoon of the remaining Tare Sauce and the vegetable oil; toss to coat.

5. For a charcoal or gas grill, place asparagus perpendicular to wires of a rack of an uncovered grill, directly over medium heat. Grill about 7 minutes or until asparagus is crisp-tender, turning occasionally. Remove from grill; cover to keep warm. Place kabobs on grill rack. Grill for 5 to 6 minutes or until meat is slightly pink in center, turning and brushing once with the remaining Tare Sauce halfway through grilling.

6. Sprinkle kabobs, asparagus, and aïoli with additional parsley and sesame seeds. Serve kabobs and asparagus with aïoli.

Tare Sauce: In a small saucepan combine 1 cup gluten-free chicken or beef broth; ½ cup sweet rice wine (mirin); ¼ cup gluten-free, reduced-sodium soy sauce; 3 tablespoons sugar; 1 tablespoon grated fresh ginger; 6 cloves garlic, minced; 1 teaspoon fish sauce; and ½ teaspoon black pepper. Bring to boiling; reduce heat. Simmer, uncovered, for 25 to 30 minutes or until reduced to 1 cup; cool. Strain sauce through a fine-mesh sieve; discard solids. Store, covered, in the refrigerator for up to 3 weeks.

PER SERVING: 461 cal., 30 g fat (7 g sat. fat), 61 mg chol., 800 mg sodium, 20 g carb., 3 g fiber, 29 g pro.

*Tip: Check the labels of these products carefully to be sure they do not contain added gluten.

**Tip: If using wooden skewers, soak in enough water to cover for at least 30 minutes before using.

Fontina-Stuffed Meatball Kabobs

PREP: 30 minutes
GRILL: 10 minutes
MAKES: 6 servings

1 egg, lightly beaten
⅓ cup grated Parmesan cheese*
2 cloves garlic, minced
1 teaspoon dried Italian seasoning, crushed*
½ teaspoon salt
⅛ teaspoon black pepper
1½ pounds lean ground beef
2 ounces gluten-free thinly sliced prosciutto, chopped
16 ½-inch cubes Fontina cheese (1½ ounces)
8 canned artichoke hearts, drained and halved lengthwise
1 8-ounce package fresh cremini mushrooms
2 cups grape tomatoes
1 recipe Balsamic Glaze Fresh basil (optional)

1. In a large bowl combine egg, Parmesan cheese, garlic, Italian seasoning, salt, and pepper. Add ground beef and prosciutto; mix well. Divide meat mixture into 16 portions. Form each portion around a Fontina cheese cube to make a meatball. For kabobs, on sixteen 8- to 10-inch skewers** thread meatballs, artichokes, mushrooms, and tomatoes, leaving a ¼ inch space between pieces. Prepare Balsamic Glaze; set aside.

2. For charcoal or gas grill, place kabobs on the grill rack of a covered grill directly over medium heat. Grill for 10 to 12 minutes or until meatballs are done (160°F), turning once and brushing with half of the Balsamic Glaze halfway through grilling.

3. To serve, drizzle kabobs with the remaining glaze. If desired, garnish with basil.

Balsamic Glaze: In a small saucepan combine ⅓ cup balsamic vinegar; 2 teaspoons olive oil; 1 clove garlic, minced; ¼ teaspoon salt; ¼ teaspoon dried Italian seasoning,* crushed; and ⅛ teaspoon black pepper. Bring to boiling; reduce heat. Simmer, uncovered, about 4 minutes or until reduced to about ¼ cup.

PER SERVING: 269 cal., 15 g fat (5 g sat. fat), 91 mg chol., 673 mg sodium, 8 g carb., 2 g fiber, 24 g pro.

*Tip: Check the labels of these products carefully to be sure they do not contain added gluten.

**Tip: If using wooden skewers, soak them in enough water to cover for at least 30 minutes before using.

Tri-Tip Roast with Grilled Avocados

PREP: 25 minutes
GRILL: 35 minutes + 10 minutes
STAND: 15 minutes
MAKES: 6 servings

1 **cup California red oak or oak wood chips**
1 **tablespoon kosher salt**
1 **tablespoon granulated garlic**
1 **teaspoon onion powder**
1 **teaspoon black pepper**
1 **teaspoon dried parsley flakes**
1 **pound boneless beef tri-tip roast (bottom sirloin roast)**
1 **recipe Red Wine Vinegar Baste**
3 **tablespoons olive oil**
2 **tablespoons lemon juice**
3 **firm medium avocados, halved and seeded**
  Purchased gluten-free pico de gallo (optional)

1. Soak wood chips in enough water to cover for 1 hour. For the rub, in a small bowl combine the salt, garlic, onion powder, pepper, and parsley flakes.

2. Trim fat from roast. Place roast in a shallow dish. Generously sprinkle rub evenly over all sides of the roast; rub in with your fingers.

3. For a charcoal grill, arrange medium-hot coals around a drip pan. Drain wood chips and sprinkle over the coals. Test for medium heat above pan. Place roast on grill rack over pan. Cover and grill to desired doneness, turning once halfway through grilling and brushing with the Red Wine Vinegar Baste three times during the first 30 minutes of grilling. Allow 35 to 40 minutes for medium rare (135°F) or 40 to 45 minutes for medium (150°F). (For a gas grill, preheat grill. Reduce heat to medium. Adjust for indirect cooking. Add wood chips according to the manufacturer's directions. Place roast on grill rack over the burner that is turned off. Grill as directed.) Discard any remaining Red Wine Vinegar Baste.

4. Remove roast from grill. Cover roast with foil; let stand for 15 minutes.

5. Meanwhile, in a small bowl combine oil and lemon juice; brush over cut sides of avocados. Sprinkle with additional salt. Grill avocado halves about 10 minutes or until grill marks form, turning once halfway through grilling.

6. Cut roast diagonally against the grain. Peel and slice avocados; serve with meat. If desired, top with pico de gallo.

Red Wine Vinegar Baste: In a small bowl whisk together ¼ cup red wine vinegar, ¼ cup olive oil, and 6 cloves garlic, minced.

PER SERVING: 511 cal., 39 g fat (8 g sat. fat), 98 mg chol., 1,131 mg sodium, 8 g carb., 5 g fiber, 33 g pro.

Argentinean Rolled Flank Steak

PREP: 40 minutes   **GRILL:** 40 minutes   **STAND:** 10 minutes   **MAKES:** 6 servings

1   1¼- to 1½-pound beef flank
    steak
2   medium Anaheim peppers,
    chopped (see tip, page 21)
½   cup chopped sweet onion
2   cloves garlic, minced
1   tablespoon vegetable oil
1   tablespoon snipped fresh
    oregano
½   teaspoon salt
¼   teaspoon black pepper
4   ounces gluten-free sliced
    Black Forest ham or gluten-
    free cooked ham
2   ounces Fontina cheese,
    shredded (½ cup)
12 corn tortillas,* warmed**
1   recipe Chimichurri Sauce
    Grilled vegetables (optional)

1. Score both sides of steak in a diamond pattern by making shallow diagonal cuts at 1-inch intervals. Place steak between two pieces of plastic wrap. Using the flat side of a meat mallet, pound steak lightly to about ¼-inch thickness, working from the center to the edges (about a 12×8-inch rectangle). Discard plastic wrap.

2. In a large skillet cook Anaheim peppers, onion, and garlic in hot oil over medium heat about 3 minutes or until tender. Stir in oregano, salt, and pepper.

3. Arrange ham slices evenly over the steak. Spread pepper mixture over the ham. Sprinkle with cheese. Starting from a long side, roll meat into a spiral. Tie in three or four places with heavy 100%-cotton kitchen string.

4. For a charcoal grill, arrange medium-hot coals around a drip pan. Test for medium heat above the pan. Place rolled flank steak on grill rack over pan. Cover and grill for 40 to 45 minutes or until thermometer registers 150°F, tuning once halfway through grilling. (For a gas grill, preheat grill. Reduce heat to medium. Adjust for indirect cooking. Place rolled steak on grill rack over the burner that is turned off. Grill as directed.)

5. Remove steak roll. Cover with foil; let stand for 10 minutes. (Meat temperature after standing should be 155°F.) Remove string. Cut steak roll crosswise into 1-inch slices. Serve with tortillas, Chimichurri Sauce, and, if desired, grilled vegetables.

Chimichurri Sauce: In a food processor or blender combine 1¼ cups fresh Italian parsley leaves, ¼ cup olive oil, 1 medium shallot, 2 tablespoons fresh oregano leaves, 2 tablespoons red wine vinegar, 1 tablespoon lemon juice, 4 cloves garlic, ½ teaspoon salt, and ½ teaspoon crushed red pepper. Cover and process just until chopped and a few parsley leaves are still visible. Cover and chill for 2 hours before serving.

PER SERVING: 631 cal., 28 g fat (7 g sat. fat), 61 mg chol., 1,273 mg sodium, 58 g carb., 1 g fiber, 36 g pro.

*Tip: Check the label of this product carefully to be sure it does not contain added gluten.

**Tip: If desired, wrap tortillas in foil and place on side of grill rack for 10 minutes to warm, turning once.

Cuban-Style Pork Roast

PREP: 15 minutes
MARINATE: 3 hours
GRILL: 45 minutes
STAND: 15 minutes
MAKES: 4 servings

- 1 1½-pound boneless pork top loin roast (single loin)
- ½ cup orange juice
- 3 tablespoons lemon juice
- 1 tablespoon gluten-free soy sauce or tamari
- 4 cloves garlic, minced
- 1 teaspoon dried oregano, crushed
- ½ teaspoon salt
- ¼ teaspoon black pepper
- 1 recipe Grilled Plantains and Sweet Potatoes (optional)

1. Trim the fat from pork. Place pork in a large resealable plastic bag set in a shallow dish. For marinade, in a small bowl whisk together orange juice, lemon juice, soy sauce, garlic, oregano, salt, and pepper. Pour marinade over pork; seal bag. Marinate in the refrigerator for 3 to 6 hours, turning bag occasionally. Drain pork, discarding marinade.

2. For a charcoal grill, arrange medium-hot coals around a drip pan. Test for medium heat above the pan. Place pork, fat side up, on grill rack over drip pan. Cover and grill for 45 to 60 minutes or until a thermometer registers 150°F. (For a gas grill, preheat grill. Reduce heat to medium. Adjust for indirect cooking. Place pork on grill rack over burner that is turned off. Grill as directed.) Remove pork from grill. Cover and let stand for 15 minutes. If desired, prepare Grilled Plantains and Sweet Potatoes while roast stands.

PER SERVING: 217 cal., 11 g fat (4 g sat. fat), 82 mg chol., 162 mg sodium, 1 g carb., 0 g fiber, 27 g pro.

Grilled Plantains and Sweet Potatoes: Bias-cut 2 to 3 ripe plantains into ½-inch slices or cut four to six ½-inch slices from a peeled and cored pineapple. Cut 2 medium sweet potatoes into ½- to ¾-inch slices. Brush fruit, sweet potatoes, and 6 to 8 green banana peppers with vegetable oil; sprinkle with salt and black pepper. For a charcoal or gas grill, place sweet potatoes on the rack of a covered grill directly over medium heat. Grill for 6 minutes. Turn sweet potatoes. Add plantain or pineapple and banana peppers to grill rack. Grill for 6 to 8 minutes more or until sweet potato and plantain centers are soft and pineapple and peppers are heated through, turning once halfway through grilling. Serve warm.

Grilled Pork and Pineapple

PREP: 15 minutes
GRILL: 6 minutes
STAND: 3 minutes
MAKES: 4 servings

1 fresh pineapple, peeled and cored
4 boneless top loin pork chops, cut ¾ inch thick
  Salt
  Black pepper
3 tablespoons orange marmalade*
½ cup plain Greek yogurt*
2 teaspoons snipped fresh thyme

1. Cut pineapple into ½-inch slices; set aside. Trim fat from pork chops. Sprinkle chops lightly with salt and pepper.

2. For a charcoal or gas grill, place chops on the rack of a covered grill directly over medium heat. Grill for 4 minutes. Turn chops; add pineapple to grill rack. Brush chops and pineapple with 2 tablespoons of the marmalade. Grill for 2 to 4 minutes more or until a thermometer registers 145°F, turning pineapple halfway through grilling. Remove pork and pineapple from grill; let stand for 3 minutes.

3. Meanwhile, for sauce, in a small bowl combine yogurt and the remaining 1 tablespoon marmalade. Arrange pineapple and chops on plates. Sprinkle with thyme; serve with sauce.

PER SERVING: 301 cal., 6 g fat (3 g sat. fat), 97 mg chol., 220 mg sodium, 27 g carb., 2 g fiber, 35 g pro.

*Tip: Check the labels of these products carefully to be sure they do not contain added gluten.

Smoked Pork Chops with Onion-Blackberry Relish

PREP: 20 minutes
STAND: 1 hour
GRILL: 5 minutes
MAKES: 6 servings

2 cups coarsely chopped Vidalia, Walla Walla, or other sweet onions
1 cup water
¼ teaspoon salt
2 tablespoons red wine vinegar
1 canned gluten-free chipotle chile pepper in adobo sauce, chopped
¼ teaspoon salt
1 cup fresh blackberries or raspberries
6 gluten-free cooked smoked boneless pork chops
¼ cup snipped fresh Italian parsley
¼ cup sliced green onions
 Fresh Italian parsley sprigs (optional)

1. In a small saucepan combine onions, the water, and ¼ teaspoon salt. Bring to boiling; reduce heat. Simmer, uncovered, for 3 minutes; drain. Cool slightly.

2. For relish, in a serving bowl whisk together vinegar, chipotle pepper, and ¼ teaspoon salt. Stir in the onions and blackberries. If desired, cover and chill up to 24 hours. Let stand at room temperature for 1 hour before serving.

3. For a charcoal or gas grill, place chops on the rack of an uncovered grill directly over medium heat. Grill about 5 minutes or until heated through, turning once halfway through grilling.

4. To serve, stir the snipped parsley and the green onions into relish. Serve chops with relish. If desired, garnish with parsley sprigs.

PER SERVING: 198 cal., 7 g fat (2 g sat. fat), 60 mg chol., 1,752 mg sodium, 13 g carb., 3 g fiber, 21 g pro.

Grilled Mahi Mahi with Pineapple Green Rice

PREP: 25 minutes
MARINATE: 15 minutes
COOK: 20 minutes
STAND: 5 minutes
GRILL: 4 minutes per ½-inch thickness
MAKES: 4 servings

- 4 4- to 5-ounce fresh or frozen skinless mahi mahi fillets
- ¾ teaspoon kosher salt
- ⅛ teaspoon black pepper
- 1 cup Salsa Verde (recipe, page 289) or purchased gluten-free salsa verde
- 2 tablespoons mayonnaise*
- 1 to 2 tablespoons lime juice
- 1 tablespoon vegetable oil
- ½ cup chopped onion
- ½ cup chopped green sweet pepper
- 2 cloves garlic, minced
- 1½ cups gluten-free vegetable or chicken broth
- 1 cup uncooked long grain white rice
- ⅔ cup chopped fresh pineapple
- ½ cup snipped fresh cilantro
- 1 large tomato, cut into wedges and seasoned with salt and pepper
  Lime wedges

1. Thaw fish, if frozen. Rinse fish; pat dry with paper towels. Measure thickness of fish. Sprinkle fish with ¼ teaspoon of the salt and the black pepper. Place fish in a resealable plastic bag set in a shallow dish. In a small bowl combine ¼ cup of the salsa verde, the mayonnaise, and lime juice; add to bag. Seal bag; turn to coat fish. Marinate in the refrigerator for 15 minutes.

2. Meanwhile, in a medium saucepan heat the oil over medium heat. Add onion, sweet pepper, and the remaining ½ teaspoon salt; cook for 2 minutes. Add the garlic; cook 30 seconds more. Stir in broth and the remaining ¾ cup salsa verde; bring to boiling. Stir in rice; reduce heat to low. Simmer, covered, for 20 to 25 minutes or until rice is tender.

3. Remove saucepan from heat; remove lid. Cover saucepan with a clean kitchen towel; replace lid. Let stand for 5 minutes to let the towel absorb any excess moisture. Remove lid and towel. Add pineapple and cilantro, fluffing with a fork; keep warm.

4. For a charcoal or gas grill, place fish on the greased rack of a covered grill directly over medium heat. Grill until fish flakes when tested with a fork (allow 4 to 6 minutes per ½-inch thickness of fish). Serve fish with the pineapple green rice, tomato wedges, and lime wedges.

PER SERVING: 414 cal., 11 g fat (2 g sat. fat), 85 mg chol., 1,228 mg sodium, 53 g carb., 4 g fiber, 26 g pro.

***Tip:** Check the label of this product carefully to be sure it does not contain added gluten.

Catfish with Black Bean and Avocado Relish

PREP: 20 minutes
GRILL: 4 minutes
MAKES: 6 servings

6 4- to 5-ounce fresh or frozen catfish fillets, about ½ inch thick
1 teaspoon finely shredded lime peel
3 tablespoons lime juice
2 tablespoons snipped fresh cilantro
2 tablespoons snipped fresh oregano
2 tablespoons finely chopped green onion
1 tablespoon olive oil
¼ teaspoon salt
¼ teaspoon cayenne pepper
1 15-ounce can black beans, rinsed and drained*
1 medium avocado, halved, seeded, peeled, and diced
½ cup chopped tomato
Lime wedges
Fresh cilantro sprigs (optional)

1. Thaw fish, if frozen. Rinse fish; pat dry with paper towels. Set aside.

2. For relish, in a small bowl stir together lime peel, lime juice, the snipped cilantro, oregano, green onion, olive oil, salt, and cayenne pepper. In a medium bowl combine beans, avocado, and tomato; stir in half of the cilantro mixture. Cover and chill until serving time.

3. For a charcoal or gas grill, grill fish on the greased rack of an uncovered grill directly over medium heat for 4 to 6 minutes or until fish flakes when tested with a fork, turning once and brushing with the remaining cilantro mixture halfway through grilling. Discard any remaining cilantro mixture. Serve fish with relish and lime wedges. If desired, garnish with cilantro sprigs.

PER SERVING: 273 cal., 15 g fat (3 g sat. fat), 53 mg chol., 337 mg sodium, 14 g carb., 6 g fiber, 23 g pro.

***Tip:** Check the label of this product carefully to be sure it does not contain added gluten.

Thai-Style Sea Bass

PREP: 25 minutes
MARINATE: 1 hour
GRILL: 4 minutes per ½-inch thickness
MAKES: 4 servings

- 4 5- to 6-ounce fresh or frozen skinless sea bass fillets
- ¼ teaspoon salt
- ½ cup lime juice
- 2 tablespoons fish sauce or gluten-free soy sauce
- 1 tablespoon toasted sesame oil
- 1 teaspoon sugar
- 1 teaspoon grated fresh ginger
- ¼ teaspoon crushed red pepper
- 1 tablespoon minced fresh garlic
- 2 cups hot cooked rice noodles or rice
  Snipped fresh cilantro (optional)

1. Thaw fish, if frozen. Rinse fish; pat dry with paper towels. Measure thickness of fish. Sprinkle fish with salt. Place fish in a large resealable plastic bag set in a shallow dish; set aside.

2. For marinade, in a small bowl stir together lime juice, fish sauce, sesame oil, sugar, ginger, crushed red pepper, and garlic. Pour half of the marinade over fish in bag; seal bag. Turn to coat fish. Marinate in the refrigerator for 1 hour, turning bag occasionally. Chill the remaining marinade.

3. Drain fish, discarding marinade. For a charcoal or gas grill, place fish on the greased rack of an uncovered grill directly over medium coals. Grill until fish flakes when tested with a fork (allow 4 to 6 minutes per ½-inch thickness of fish).

4. Serve fish with rice noodles. Drizzle the reserved marinade over fish and noodles. If desired, sprinkle with cilantro.

PER SERVING: 270 cal., 6 g fat (1 g sat. fat), 58 mg chol., 781 mg sodium, 26 g carb., 1 g fiber, 28 g pro.

Salmon-Pepper Kabobs with Mango-Avocado Salsa

PREP: 35 minutes   **GRILL:** 10 minutes   **MAKES:** 4 servings

1½ pounds fresh or frozen skinless salmon fillets
 8 miniature sweet peppers, halved lengthwise and seeded
 8 green onions, cut into 2-inch pieces
 ½ cup pineapple marmalade* or preserves*
 1 tablespoon unsweetened pineapple juice
 ½ teaspoon ground ginger
 1 tablespoon rum or unsweetened pineapple juice
 1 cup chopped fresh mango
 1 cup chopped avocado
 ½ cup chopped red sweet pepper
 ¼ cup finely chopped red onion
 ¼ cup snipped fresh cilantro
 2 tablespoons lime juice
 1 small fresh jalapeño chile pepper, seeded and finely chopped (see tip, page 21)
   Salt
   Roasted pumpkin seeds (pepitas) (optional)

1. Thaw salmon, if frozen. Rinse salmon; pat dry with paper towels. Cut into 2-inch pieces. On four 12-inch skewers** alternately thread salmon, sweet peppers, and green onions, leaving ¼ inch between pieces.

2. For glaze, snip any large pieces of fruit in marmalade. In a small saucepan combine marmalade, 1 tablespoon pineapple juice, and ginger. Cook and stir over medium heat until bubbly. Remove from heat; stir in rum.

3. For a charcoal or gas grill, place salmon kabobs on the rack of an uncovered grill directly over medium heat. Grill for 10 to 14 minutes or until salmon flakes when tested with a fork, turning occasionally to cook evenly and brushing with glaze for the last 2 minutes of grilling.

4. For salsa, in a small bowl combine mango, avocado, sweet pepper, onion, cilantro, lime juice, and jalapeño pepper. Season to taste with salt.

5. If desired, sprinkle salmon kabobs with pumpkin seeds. Serve with salsa.

PER SERVING: 511 cal., 20 g fat (3 g sat. fat), 94 mg chol., 257 mg sodium, 47 g carb., 8 g fiber, 37 g pro.

*Tip: Check the labels of these products carefully to be sure they do not contain added gluten.

**Tip: If using wooden skewers, soak in water for at least 30 minutes before using.

Barbecued Salmon with Fresh Nectarine Salsa

START TO FINISH: 20 minutes
MAKES: 4 servings

4   **4- to 5-ounce fresh or frozen skinless salmon fillets, about 1 inch thick**
   Salt
   Black pepper
3   **tablespoons Kansas City Barbecue Sauce (recipe, page 290) or purchased gluten-free barbecue sauce**
1½ **cups chopped nectarines**
¾ **cup fresh blueberries**
¼ **cup coarsely chopped pecans, toasted***
   Lemon wedges

1. Thaw salmon, if frozen. Rinse salmon; pat dry with paper towels. Lightly sprinkle salmon with salt and pepper. Place 2 tablespoons of the barbecue sauce in a small bowl; brush sauce onto both sides of the salmon.

2. For a charcoal or gas grill, place salmon on the greased rack of a covered grill directly over medium heat. Grill for 8 to 12 minutes or until salmon flakes when tested with a fork, turning once halfway through grilling.

3. For nectarine salsa, in a medium bowl combine nectarines, blueberries, toasted pecans, and the remaining 1 tablespoon barbecue sauce. Season to taste with salt. Serve salmon with salsa and lemon wedges.

PER SERVING: 318 cal., 17 g fat (3 g sat. fat), 66 mg chol., 344 mg sodium, 17 g carb., 3 g fiber, 24 g pro.

***Tip:** To toast nuts, preheat oven to 350°F. Spread nuts in a shallow baking pan. Bake for 5 to 10 minutes or until lightly browned, shaking the pan once or twice. Watch carefully to prevent nuts from burning.

Grilled Cod with Red Pepper Sauce

PREP: 30 minutes
GRILL: 4 minutes per ½-inch thickness
MAKES: 4 servings

4   **4- to 6-ounce fresh or frozen skinless cod fillets**
1¼   **cups chopped red sweet peppers**
2   **tablespoons olive oil**
1   **cup chopped, seeded, peeled tomatoes**
2   **tablespoons white wine vinegar**
¼   **teaspoon salt**
    Dash cayenne pepper
1   **tablespoon snipped fresh basil or oregano or ½ teaspoon dried basil or oregano, crushed**
    Red and/or yellow cherry tomatoes (optional)
    Fresh basil or oregano sprigs (optional)

1. Thaw fish, if frozen. Rinse fish; pat dry with paper towels. Measure thickness of fish; set aside.

2. For sauce, in a small skillet cook sweet peppers in 1 tablespoon of the oil over medium heat for 3 to 5 minutes or until tender, stirring occasionally. Stir in chopped tomatoes, 1 tablespoon of the vinegar, the salt, and cayenne pepper. Cook about 5 minutes or until tomatoes are softened, stirring occasionally. Cool slightly. Transfer to a blender or food processor. Cover and blend or process until smooth. Return sauce to skillet; cover and keep warm.

3. In a small bowl stir together the remaining 1 tablespoon oil, remaining 1 tablespoon vinegar, and the snipped fresh or dried basil; brush over both sides of fish. Place fish in a greased grill basket, tucking under any thin edges.

4. For a charcoal or gas grill, place fish in basket on the rack of an uncovered grill directly over medium heat. Grill until fish flakes when tested with a fork, turning basket once halfway through grilling (allow 4 to 6 minutes per ½-inch thickness of fish).

5. Serve fish with sauce. If desired, serve with cherry tomatoes and fresh basil sprigs.

PER SERVING: 194 cal., 8 g fat (1 g sat. fat), 41 mg chol., 223 mg sodium, 4 g carb., 1 g fiber, 26 g pro.

Shrimp-Olive Skewers with Orange Compote and Fennel

PREP: 30 minutes **GRILL:** 10 minutes **MAKES:** 4 servings

32 **fresh or frozen large shrimp in shells (about 1¾ pounds total)**
 1 **navel orange, quartered**
 ½ **cup sugar**
 ¼ **teaspoon salt**
 1 **tablespoon snipped fresh fennel leaves or tarragon**
32 **pimiento-stuffed green olives**
    Olive oil
    Salt
    Black pepper
 2 **large fennel bulbs, each cut into 8 wedges**
    Fresh tarragon (optional)

1. Thaw shrimp, if frozen. Peel and devein shrimp, leaving tails intact if desired. Rinse shrimp; pat dry with paper towels. Cover and chill until needed.

2. For orange compote, place orange quarters in a food processor. Cover and process with on/off pulses until finely chopped. Transfer to a medium saucepan. Stir in sugar and ¼ teaspoon salt. Cook over medium-low heat about 15 minutes or until thickened, stirring frequently. Remove from heat. Stir in 1 tablespoon snipped fennel or tarragon; set aside.

3. On four 12- to 15-inch skewers* alternately thread shrimp and olives, allowing a ¼ inch between pieces. Brush lightly with oil; sprinkle with additional salt and pepper. Brush fennel wedges lightly with oil; sprinkle with additional salt and pepper.

4. For a charcoal or gas grill, place fennel wedges on the rack of the uncovered grill directly over medium heat. Grill for 10 to 12 minutes or just until fennel is tender, turning once halfway through grilling. Add shrimp kabobs to the grill for the last 5 to 8 minutes of grilling or until shrimp are opaque, turning once.

5. If desired, sprinkle shrimp kabobs, fennel wedges, and orange compote with additional tarragon. Serve shrimp and fennel with orange compote.

PER SERVING: 240 cal., 6 g fat (1 g sat. fat), 71 mg chol., 884 mg sodium, 39 g carb., 5 g fiber, 10 g pro.

***Tip:** If using wooden skewers, soak in enough water to cover for at least 30 minutes before using.

Grilled Eggplant Stacks with Basil Chiffonade

PREP: 25 minutes
COOL: 1 hour
GRILL: 8 minutes
MAKES: 5 servings

½ cup extra-virgin olive oil
½ cup packed fresh basil leaves
1 large eggplant, cut crosswise into ½-inch slices (10 to 12 slices)
½ teaspoon salt
½ teaspoon black pepper
1 19-ounce can cannellini (white kidney) beans,* rinsed and drained
4 ounces feta cheese, crumbled
½ teaspoon finely shredded lemon peel
2 tablespoons lemon juice
1 clove garlic, minced
½ cup roasted red sweet peppers, cut into bite-size strips
¼ cup fresh basil leaves

1. For basil-infused olive oil, in a blender combine olive oil and the ½ cup basil leaves. Cover and blend until finely chopped. Transfer to a small saucepan. Cook over medium heat just until bubbles appear around the edges. Remove from heat. Cool to room temperature, about 1 hour. Strain oil. Brush eggplant slices with 2 tablespoons of the basil-infused olive oil. Sprinkle with the salt and pepper.

2. For a charcoal or gas grill, place eggplant slices on a grill rack directly over medium-high heat. Grill for 8 to 10 minutes or until very tender and lightly charred, turning frequently.

3. In a blender or food processor combine beans, feta cheese, lemon peel, lemon juice, 2 tablespoons of the basil-infused olive oil, and the garlic. Cover and blend or process just until combined but still chunky. Season to taste with salt and pepper.

4. Arrange eggplant slices on plates. Top with bean mixture and roasted pepper strips. Drizzle with the remaining 1 tablespoon basil-infused olive oil.** For basil chiffonade, roll up basil leaves and cut across the roll; sprinkle over eggplant stacks.

PER SERVING: 302 cal., 19 g fat (5 g sat. fat), 20 mg chol., 771 mg sodium, 27 g carb., 10 g fiber, 11 g pro.

*Tip: Check the label of this product carefully to be sure it does not contain added gluten.

**Tip: Store leftover basil-infused olive oil in a covered container in the refrigerator up to 3 days.

Grilled Summer Squash Caprese

PREP: 20 minutes
GRILL: 6 minutes
MAKES: 12 servings

- 3 **pounds yellow summer squash, cut lengthwise into ¼-inch slices**
- 5 **tablespoons olive oil**
- 1 **teaspoon salt**
- ½ **teaspoon freshly ground black pepper**
- 1 **pint grape or cherry tomatoes, halved**
- ½ **cup fresh small basil leaves**

1. Brush both sides of squash slices with 3 tablespoons of the oil; sprinkle with salt and pepper.

2. For a charcoal or gas grill, place squash, on the rack of a covered grill directly over medium heat. Grill about 6 minutes or until crisp-tender, turning once halfway through grilling.

3. On a platter arrange squash, tomatoes, and basil. Drizzle the remaining 2 tablespoons oil over vegetables just before serving.

PER SERVING: 80 cal., 6 g fat (1 g sat. fat), 0 mg chol., 200 mg sodium, 6 g carb., 2 g fiber, 1 g pro.

Grilled Squash and Manchego Quesadillas with Nectarine-Tomato Salsa

PREP: 40 minutes   **GRILL:** 10 minutes   **MAKES:** 8 servings

1½ cups chopped firm, ripe nectarines
 1 cup chopped, seeded tomatoes
 ½ cup snipped fresh cilantro
 ¼ cup finely chopped onion
 3 tablespoons lime juice
 1 fresh jalapeño or serrano chile pepper, seeded and finely chopped (see tip, page 21)
 2 to 3 teaspoons green hot pepper sauce*
 ¾ teaspoon kosher salt
12 ounces yellow summer squash and/or zucchini Nonstick cooking spray*
 ¼ teaspoon dried oregano, crushed
 ¼ teaspoon black pepper
12 6-inch corn tortillas*
 3 ounces Manchego or aged white cheddar cheese, shredded (¾ cup)
 ¼ cup light sour cream* Fresh cilantro sprigs (optional)

1. For nectarine-tomato salsa, in a medium bowl combine nectarines, tomatoes, the ½ cup cilantro, the onion, lime juice, chile pepper, hot pepper sauce, and ½ teaspoon of the salt; set aside.

2. Cut squash lengthwise into about ⅓-inch slices. Coat squash with cooking spray; sprinkle with the remaining ¼ teaspoon salt, the oregano, and black pepper.

3. For a charcoal or gas grill, place squash slices on the rack of a covered grill directly over medium heat. Grill about 7 minutes or until squash is crisp-tender, turning once halfway through grilling. Coarsely chop squash.

4. Place six of the tortillas on a work surface. Divide squash among tortillas; sprinkle with cheese. Top with the remaining tortillas, pressing firmly. Coat tortillas with cooking spray.

5. Place filled tortillas on the grill rack. Grill for 3 to 5 minutes or until golden and crisp, turning once halfway through grilling. Cut quesadillas into quarters. Serve with nectarine-tomato salsa and sour cream. If desired, garnish with cilantro sprigs.

PER SERVING: 160 cal., 5 g fat (2 g sat. fat), 13 mg chol., 287 mg sodium, 24 g carb., 4 g fiber, 6 g pro.

*Tip: Check the labels of these products carefully to be sure they do not contain added gluten.

Main-Dish Salads

Big, hearty salads are popular dinner choices for those on a gluten-free diet, but it's not always easy to think up new combinations. Whether you're in the mood for a Mexican-style toss-together or an elegant seafood salad, let these fresh recipes inspire your next one-bowl meal.

Chicken, Pineapple, Avocado, and Rice Salad

START TO FINISH: 30 minutes   **MAKES:** 4 servings

5 tablespoons lime juice
5 teaspoons canola oil
2 cloves garlic, minced
⅛ teaspoon crushed red pepper
1 pound skinless, boneless chicken breast halves, cut into ½- to ¾-inch pieces
  Nonstick cooking spray*
1 teaspoon sugar
½ teaspoon ground ginger
½ teaspoon salt
¼ teaspoon black pepper
1 ripe avocado, halved, seeded, and peeled
2 cups cooked brown rice or one 8.8-ounce package cooked brown rice
2 cups fresh or juice-pack canned pineapple chunks, drained
4 cups torn fresh spinach

1. For marinade, in a medium bowl whisk together 1 tablespoon of the lime juice, 2 teaspoons of the oil, the garlic, and the crushed red pepper. Add chicken pieces and toss to coat.

2. Coat a large nonstick skillet with cooking spray. Add chicken and marinade to the skillet and cook over medium-high heat until browned and cooked through (170°F), about 5 to 7 minutes. Remove from heat; set aside.

3. For avocado dressing, in a medium bowl whisk together the remaining oil, remaining lime juice, sugar, ginger, salt, and black pepper. Chop half of the avocado. Gently stir chopped avocado into the dressing.

4. In a large bowl combine rice, pineapple, cooled chicken, and avocado dressing. Serve over fresh spinach. Slice remaining avocado half and serve with salad.

PER SERVING: 402 cal., 15 g fat (2 g sat. fat), 72 mg chol., 429 mg sodium, 40 g carb., 6 g fiber, 29 g pro.

*Tip: Check the label of this product carefully to be sure it does not contain added gluten.

Superfoods Chicken Salad

START TO FINISH: 25 minutes
MAKES: 4 servings

PER SERVING: 303 cal., 13 g fat (2 g sat. fat), 63 mg chol., 249 mg sodium, 22 g carb., 3 g fiber, 26 g pro.

⅓ cup raspberry vinegar
2 tablespoons snipped fresh mint
2 tablespoons honey
1 tablespoon canola oil
¼ teaspoon salt
4 cups packaged fresh baby spinach
2 cups chopped cooked chicken breast (about 10 ounces)
2 cups fresh strawberries, sliced
½ cup fresh blueberries
¼ cup walnuts, toasted and coarsely chopped
1 ounce semisoft goat cheese (chèvre), crumbled (¼ cup)
½ teaspoon freshly ground black pepper

1. For vinaigrette, in a screw-top jar combine vinegar, mint, honey, oil, and salt. Cover and shake well.

2. In a large bowl toss together spinach, chicken, strawberries, blueberries, walnuts, and cheese. Divide among four plates. Shake vinaigrette; drizzle over salads. Sprinkle with pepper.

Picadillo-Style Chicken Taco Salad

START TO FINISH: 30 minutes
MAKES: 4 servings

- 12 **ounces ground chicken**
- ⅓ **cup chopped onion**
- 2 **teaspoons ground coriander**
- 2 **teaspoons ground cumin**
- ½ **teaspoon salt**
- 1 **14.5-ounce can no-salt-added diced tomatoes, undrained**
- ⅔ **cup finely chopped, peeled potato**
- ¼ **cup snipped pitted dried plums (prunes)**
- ¼ **cup chopped pimiento-stuffed green olives**
- 2 **corn tostada shells* or ⅔ cup crushed tortilla chips***
- 6 **cups shredded romaine or iceberg lettuce**
- 1 **ounce reduced-fat Monterey Jack cheese (¼ cup)**
  Sliced green onions and/or snipped fresh cilantro (optional)
- 1 **cup Salsa Verde (recipe, page 289) or purchased gluten-free salsa verde**
  Lime wedges

1. In a large skillet cook ground chicken and chopped onion over medium heat until chicken is browned, using a wooden spoon to break up chicken as it cooks. Drain off fat. Add coriander, cumin, and salt to chicken mixture; cook and stir for 1 to 2 minutes. Stir in tomatoes, potato, dried plums, and olives. Bring to boiling; reduce heat. Simmer, covered, about 10 minutes or until potato is tender. Cook, uncovered, about 3 minutes more or until most of the liquid has evaporated.

2. Meanwhile, heat tostada shells according to package directions until crisp.

3. Arrange shredded lettuce on a platter. Top with chicken salad; sprinkle with cheese. Coarsely crush the tostada shells; sprinkle over salad. If desired, top with green onions and/or cilantro. Serve with salsa and lime wedges.

PER SERVING: 295 cal., 12 g fat (4 g sat. fat), 78 mg chol., 956 mg sodium, 29 g carb., 6 g fiber, 21 g pro.

***Tip:** Check the labels of these products carefully to be sure they do not contain added gluten.

Honey-Lime Rice Chicken Salad

START TO FINISH: 20 minutes   MAKES: 4 servings

¼ cup snipped fresh cilantro
1 teaspoon finely shredded lime peel
2 tablespoons lime juice
2 tablespoons honey
4 teaspoons olive oil or canola oil
¼ to ½ teaspoon crushed red pepper
½ teaspoon salt
¼ of a medium red onion, thinly sliced
1½ cups cooked long grain brown rice
1⅓ cups cooked wild rice
1 cup chopped cooked chicken breast (5 ounces)
2 large oranges or 1 large grapefruit, peeled, seeded, and sectioned
4 cups packaged fresh baby spinach
1 medium avocado, halved, seeded, peeled, and thinly sliced

1. For dressing, in a large bowl whisk together cilantro, lime peel, lime juice, honey, oil, crushed red pepper, and the salt. Remove 2 tablespoons of the dressing and set aside until ready to serve. Add red onion to the remaining dressing in bowl; toss to coat. Add rice and chicken; toss to coat. Gently stir in orange sections.

2. To serve, divide spinach among four plates. Spoon rice salad onto spinach. Top with avocado and drizzle with the reserved dressing.

PER SERVING: 393 cal., 12 g fat (2 g sat. fat), 30 mg chol., 658 mg sodium, 56 g carb., 7 g fiber, 19 g pro.

Chicken Salad Lettuce Cups

START TO FINISH: 25 minutes
MAKES: 4 servings

¼ cup light mayonnaise*
2 tablespoons plain low-fat yogurt*
2 tablespoons white balsamic vinegar or regular balsamic vinegar
1 large clove garlic, minced
⅛ teaspoon salt
3 cups coarsely chopped cooked chicken breast
1 large red-skin apple, cored and coarsely chopped
1 cup coarsely chopped, seeded cucumber
1 cup chopped Bibb or Boston lettuce or red leaf lettuce
½ cup chopped roasted red sweet peppers
¼ cup thinly sliced green onions
12 large leaves Bibb or Boston lettuce or red leaf lettuce
2 tablespoons pine nuts, toasted

1. In a large bowl whisk together mayonnaise, yogurt, vinegar, garlic, and salt. Add chicken, apple, cucumber, chopped lettuce, roasted sweet peppers, and green onions. Toss to coat.

2. To serve, divide lettuce leaves among four plates. Spoon about ½ cup of the chicken salad into each lettuce leaf. Sprinkle with pine nuts.

PER SERVING: 302 cal., 12 g fat (2 g sat. fat), 95 mg chol., 263 mg sodium, 14 g carb., 2 g fiber, 35 g pro.

*Tip: Check the labels of these products carefully to be sure they do not contain added gluten.

Papaya and Coconut Chicken Salad

PREP: 20 minutes
BAKE: 12 minutes at 450°F
MAKES: 4 servings

- 1 **pound skinless, boneless chicken breast halves**
- ¾ **teaspoon salt**
- 1½ **cups flaked coconut**
- 1 **medium papaya (about 12 ounces)**
- ¼ **cup vegetable oil**
- ¼ **cup cider vinegar**
- 1 **tablespoon honey**
  Dash cayenne pepper
- 1 **5-ounce package mixed salad greens**
- ¾ **cup fresh blueberries**

1. Preheat oven to 450°F. Line a baking sheet with foil; set aside. Cut chicken into strips; sprinkle with ½ teaspoon of the salt. Place coconut in a shallow dish. Roll chicken in coconut to coat, pressing lightly to adhere. Place chicken on prepared baking sheet. Bake about 12 minutes or until coconut is golden and chicken is no longer pink (170°F).

2. Meanwhile, peel and seed papaya; cut into cubes. For dressing, in a food processor or blender combine ¼ cup of the papaya cubes, the oil, vinegar, honey, cayenne pepper, and the remaining ¼ teaspoon salt. Cover and process or blend until smooth. In a large bowl toss greens with ¼ cup of the dressing; divide greens among four plates.

3. Top greens with chicken, the remaining papaya cubes, and blueberries. Serve salads with the remaining dressing.

PER SERVING: 526 cal., 30 g fat (15 g sat. fat), 66 mg chol., 639 mg sodium, 35 g carb., 6 g fiber, 30 g pro.

Turkey Taco Salad

START TO FINISH: 25 minutes
MAKES: 4 servings

Nonstick cooking spray*
12 **ounces ground uncooked turkey breast**
1 **15-ounce can pinto beans,* rinsed and drained**
1 **cup frozen whole kernel corn**
1 **cup salsa**
¼ **cup water**
4 **to 6 cups coarsely torn or shredded romaine lettuce**
1 **ounce reduced-fat cheddar cheese, shredded (¼ cup)**
2 **ounces baked tortilla chips***

1. Lightly coat a large nonstick skillet with cooking spray; heat skillet over medium heat. Cook ground turkey in hot skillet about 5 minutes or until no longer pink, using a wooden spoon to break up turkey as it cooks. Drain off any fat.

2. Stir in beans, corn, salsa, and the water. Bring to boiling; reduce heat. Simmer, covered, for 2 to 3 minutes to blend flavors.

3. Line four plates with lettuce. Top with hot turkey mixture; sprinkle with cheese. Serve with tortilla chips.

PER SERVING: 317 cal., 7 g fat (2 g sat. fat), 46 mg chol., 857 mg sodium, 37 g carb., 8 g fiber, 30 g pro.

To Make Ahead: Prepare as directed through Step 2. Cool turkey mixture; transfer to an airtight container. Cover and store in the refrigerator for up to 3 days. To serve, transfer turkey mixture to a large saucepan. Bring to boiling; reduce heat. Simmer, covered, for 5 to 10 minutes or until heated through. Continue as directed in Step 3.

***Tip:** Check the labels of these products carefully to be sure they do not contain added gluten.

Turkey Salad with Oranges

START TO FINISH: 30 minutes
MAKES: 4 servings

1 **5-ounce package arugula or baby spinach**
12 **ounces cooked turkey or chicken, shredded**
1 **red sweet pepper, cut into strips**
¼ **cup snipped fresh cilantro**
3 **tablespoons orange juice**
2 **tablespoons peanut oil or canola oil**
1 **tablespoon honey**
2 **teaspoons lemon juice**
2 **teaspoons gluten-free Dijon-style mustard**
¼ **teaspoon ground cumin**
¼ **teaspoon salt**
¼ **teaspoon black pepper**
4 **oranges, peeled and sectioned**

1. In a large bowl toss together arugula, turkey, sweet pepper, and cilantro.

2. For vinaigrette, in a small bowl whisk together orange juice, oil, honey, lemon juice, mustard, cumin, salt, and black pepper. Drizzle vinaigrette over salad; toss gently to coat. Just before serving, add orange sections to salad.

PER SERVING: 281 cal., 8 g fat (1 g sat. fat), 71 mg chol., 263 mg sodium, 25 g carb., 5 g fiber, 28 g pro.

Turkey Steaks with Spinach, Pears, and Blue Cheese

START TO FINISH: 20 minutes **MAKES:** 4 servings

2 **turkey breast tenderloins (1 to 1¼ pounds total)**
1 **teaspoon dried sage, crushed Salt and freshly ground black pepper**
2 **tablespoons butter**
1 **6-ounce package fresh baby spinach**
1 **large pear, cored and thinly sliced**
2 **ounces blue cheese, crumbled**

1. Using a sharp knife, split turkey tenderloins in half horizontally to make four steaks, each about ½ inch thick. Rub turkey with sage; sprinkle with salt and pepper.

2. In an extra-large skillet melt 1 tablespoon of the butter over medium-high heat. Add turkey; cook for 14 to 16 minutes or until no longer pink (170°F), turning once. (Reduce heat to medium if turkey browns too quickly.) Remove turkey from skillet. Add spinach to skillet. Cook and stir just until spinach is wilted.

3. Meanwhile, in a small skillet melt the remaining 1 tablespoon butter. Add pear slices; cook over medium to medium-high heat about 5 minutes or until lightly browned, stirring occasionally.

4. Arrange turkey, spinach, and pear slices on plates. Top with blue cheese.

PER SERVING: 240 cal., 9 g fat (5 g sat. fat), 92 mg chol., 380 mg sodium, 8 g carb., 2 g fiber, 31 g pro.

Flank Steak and Plum Salad with Creamy Chimichurri Dressing

PREP: 15 minutes
GRILL: 10 minutes
STAND: 5 minutes
MAKES: 4 servings

- 8 ounces beef flank steak
- 1 teaspoon ground cumin
- ¼ teaspoon salt
- 1 medium sweet onion, such as Vidalia or Maui, sliced horizontally into ½-inch slices
- 2 teaspoons olive oil
- ¼ teaspoon freshly ground black pepper
- 6 cups fresh mâche (lamb's lettuce) or baby greens
- 4 ripe plums, pitted and cut into thin wedges
- 1 recipe Creamy Chimichurri Dressing

1. Sprinkle meat with cumin and salt. Brush onion slices on both sides with oil; sprinkle with pepper.

2. For a charcoal or gas grill, place meat and onion slices on the rack of a covered grill directly over medium-hot heat. Grill meat for 10 to 14 minutes for medium-rare to medium (145°F to 160°F) and onion slices about 10 minutes or until tender, turning both meat and onion slices once halfway through grilling. Let meat stand for 5 minutes. Thinly slice meat. Coarsely chop onion.

3. Place mâche in a large salad bowl or arrange on a large platter. Top with meat, onion, and plums. Drizzle with half of the Creamy Chimichurri Dressing. If desired, pass remaining dressing.

PER SERVING: 336 cal., 22 g fat (5 g sat. fat), 53 mg chol., 546 mg sodium, 19 g carb., 2 g fiber, 16 g pro.

Creamy Chimichurri Dressing:
In a small bowl stir together ¾ cup light mayonnaise,* ¼ cup plain Greek yogurt* or sour cream,* 1 tablespoon white vinegar, and 3 cloves garlic, minced. Stir in 3 tablespoons snipped fresh Italian parsley, ½ teaspoon crushed red pepper, and ⅛ teaspoon salt. Serve immediately or cover and chill for up to 1 week. Before serving, stir in enough milk to reach desired consistency if necessary.

*Tip: Check the labels of these products carefully to be sure they do not contain added gluten.

Beef and Fruit Salad

PREP: 20 minutes
MARINATE: 30 minutes
GRILL: 8 minutes
MAKES: 4 servings

- 12 **ounces boneless beef sirloin steak, cut 1 inch thick**
- ⅓ **cup gluten-free, reduced-sodium teriyaki sauce or gluten-free soy sauce**
- ¼ **cup lemon juice**
- ¼ **cup water**
- 2 **teaspoons toasted sesame oil**
- ⅛ **teaspoon hot pepper sauce***
- 3 **cups shredded napa cabbage**
- 1 **cup torn or shredded sorrel or spinach**
- 2 **cups fresh fruit (sliced plums, nectarines, or kiwifruit; halved seedless grapes or strawberries; raspberries; and/or blueberries)**

1. Trim fat from steak. Place steak in a plastic bag set in a shallow dish. For marinade, combine the teriyaki sauce, lemon juice, water, toasted sesame oil, and hot pepper sauce. Reserve ⅓ cup for dressing. Pour remaining marinade over steak; close bag. Marinate in refrigerator for 30 minutes to 8 hours, turning bag occasionally.

2. Drain steak, reserving marinade. For a charcoal or gas grill, place steak on the rack of a covered grill directly over medium heat. Grill to desired doneness, turning once and brushing occasionally with marinade up to the last 5 minutes of grilling. Allow 8 to 12 minutes for medium rare (145°F) or 12 to 15 minutes for medium (160°F). Discard any remaining marinade.

3. To serve, divide cabbage and sorrel among four plates. Thinly slice steak diagonally. Arrange steak and fruit on greens. Drizzle with the dressing.

PER SERVING: 248 cal., 10 g fat (3 g sat. fat), 57 mg chol., 307 mg sodium, 19 g carb., 2 g fiber, 22 g pro.

*Tip: Check the label of this product carefully to be sure it does not contain added gluten.

Sesame-Crusted Beef and Spinach Salad

PREP: 20 minutes   **BROIL:** 15 minutes   **MAKES:** 4 servings

- 1   12-ounce boneless beef top sirloin steak, cut 1 inch thick
- ⅛   teaspoon salt
- ⅛   teaspoon black pepper
- 1   tablespoon gluten-free Dijon-style mustard
- 2   tablespoons sesame seeds
- 6   cups fresh baby spinach
- 1   15-ounce can garbanzo beans (chickpeas),* rinsed and drained
- ¼   cup chopped dried apricots
- ¼   of a medium red onion, thinly sliced
- 1   recipe Orange-Mint Vinaigrette

1. Preheat broiler. Trim fat from steak. Sprinkle steak with salt and pepper. Place steak on the unheated rack of a broiler pan. Broil 3 to 4 inches from the heat until almost desired doneness, turning once halfway through broiling time. Allow 11 to 13 minutes for medium rare (145°F) or 16 to 18 minutes for medium (160°F).

2. Brush half of the mustard on top of the steak; sprinkle with half of the sesame seeds. Turn steak over; brush with the remaining mustard and sprinkle with the remaining sesame seeds. Broil about 4 minutes more or until steak is desired doneness and sesame seeds are lightly browned, turning once halfway through broiling time.

3. Divide spinach among four shallow serving bowls or plates. Thinly slice steak across the grain; arrange on spinach. Top with garbanzo beans, apricots, and red onion. Drizzle with Orange-Mint Vinaigrette.

Orange-Mint Vinaigrette: In a screw-top jar combine ¼ cup snipped fresh mint, 3 tablespoons orange juice, 3 tablespoons white wine vinegar, 2 tablespoons olive oil or untoasted sesame oil, ¼ teaspoon salt, and ⅛ teaspoon black pepper. Cover and shake well.

PER SERVING: 379 cal., 13 g fat (3 g sat. fat), 36 mg chol., 638 mg sodium, 36 g carb., 8 g fiber, 27 g pro.

*Tip: Check the label of this product carefully to be sure it does not contain added gluten.

Asian Pork and Cabbage Salad

PREP: 20 minutes
COOK: 5 minutes
MAKES: 4 servings

¼ cup low-sugar orange marmalade* or apricot preserves*

2 tablespoons gluten-free, reduced-sodium soy sauce or gluten-free tamari

2 tablespoons rice vinegar

1 tablespoon toasted sesame oil

1 clove garlic, minced
Nonstick cooking spray*

12 ounces boneless pork loin chops, cut into bite-size pieces

1 cup yellow or red sweet pepper thin bite-size strips

6 cups shredded napa cabbage

1 cup chopped cucumber

4 green onions, bias-sliced

¼ cup slivered almonds, toasted

1. For dressing, in a small bowl stir together orange marmalade, soy sauce, vinegar, toasted sesame oil, and garlic. Set aside.

2. Lightly coat an unheated wok or large nonstick skillet with cooking spray. Heat over medium-high heat. Add pork and cook for 2 minutes. Add sweet pepper and continue to cook about 3 minutes or until pork is no longer pink and sweet pepper is crisp-tender, stirring occasionally. Add one-fourth of the dressing to the pan; stir until well coated. Remove pan from heat.

3. Place cabbage in a large bowl; drizzle remaining dressing over cabbage and toss to coat. On a platter layer cabbage, pork mixture, and cucumber. Sprinkle with green onions and almonds. Serve immediately.

PER SERVING: 242 cal., 10 g fat (2 g sat. fat), 59 mg chol., 352 mg sodium, 16 g carb., 3 g fiber, 23 g pro.

*Tip: Check the labels of these products carefully to be sure they do not contain added gluten.

Frisée Salad with Bacon and Poached Egg

START TO FINISH: 20 minutes
MAKES: 6 servings

- 1 **tablespoon white wine vinegar**
- ¾ **teaspoon gluten-free Dijon-style mustard**
- ½ **teaspoon light mayonnaise***
- ⅛ **teaspoon salt**
- ⅛ **teaspoon black pepper**
- 3 **tablespoons extra-virgin olive oil**
- 5 **slices gluten-free turkey bacon**
- 8 **cups chopped frisée (2 large heads)**
- 12 **radishes, thinly sliced**
- 6 **eggs**

1. For dressing, in a small bowl whisk together vinegar, mustard, mayonnaise, salt, and pepper. Slowly whisk in olive oil. Set aside.

2. Cut turkey bacon crosswise into ½-inch pieces. In a large nonstick skillet cook turkey bacon over medium-high heat about 7 minutes or until crisp. Remove bacon from skillet; drain on paper towels.

3. In a large bowl combine frisée, radishes, and the bacon. Drizzle dressing over salad; toss to coat. Divide salad among six plates.

4. To poach eggs, fill a large skillet three-fourths full with water. Bring water to boiling; reduce heat to simmering. Break an egg into a cup and slip it into simmering water. Repeat with remaining eggs. Simmer eggs, uncovered, for 3 to 5 minutes or until whites are completely set and yolks begin to thicken but are not hard. Remove eggs with a slotted spoon and place on salad.

PER SERVING: 250 cal., 18 g fat (4 g sat. fat), 235 mg chol., 544 mg sodium, 13 g carb., 10 g fiber, 14 g pro.

***Tip:** Check the label of this product carefully to be sure it does not contain added gluten.

Shrimp and Quinoa Salad

START TO FINISH: 45 minutes
MAKES: 4 servings

12 **ounces fresh or frozen large shrimp**
1 **cup quinoa**
2 **Cara Cara oranges**
3 **tablespoons white balsamic vinegar**
¼ **teaspoon salt**
¼ **teaspoon black pepper**
1 **5- to 6-ounce package baby spinach or arugula**

1. Thaw shrimp, if frozen. Peel and devein shrimp, leaving tails intact if desired. Rinse shrimp: pat dry with paper towels. Thread shrimp on four 8-inch skewers.* For a charcoal or gas grill, place skewers on the rack of a covered grill directly over medium heat. Grill for 4 to 6 minutes or until shrimp are opaque, turning once halfway through grilling.**

2. Meanwhile, rinse quinoa; drain. In a medium saucepan bring 2 cups water to boiling. Add quinoa. Return to boiling; reduce heat. Simmer, covered, about 15 minutes or until water is absorbed. Remove from heat.

3. Finely shred 1 teaspoon peel from one orange; set aside. Using a paring knife, cut remaining peel and white pith from oranges; discard. Holding each orange over a very large bowl to catch juices, cut sections from oranges (set sections aside). Squeeze juice from membranes into bowl. Stir in finely shredded orange peel, balsamic vinegar, salt, and pepper. Add grilled shrimp, orange sections, quinoa, and spinach; toss gently to combine. To serve, divide salad among four shallow bowls or plates.

PER SERVING: 281 cal., 3 g fat (0 g sat. fat), 119 mg chol., 263 mg sodium, 42 g carb., 5 g fiber, 22 g pro.

*Tip: If using wooden skewers, soak them in enough water to cover for at least 30 minutes before using.

**Tip: To use a grill pan, lightly brush olive oil on grill pan. Preheat over medium-high heat. Add skewers; grill for 4 to 6 minutes or until shrimp are opaque, turning once halfway through cooking.

Shrimp Ceviche Tostada with Fennel and Grapefruit

PREP: 35 minutes
CHILL: 2 hours
MAKES: 6 servings

1 pound fresh or frozen shrimp, peeled and deveined
4 cups water
Salt
¼ cup orange juice
¼ cup lime juice
1 bulb fennel, cut into julienne strips (fronds reserved)
¼ cup finely chopped red onion
1 ruby red grapefruit, peeled, sectioned, and chopped
1 medium orange, peeled, sectioned, and chopped
2 tablespoons fresh snipped fennel fronds or fresh tarragon leaves
1 fresh red Anaheim chile pepper, seeded and finely chopped (see tip, page 21)
2 avocados, halved, seeded, and peeled
Hot pepper sauce*
6 tostada shells*
4 cups shredded iceberg lettuce
⅓ cup pumpkin seeds (pepitas), toasted

1. Thaw shrimp, if frozen. Rinse shrimp; pat dry with paper towels. Cut shrimp in half lengthwise. In a large saucepan bring water and 1 teaspoon salt to boiling. Add shrimp. Simmer, uncovered, 1 to 2 minutes or until shrimp turn opaque, stirring occasionally. Rinse shrimp under cold running water; drain. For shrimp ceviche, transfer shrimp to a large bowl. Immediately add the orange juice and lime juice.

2. Stir in the sliced fennel, red onion, grapefruit, orange, fennel fronds, and chile. Cover and chill for 2 to 4 hours. Season to taste with salt before serving.

3. In another bowl use a fork to mash the avocados; season to taste with salt and hot pepper sauce.

4. Spread the tostada shells with the avocado mixture. Top with lettuce and ceviche. Garnish with pumpkin seeds and, if desired, additional fennel fronds.

PER SERVING: 316 cal., 17 g fat (3 g sat. fat), 95 mg chol., 739 mg sodium, 28 g carb., 8 g fiber, 17 g pro.

*Tip: Check the labels of these products carefully to be sure they do not contain added gluten.

Iceberg Wedges with Shrimp and Blue Cheese Dressing

START TO FINISH: 35 minutes
MAKES: 6 servings

1½ **pounds fresh or frozen large shrimp in shells**
 3 **tablespoons lemon juice**
 ¼ **teaspoon black pepper**
 ½ **cup light mayonnaise***
 ¼ **to ½ teaspoon hot pepper sauce***
 2 **tablespoons crumbled blue cheese***
 3 **to 4 tablespoons fat-free milk Nonstick cooking spray***
 1 **large head iceberg lettuce, cut into 12 wedges**
 1 **large tomato, chopped**
 ⅓ **cup thinly sliced, quartered red onion**
 2 **slices gluten-free turkey bacon, cooked and crumbled**

1. Thaw shrimp, if frozen. Peel and devein shrimp, leaving tails intact if desired. Rinse shrimp; pat dry with paper towels. In a medium bowl combine shrimp, 2 tablespoons of the lemon juice, and ⅛ teaspoon of the black pepper. Toss to coat. Set aside.

2. For dressing, in a small bowl combine the remaining 1 tablespoon lemon juice, the remaining ⅛ teaspoon black pepper, the mayonnaise, and hot pepper sauce. Stir in blue cheese. Stir in enough of the milk to make desired consistency.

3. Coat an unheated grill pan with cooking spray. Preheat grill pan over medium-high heat. Thread shrimp onto six 10- to 12-inch-long skewers.** Place skewers on grill pan. Cook for 3 to 5 minutes or until shrimp are opaque, turning once halfway through cooking. (If necessary, cook shrimp skewers half at a time.)

4. Place two of the lettuce wedges on each of six plates. Top with shrimp, tomato, red onion, and bacon. Serve with dressing.

PER SERVING: 190 cal., 10 g fat (2 g sat. fat), 129 mg chol., 360 mg sodium, 8 g carb., 1 g fiber, 18 g pro.

***Tip:** Check the labels of these products carefully to be sure they do not contain added gluten.

****Tip:** If using wooden skewers, soak them in enough water to cover for at least 30 minutes before using.

Grilled Shrimp and Romaine

PREP: 15 minutes
GRILL: 7 minutes
MAKES: 4 servings

1 pound fresh or frozen large shrimp, peeled and deveined
¼ cup olive oil
½ teaspoon kosher salt or ¼ teaspoon salt
2 hearts of romaine lettuce, halved lengthwise
1 ounce Parmesan cheese, finely shredded (¼ cup)
2 lemons
  Olive oil
  Kosher salt or sea salt
  Freshly ground black pepper

1. Thaw shrimp, if frozen. Rinse shrimp; pat dry with paper towels. On four 10-inch metal skewers thread shrimp, leaving ¼ inch between shrimp.* In a small bowl whisk together the ¼ cup olive oil and the ½ teaspoon salt. Brush oil mixture over shrimp and cut sides of lettuce.

2. For a charcoal or gas grill, place shrimp on the rack of a covered grill directly over medium heat. Grill for 5 to 8 minutes or until shrimp are opaque, turning once halfway through grilling. Grill lettuce, cut sides down, for 2 to 4 minutes or until grill marks appear and lettuce is slightly wilted.

3. Place lettuce in serving bowl. Remove shrimp from the skewers. Place in bowl with lettuce and sprinkle with the Parmesan cheese. Squeeze the juice of one of the lemons over the shrimp and lettuce and drizzle with additional olive oil. Sprinkle with additional salt and freshly ground black pepper. Cut the remaining lemon into wedges and serve with the salad.

PER SERVING: 267 cal., 20 g fat (3 g sat. fat), 133 mg chol., 514 mg sodium, 2 g carb., 19 g pro.

*Tip: If you like, rather than skewering shrimp, you can cook them on the grill in a grill wok. Preheat the grill wok on the grill for 5 minutes. Add shrimp to the wok; cook and stir for 5 to 8 minutes or until shrimp are opaque.

Seared Scallops with Beurre Blanc and Savoy Slaw

PREP: 20 minutes
COOK: 30 minutes
MAKES: 4 servings

20 fresh or frozen large sea scallops
1 cup Sauvignon Blanc or other dry white wine
¼ cup Meyer lemon juice
¼ cup finely chopped shallots
1 tablespoon heavy cream
12 tablespoons cold butter, cubed
¼ teaspoon salt
2 tablespoons olive oil
2 ounces gluten-free pancetta, cut into ¼-inch cubes
½ cup thinly sliced green onions
¼ cup white wine vinegar
4 cups tightly packed savoy cabbage, thinly sliced
1 large orange, peeled and sectioned
1 small red grapefruit, peeled and sectioned
¼ cup snipped fresh chives or sliced green onions

1. Thaw scallops, if frozen. Rinse scallops; pat dry with paper towels. Set scallops aside.

2. For beurre blanc, in a medium saucepan combine wine, lemon juice, and shallots. Bring to boiling; reduce heat. Simmer, uncovered, until reduced to 2 tablespoons. Add cream to saucepan. Return to simmering; reduce heat to low. Add butter, one cube at a time and whisking between additions, until a rich sauce forms. Stir in salt. Ladle sauce into a wide-mouth thermos; close tightly and set aside.

3. In a large skillet heat oil over medium-high heat. Working in batches, add scallops; sear about 1 minute on each side or until golden brown. Transfer scallops to a oven-proof platter; keep warm in a 200°F oven.

4. Meanwhile, for savoy slaw, in a large skillet cook and stir pancetta over medium heat for 6 to 8 minutes or until crisp. Using a slotted spoon, transfer pancetta to paper towels to drain. Add green onions to drippings in skillet; cook for 1 to 2 minutes or until tender. Stir in vinegar. Bring to boiling, stirring constantly and scraping up any browned bits from bottom of skillet. Add cabbage; cook and stir for 2 to 3 minutes or until cabbage is lightly wilted. Add orange and grapefruit sections; toss gently to combine.

5. To serve, divide slaw among plates; top with scallops. Spoon beurre blanc over scallops. Garnish with pancetta cubes and chives.

PER SERVING: 502 cal., 38 g fat (20 g sat. fat), 103 mg chol., 803 mg sodium, 18 g carb., 4 g fiber, 16 g pro.

Quick Scallop and Noodle Salad

START TO FINISH: 30 minutes
MAKES: 4 servings

12   **fresh or frozen sea scallops (about 18 ounces total)**
4   **ounces banh pho (Vietnamese wide rice noodles) or dried brown rice fettuccine**
¼   **cup orange juice**
2   **tablespoons rice vinegar**
2   **tablespoons toasted sesame oil**
1   **teaspoon finely shredded lime peel**
1   **teaspoon grated fresh ginger**
½   **teaspoon salt**
1½   **cups torn fresh spinach leaves**
1   **cup chopped cucumber**
⅔   **cup thinly sliced radishes**
¼   **teaspoon black pepper**
    Nonstick cooking spray*
2   **tablespoons sesame seeds, toasted****

1. Thaw scallops, if frozen. Cook noodles according to package directions; drain. Rinse with cold water; drain again. In a large bowl combine orange juice, vinegar, sesame oil, lime peel, ginger, and ¼ teaspoon of the salt. Add cooked noodles, the spinach, cucumber, and radishes; toss gently to mix. Set aside.

2. Rinse scallops with cold water; pat dry with paper towels. Sprinkle with the remaining ¼ teaspoon salt and the pepper.

3. Coat a large nonstick skillet with cooking spray; heat skillet over medium-high heat. Add scallops. Cook for 3 to 5 minutes or until scallops are opaque, turning once. Serve scallops with noodle salad. Sprinkle with toasted sesame seeds.

PER SERVING: 297 cal., 10 g fat (2 g sat. fat), 31 mg chol., 817 mg sodium, 31 g carb., 2 g fiber, 19 g pro.

***Tip:** Check the label of this product carefully to be sure it does not contain added gluten.

****Tip:** To toast sesame seeds, spread seeds in a small dry skillet. Cook over medium heat until lightly browned, stirring often to prevent burning.

Layered Southwestern Salad with Tortilla Strips

PREP: 15 minutes
BAKE: 15 minutes at 350°F
MAKES: 6 servings

2 6-inch corn tortillas*
  Nonstick cooking spray*
½ cup light sour cream*
¼ cup snipped fresh cilantro
2 tablespoons fat-free milk
1 teaspoon olive oil
1 large clove garlic, minced
½ teaspoon chili powder*
½ teaspoon finely shredded
  lime peel
¼ teaspoon salt
¼ teaspoon black pepper
6 cups torn romaine lettuce
4 roma tomatoes, chopped
  (2 cups)
1 15-ounce can black beans,
  rinsed and drained*
1 cup fresh corn kernels**
2 ounces reduced-fat cheddar
  cheese, shredded (½ cup)
1 avocado, halved, seeded,
  peeled, and chopped
  Snipped fresh cilantro
  (optional)

1. Preheat oven to 350°F. Cut tortillas into ½-inch strips; place in a 15×10×1-inch baking pan. Coat tortillas lightly with cooking spray. Bake for 15 to 18 minutes or just until crisp, stirring once. Cool on wire rack.

2. Meanwhile, for dressing, in a small bowl stir together sour cream, the ¼ cup cilantro, the milk, oil, garlic, chili power, lime peel, salt, and pepper.

3. Place lettuce in a large glass serving bowl. Layer with tomatoes, then beans, corn, cheese, and avocado. Add dressing and sprinkle with tortilla strips. If desired, garnish with additional cilantro.

PER SERVING: 227 cal., 11 g fat (3 g sat. fat), 12 mg chol., 386 mg sodium, 29 g carb., 9 g fiber, 11 g pro.

*Tip: Check the labels of these products carefully to be sure they do not contain added gluten.

**Tip: It isn't necessary to cook the corn. However, for a roasted flavor and soft texture, bake it with the tortilla strips. Place the strips and corn at opposite ends of the baking pan.

Roasted Root Vegetable and Wilted Romaine Salad

PREP: 30 minutes
BAKE: 30 minutes at 375°F + 30 minutes at 425°F
MAKES: 12 servings

- 2 fresh medium beets (about 12 ounces)
- 8 tablespoons olive oil
  Salt and black pepper
- 1¾ pounds carrots, turnips, and/or parsnips
- 4 medium shallots, peeled and quartered
- 6 tablespoons olive oil
- 2 tablespoons white wine vinegar
- 1 tablespoon snipped fresh thyme
- 1 teaspoon gluten-free Dijon-style mustard
- 1 teaspoon honey
- 1 clove garlic, minced
- 8 cups torn romaine lettuce
- ½ cup chopped pecans, toasted
- ¼ cup snipped fresh Italian parsley

1. Preheat oven to 375°F. Wash and peel beets; cut into 1-inch pieces. Place in a 2-quart baking dish. Toss with 1 tablespoon of the olive oil and salt and pepper to taste. Cover dish tightly with foil and bake for 30 minutes.

2. Meanwhile, peel carrots, turnips, and/or parsnips. Cut carrots and turnips into 1-inch pieces. Cut parsnips into ¾-inch pieces. Place in a 15×10×1-inch baking pan. Add shallots. Toss with 1 tablespoon of the olive oil. Sprinkle with additional salt and pepper.

3. Remove foil from dish with beets; stir beets gently. Increase oven temperature to 425°F. Return beets to oven. Place pan with the other vegetables alongside beets. Roast, uncovered, for 30 to 40 minutes or until all vegetables are tender.

4. Meanwhile, for dressing, in a screw-top jar combine the remaining 5 tablespoons olive oil, the vinegar, thyme, mustard, honey, garlic, and salt and pepper to taste; cover and shake well.

5. To serve, toss romaine lettuce with the dressing. Transfer to a serving platter. Top with hot vegetables. Sprinkle with pecans and parsley. Serve immediately.

PER SERVING: 165 cal., 13 g fat (2 g sat. fat), 0 mg chol., 179 mg sodium, 13 g carb., 4 g fiber, 2 g pro.

To Make Ahead: Prepare and store dressing in the refrigerator up to 3 days. To serve, bring dressing to room temperature; shake well before using.

Noodles

When pasta cravings hit, look no further. Enjoy noodles the gluten-free way by letting spiralized vegetables, rice pasta, soba noodles, and other wheat-free noodles take the place of traditional pasta.

Chicken Soba Noodle Bowl

START TO FINISH: 25 minutes **MAKES:** 4 servings

2 **14.5-ounce cans gluten-free, reduced-sodium chicken broth**
1 **cup water**
2 **skinless, boneless chicken breast halves (about 12 ounces total)**
8 **ounces fresh sugar snap peas or frozen peas**
6 **ounces gluten-free dried soba (buckwheat noodles)**
2 **medium carrots, thinly bias-sliced**
1 **red or green fresh jalapeño chile pepper, thinly sliced and seeded (see tip, page 21) (optional)**
2 **tablespoons gluten-free, reduced-sodium soy sauce or gluten-free tamari**
   Crushed red pepper (optional)
   Snipped fresh parsley or cilantro (optional)

1. In a large saucepan combine the broth and water; bring to boiling. Meanwhile, very thinly slice the chicken and halve any large sugar snap peas.

2. Add chicken, noodles, carrots, chile pepper, and soy sauce to boiling broth mixture. Cover and cook over medium heat about 7 minutes or until chicken is cooked through and noodles are tender. Add sugar snap peas; cook, covered, about 3 minutes more or just until peas are tender.

3. If desired, sprinkle with crushed red pepper and/or fresh parsley before serving.

PER SERVING: 295 cal., 1 g fat (0 g sat. fat), 49 mg chol., 1,172 mg sodium, 41 g carb., 4 g fiber, 30 g pro.

Chicken Meatball Noodle Bowl

START TO FINISH: 25 minutes
MAKES: 4 servings

 4 ounces thin rice noodles
12 ounces uncooked ground chicken
 2 tablespoons snipped fresh cilantro (optional)
 1 tablespoon grated fresh ginger or 1 teaspoon dried ginger
 ½ teaspoon salt
 3 tablespoons canola oil
 1 red Fresno chile pepper, seeded and finely chopped (see tip, page 21) (optional)
 ⅓ cup rice vinegar
 2 tablespoons honey
 1 tablespoon lime juice
 3 cups shredded leaf lettuce
 ½ cup finely shredded carrot
    Fresh cilantro, sliced Fresno chile peppers (see tip, page 21), lime wedges, and/or sliced green onions (optional)

1. Prepare noodles according to package directions; drain and set aside.

2. Meanwhile, in a large bowl combine ground chicken, cilantro, ginger, and salt. Form chicken mixture into 16 meatballs. In a large skillet heat 1 tablespoon of the oil over medium heat. Add meatballs. Cook about 10 minutes or until browned and cooked through (165°F),* turning to brown evenly. Transfer meatballs to a plate. Turn off heat.

3. Add the remaining 2 tablespoons oil and, if desired, the finely chopped chile pepper to the warm pan. Stir in rice vinegar, honey, and lime juice; set aside.

4. Divide noodles, lettuce, and carrot among four bowls. Top with meatballs; drizzle with the warm vinegar-honey mixture.

PER SERVING: 369 cal., 17 g fat (3 g sat. fat), 73 mg chol., 413 mg sodium, 36 g carb., 1 g fiber, 16 g pro.

*Tip: The internal color of a meatball is not a reliable doneness indicator. A chicken meatball cooked to 165°F is safe, regardless of color. To measure the doneness of a meatball, insert an instant-read thermometer into the center of the meatball.

Chicken Curry Skillet with Rice Noodles

START TO FINISH: 30 minutes
MAKES: 6 servings

8 ounces dried wide rice noodles, broken
2 tablespoons vegetable oil
1½ pounds skinless, boneless chicken breast halves, cut into 1-inch pieces
1 16-ounce package frozen stir-fry vegetables, thawed
1 14-ounce can unsweetened light coconut milk*
½ cup water
1 tablespoon sugar
1 tablespoon fish sauce
½ to 1 teaspoon gluten-free red curry paste
¼ teaspoon salt
¼ teaspoon black pepper
¼ cup snipped fresh basil

1. Soak rice noodles according to package directions; drain.

2. In an extra-large skillet heat oil over medium-high heat. Add chicken; cook and stir for 8 to 10 minutes or until chicken is no longer pink, adding stir-fry vegetables the last 4 minutes of cooking. Remove chicken mixture from skillet.

3. In the same skillet combine coconut milk, the water, sugar, fish sauce, curry paste, salt, and pepper. Bring to boiling. Stir in rice noodles and chicken mixture. Return to boiling; reduce heat. Simmer, uncovered, about 2 minutes or until noodles are tender but still firm and sauce is thickened. Sprinkle with fresh basil.

PER SERVING: 386 cal., 10 g fat (3 g sat. fat), 66 mg chol., 529 mg sodium, 42 g carb., 2 g fiber, 28 g pro.

*Tip: Check the label of this product carefully to be sure it does not contain added gluten.

Chicken Pad Thai

START TO FINISH: 45 minutes   MAKES: 4 servings

8   **ounces dried linguine-style rice noodles**

¼   **cup salted peanuts,* finely chopped**

½   **teaspoon finely shredded lime peel**

2   **tablespoons lime juice**

¼   **cup fish sauce**

2   **tablespoons packed brown sugar**

2   **tablespoons rice vinegar**

1   **tablespoon water**

1   **tablespoon Asian chili sauce with garlic***

3   **tablespoons vegetable oil**

1   **pound skinless, boneless chicken breast halves, cut into bite-size strips**

1   **tablespoon minced garlic (6 cloves)**

1   **egg, lightly beaten**

1   **cup fresh bean sprouts, rinsed and drained**

⅓   **cup sliced green onions**

2   **tablespoons snipped fresh cilantro**
    Lime wedges (optional)

1. Place rice noodles in a large bowl. Add enough boiling water to cover; let stand for 10 to 15 minutes or until softened but still slightly chewy (al dente), using tongs to stir occasionally. Drain well in a colander set in a sink.

2. Meanwhile, for peanut topping, in a small bowl combine peanuts and lime peel; set aside. For sauce, in another small bowl whisk together lime juice, fish sauce, brown sugar, rice vinegar, the water, and chili sauce until smooth; set aside.

3. In an extra-large nonstick skillet heat 1 tablespoon of the oil over medium-high heat. Add chicken and garlic; cook and stir about 6 minutes or until chicken is no longer pink. Transfer chicken to a bowl.

4. Add egg to the hot skillet; tilt skillet to spread egg in an even layer (egg may not fill bottom of skillet). Cook, without stirring, for 30 seconds. Using a wide spatula, carefully turn egg over; cook for 30 to 60 seconds more or just until set. Transfer egg to a plate. Using a sharp knife, cut egg round into bite-size strips; set aside.

5. In the same skillet heat the remaining 2 tablespoons oil over medium-high heat for 30 seconds. Add sprouts; stir-fry for 2 minutes. Add chicken and drained noodles (noodles may clump together but will separate when sauce is added). Stir in sauce; cook for 1 to 2 minutes more or until heated through. Transfer chicken pad Thai to a serving plate. Top with egg strips and peanut topping. Sprinkle with green onions and cilantro. If desired, serve with lime wedges.

PER SERVING: 549 cal., 19 g fat (3 g sat. fat), 119 mg chol., 1,816 mg sodium, 60 g carb., 2 g fiber, 32 g pro.

*Tip: Check the labels of these products carefully to be sure they do not contain added gluten.

Warm Glass Noodles with Edamame, Basil, and Chicken

START TO FINISH: 25 minutes
MAKES: 4 servings

1 **3.75-ounce package bean threads (cellophane noodles)**
1½ **cups frozen sweet soybeans (edamame)**
½ **cup gluten-free soy sauce or gluten-free tamari**
⅓ **cup thinly sliced green onions**
¼ **cup chicken broth**
2 **tablespoons packed brown sugar**
4 **teaspoons grated fresh ginger**
4 **teaspoons sesame seeds, toasted***
2 **tablespoons toasted sesame oil**
2 **cloves garlic, minced**
3 **cups shredded cooked chicken (about 1 pound)**
½ **cup small fresh basil leaves Sriracha sauce** (optional)

1. Cook noodles according to package directions, adding edamame for the last 1 minute of cooking. Drain and set aside.

2. Meanwhile, for sauce, in a medium bowl stir together soy sauce, green onions, chicken broth, brown sugar, ginger, sesame seeds, sesame oil, and garlic. Set aside.

3. Transfer noodles and edamame to a large serving bowl. If desired, use kitchen shears to snip noodles into short lengths. Add chicken, basil, and sauce to noodle mixture; toss to combine. If desired, serve with sriracha sauce.

PER SERVING: 327 cal., 13 g fat (2 g sat. fat), 63 mg chol., 872 mg sodium, 26 g carb., 3 g fiber, 26 g pro.

***Tip:** To toast sesame seeds, place them in a small skillet. Cook over medium heat for 2 minutes or until golden, stirring often.

****Tip:** Check the label of this product carefully to be sure it does not contain added gluten.

Asian Beef and Noodle Bowl

PREP: 30 minutes
COOK: 50 minutes
MAKES: 6 servings

- 1 **pound boneless beef chuck roast**
- 2 **14.5-ounce cans gluten-free, reduced-sodium beef broth**
- 1 **cup sliced onion**
- ½ **cup water**
- 2 **tablespoons gluten-free soy sauce or liquid aminos**
- 1 **tablespoon fish sauce (optional)**
- 1 **small fresh serrano chile pepper, seeded and finely chopped (see tip, page 21)**
- 4 **cloves garlic, minced**
- 1 **star anise**
- 3 **ounces dried rice noodles, broken**
- 2 **cups fresh shiitake mushrooms, stemmed and sliced, or cremini or button mushrooms, sliced**
- 2 **cups shredded napa cabbage**
- 1 **cup sugar snap pea pods, halved diagonally**
- 1 **8-ounce can water chestnuts, drained and chopped**
- 1 **tablespoon cornstarch***
- 1 **tablespoon cold water**

1. Trim fat from meat. Cut meat into 1-inch pieces. In a 4- to 5-quart Dutch oven combine meat, broth, onion, the ½ cup water, the soy sauce, fish sauce (if using), serrano pepper, garlic, and star anise. Bring to boiling; reduce heat. Simmer, covered, for 45 minutes.

2. Meanwhile, prepare rice noodles according to package directions; drain.

3. Remove and discard star anise from broth mixture. Stir in mushrooms, cabbage, pea pods, and water chestnuts. Return to boiling; reduce heat. Simmer about 5 minutes or until pea pods are crisp-tender. In a small bowl stir together cornstarch and the 1 tablespoon cold water; stir into broth. Cook and stir until thickened and bubbly; cook and stir for 2 minutes more.

4. To serve, divide noodles among bowls and ladle soup over noodles.

PER SERVING: 207 cal., 5 g fat (2 g sat. fat), 52 mg chol., 654 mg sodium, 21 g carb., 2 g fiber, 20 g pro.

***Tip:** Check the label of this product carefully to be sure it does not contain added gluten.

Zesty Meat Sauce with Spaghetti Squash

PREP: 50 minutes   BAKE: 45 minutes at 350°F   MAKES: 6 servings

- 1 medium spaghetti squash (about 2½ pounds)
- 1 medium red or green sweet pepper,* seeded and cut into thin strips
- 4 ounces fresh mushrooms, quartered
- 1 small onion, cut into thin wedges
  Nonstick cooking spray**
- 12 ounces extra-lean ground beef
- ½ cup chopped onion
- ½ cup chopped carrot
- ½ cup chopped celery
- 2 cloves garlic, minced
- 2 8-ounce cans gluten-free, no-salt-added tomato sauce
- 1 cup Fire-Roasted Tomato Salsa (recipe, page 288) or purchased gluten-free salsa
- 1 cup water
- 1 tablespoon dried Italian seasoning,** crushed
- ¼ teaspoon black pepper
- ⅛ to ¼ teaspoon crushed red pepper
- 1 ounce Parmesan cheese, finely shredded (¼ cup)

1. Preheat oven to 350°F. Line a 15×10×1-inch baking pan with foil. Halve squash lengthwise. Remove seeds. Place squash, cut sides down, in the prepared baking pan. Using a fork, prick the skin all over. Arrange sweet pepper, mushrooms, and onion wedges around squash. Coat vegetables with cooking spray. Bake for 45 to 55 minutes or until squash is tender.

2. Meanwhile, for meat sauce, in a large skillet cook ground beef, chopped onion, carrot, celery, and garlic over medium heat until meat is browned and vegetables are tender, using a wooden spoon to break up meat as it cooks. Drain off fat.

3. Stir tomato sauce, salsa, the water, Italian seasoning, black pepper, and crushed red pepper into meat sauce in skillet. Bring to boiling; reduce heat. Simmer, uncovered, for 10 to 15 minutes or until desired consistency, stirring occasionally.

4. Using a fork, remove squash pulp from the shells. In a large bowl toss 4 cups of the squash pulp with the roasted sweet pepper, mushrooms, and onion wedges (save remaining squash pulp for another use). Serve meat sauce over squash and vegetables. Sprinkle with cheese.

PER SERVING: 181 cal., 4 g fat (2 g sat. fat), 37 mg chol., 236 mg sodium, 21 g carb., 6 g fiber, 16 g pro.

*Tip: For added color, use half of a red sweet pepper and half of a green sweet pepper.

**Tip: Check the labels of these products carefully to be sure they do not contain added gluten.

Garlicky Zucchini Noodles

START TO FINISH: 20 minutes
MAKES: 6 servings

2 medium zucchini (about 10 ounces each), trimmed

3 tablespoons walnut oil or olive oil

6 cloves garlic, smashed, peeled, and halved lengthwise

½ cup broken walnuts

½ teaspoon kosher salt

¼ teaspoon crushed red pepper

4 thin slices gluten-free prosciutto or pancetta, torn

1 cup thinly sliced tart green apple

4 ounces soft goat cheese (chèvre), broken into pieces
Gluten-free baguette slices, toasted (optional)

1. Using a spiral vegetable slicer, cut zucchini into long thin strands (or using a vegetable peeler, cut lengthwise into thin ribbons). Cut through the strands with kitchen scissors to make the strands easier to serve.

2. In an extra-large skillet heat 2 tablespoons of the oil over medium-high heat. Add garlic; cook and stir about 2 minutes or until softened and starting to brown. Add zucchini; cook and toss with tongs for 1 minute. Transfer to a serving bowl. Add walnuts to skillet; cook and stir for 1 to 2 minutes or until toasted. Add to bowl with zucchini. Sprinkle with salt and crushed red pepper.

3. Add the remaining 1 tablespoon oil to skillet. Add prosciutto; cook about 1 minute or until browned and crisp, turning once. Add to bowl with zucchini mixture. Add apple slices; toss gently to combine. Top with goat cheese. If desired, serve with gluten-free baguette slices.

PER SERVING: 217 cal., 18 g fat (4 g sat. fat), 13 mg chol., 405 mg sodium, 9 g carb., 2 g fiber, 8 g pro.

Spicy Shrimp with Cabbage-Noodle Slaw

START TO FINISH: 38 minutes
MAKES: 8 servings

1½ **pounds fresh or frozen peeled, deveined large shrimp**
1 **tablespoon vegetable oil**
4 **cloves garlic, minced**
1 **teaspoon crushed red pepper**
4 **ounces dried rice vermicelli**
4 **cups shredded napa cabbage**
1 **cup shredded bok choy**
1 **cup coarsely shredded carrots**
½ **cup thinly sliced radishes**
½ **cup bite-size strips cucumber**
½ **cup bite-size strips red sweet pepper**
¼ **cup snipped fresh cilantro**
1 **recipe Lime-Ginger Dressing**
¼ **cup sliced almonds, toasted***

1. Thaw shrimp, if frozen. Rinse shrimp; pat dry with paper towels. In a large skillet heat oil over medium heat. Add garlic and crushed red pepper; cook and stir for 30 seconds. Add shrimp; cook and stir for 3 to 4 minutes or until shrimp are opaque. Remove from heat; set aside.

2. In a large saucepan cook noodles in lightly salted boiling water for 2 to 3 minutes or just until tender; drain. Use kitchen shears to snip noodles into smaller pieces.

3. For slaw, in an extra-large bowl combine noodles, cabbage, bok choy, carrots, radishes, cucumber, sweet pepper, and cilantro. Pour Lime-Ginger Dressing over slaw; toss gently to coat.

4. To serve, arrange slaw on a serving platter. Top with shrimp and sprinkle with almonds. Serve within 2 hours.

Lime-Ginger Dressing: In a small bowl whisk together 3 tablespoons vegetable oil, 2 tablespoons lime juice, 2 tablespoons rice vinegar, 2 teaspoons grated fresh ginger, 2 teaspoons honey, 2 teaspoons gluten-free soy sauce, ½ teaspoon salt, and ¼ teaspoon cayenne pepper or paprika.

PER SERVING: 249 cal., 10 g fat (1 g sat. fat), 129 mg chol., 405 mg sodium, 20 g carb., 2 g fiber, 20 g pro.

*Tip: To toast nuts, spread them in a dry skillet and cook over medium heat until lightly browned, stirring often to prevent burning.

Shrimp and Soba Noodles

START TO FINISH: 30 minutes   MAKES: 10 servings

- 2 pounds fresh or frozen shrimp in shells
- 8 ounces gluten-free dried soba (buckwheat noodles)
- 5 cups broccoli florets (about 1½ pounds broccoli)
- ⅓ cup gluten-free creamy peanut butter
- ¼ cup gluten-free tamari or liquid aminos
- 3 tablespoons rice vinegar
- 2 tablespoons toasted sesame oil
- 1 tablespoon chile oil*
- 1 tablespoon grated fresh ginger
- 3 cloves garlic, minced
- ½ cup chopped green onions
- ⅓ cup chopped cashews or almonds

1. Thaw shrimp, if frozen. Peel and devein shrimp, leaving tails intact if desired. Rinse shrimp; pat dry with paper towels.

2. In a Dutch oven cook soba in a large amount of boiling water for 4 minutes. Stir in broccoli; cook for 2 minutes. Stir in shrimp; cook for 2 to 3 minutes more or until shrimp are opaque and noodles are tender but still firm.

3. Meanwhile, for peanut sauce, in a small bowl stir together peanut butter and tamari. Stir in vinegar, sesame oil, chile oil, ginger, and garlic.

4. Drain noodle mixture; return to Dutch oven. Add peanut sauce, green onions, and nuts; toss gently to coat.

PER SERVING: 292 cal., 12 g fat (2 g sat. fat), 112 mg chol., 739 mg sodium, 25 g carb., 3 g fiber, 23 g pro.

*Tip: If you do not have chile oil, substitute 1 tablespoon vegetable oil plus a dash of cayenne pepper for the 1 tablespoon chile oil.

Spiraled Zucchini Noodle and Crispy Potato Salad

PREP: 10 minutes
BAKE: 15 minutes at 350°F +
4 minutes at 450°F
MAKES: 4 servings

Nonstick cooking spray*
1 large potato, peeled
1 tablespoon olive oil
¼ teaspoon salt
⅛ teaspoon black pepper
1 large zucchini
1 to 1½ cups halved cherry tomatoes
2 tablespoons snipped fresh basil, Italian parsley, or tarragon
1 recipe Lemon-Dijon Dressing

1. Preheat oven to 350°F. Line a baking sheet with nonstick foil. Coat foil with cooking spray; set aside.

2. Using a spiral vegetable slicer fitted with the chipper blade (large holes),** push the potato through the blade to make long potato spirals. Break spirals into 6- to 12-inch lengths and place in a large bowl. Drizzle with oil and sprinkle with salt and pepper; toss gently to coat. Transfer potato spirals to the prepared baking sheet, spreading in a single layer. Bake for 15 to 20 minutes or until tender, stirring once. Increase oven temperature to 450°F. Bake for 5 to 10 minutes more or until potato spirals are golden brown and crisp.

3. Meanwhile, using the spiral vegetable slicer fitted with the chipper blade (large holes),** push the zucchini through the blade to make long spirals. Break spirals into 6- to 12-inch lengths.

4. In a serving bowl combine the zucchini spirals, tomatoes, and basil. Add Lemon-Dijon Dressing; toss to coat. Top with the potato spirals.

Lemon-Dijon Dressing: In a small bowl whisk together 2 tablespoons canola oil, 2 teaspoons rice vinegar, 2 teaspoons lemon juice, 1 teaspoon gluten-free Dijon-style mustard, dash salt, and dash black pepper.

PER SERVING: 160 cal., 11 g fat (1 g sat. fat), 0 mg chol., 226 mg sodium, 15 g carb., 2 g fiber, 2 g pro.

*Tip: Check the label of this product carefully to be sure it does not contain added gluten.

*Tip: If you don't have a spiral slicer, substitute 2 small potatoes for the large potato. Using a vegetable peeler, slice the potatoes and zucchini lengthwise into thin, wide ribbons. Cut the ribbons into about ¼-inch-wide strips.

Cashew Soba with Cantaloupe and Cucumber

START TO FINISH: 35 minutes
MAKES: 4 servings

- 1 tablespoon vegetable oil
- 2 cloves garlic, finely chopped
- ¼ cup gluten-free cashew butter or gluten-free peanut butter
- 3 tablespoons gluten-free, reduced-sodium soy sauce or gluten-free tamari
- 2 tablespoons lime juice
- 1½ teaspoons grated fresh ginger
- 1½ teaspoons honey
- 1 teaspoon sriracha sauce*
- 2 teaspoons toasted sesame oil
- 1 to 2 tablespoons water (optional)
- 8 ounces gluten-free dried soba (buckwheat noodles)
- 1½ cups ½-inch cubes cantaloupe
- 1½ cups ½-inch chunks peeled English cucumber
- ½ cup loosely packed fresh cilantro leaves, snipped
- ⅓ cup thinly sliced green onions
  Toasted cashews (optional)
  Coarsely snipped fresh mint (optional)
  Lime wedges

1. In a small saucepan heat vegetable oil over medium-high heat. Reduce heat to medium; add garlic. Cook and stir about 2 minutes or until garlic is toasted. Set aside.

2. For dressing, in a food processor or blender combine cashew butter, soy sauce, lime juice, ginger, honey, sriracha sauce, and 1 teaspoon of the sesame oil. Cover and process or blend until smooth. If necessary, add the water, 1 tablespoon at a time, to make dressing pouring consistency.

3. Cook soba according to package directions; drain. Transfer to a large bowl. Drizzle with the remaining 1 teaspoon sesame oil; gently toss to coat. Add cantaloupe, cucumber, cilantro, and green onions. Pour dressing over soba mixture; gently toss to combine.

4. Top each serving with toasted garlic and, if desired, cashews and mint. Serve with lime wedges.

PER SERVING: 441 cal., 18 g fat (3 g sat. fat), 0 mg chol., 925 mg sodium, 63 g carb., 5 g fiber, 14 g pro.

*Tip: Check the label of this product carefully to be sure it does not contain added gluten.

Thai Noodle-Cabbage Salad

PREP: 20 minutes **STAND:** 10 minutes **MAKES:** 4 servings

1 **3.75-ounce package bean threads (cellophane noodles)**
¼ **cup gluten-free, reduced-sodium chicken broth or vegetable broth**
3 **tablespoons gluten-free creamy peanut butter**
2 **tablespoons honey**
2 **tablespoons gluten-free, reduced-sodium soy sauce**
1 **teaspoon lime juice**
½ **teaspoon toasted sesame oil**
1 **clove garlic, minced**
3 **cups shredded red, green, and/or napa cabbage**
1 **cup coarsely shredded carrots**
½ **cup snipped fresh cilantro**
¼ **cup coarsely chopped honey-roasted peanuts***
   Lime wedges

1. In a large bowl soak bean threads in enough hot water to cover for 10 minutes. Drain well. Using kitchen shears, snip bean threads into smaller strands.

2. Meanwhile, in a large bowl combine broth, peanut butter, honey, soy sauce, lime juice, sesame oil, and garlic. Add cabbage and carrots. Toss to combine.

3. Divide noodles among four bowls. Top with cabbage mixture. Sprinkle with cilantro and peanuts. Serve with lime wedges.

PER SERVING: 278 cal., 10 g fat (2 g sat. fat), 0 mg chol., 442 mg sodium, 44 g carb., 4 g fiber, 6 g pro.

*Tip: Check the label of this product carefully to be sure it does not contain added gluten.

Glass Noodle Veggie Salad with Peanut Sauce

PREP: 20 minutes   STAND: 15 minutes   MAKES: 4 servings

1 3.75-ounce package bean threads (cellophane noodles)
2 cups frozen sweet soybeans (edamame), thawed
2 cups broccoli florets, cut up or sliced
¾ cup chopped red sweet pepper
¼ cup finely chopped shallots
2 tablespoons gluten-free peanut butter
1 tablespoon gluten-free, reduced-sodium soy sauce or gluten-free tamari
1 tablespoon rice vinegar
2 teaspoons honey
1½ teaspoons grated fresh ginger
⅛ to ¼ teaspoon crushed red pepper
¼ cup lightly salted peanuts,* chopped
Lime wedges (optional)

1. In a large glass bowl combine bean threads and thawed edamame; pour enough boiling water over to cover completely. Cover and let stand for 15 to 20 minutes or until edamame are tender. Drain well; rinse with cold water and drain again. Snip noodles five or six times. Return noodles and edamame to the bowl. Add broccoli, sweet pepper, and shallots to the noodles; toss together.

2. For dressing, place peanut butter in a small microwave-safe bowl. Microwave about 40 seconds or until melted. Whisk in soy sauce, vinegar, honey, ginger, and crushed red pepper. Pour dressing over noodle mixture; toss to combine.

3. Divide among four bowls. Sprinkle with peanuts. If desired, serve with lime wedges.

PER SERVING: 303 cal., 12 g fat (1g sat. fat), 0 mg chol., 208 mg sodium, 41 g carb., 6 g fiber, 12 g pro.

*Tip: Check the label of this product carefully to be sure it does not contain added gluten.

Pizzas, Wraps & Tacos

Foods you can eat with your hands always make fun meals, but a no-gluten diet can limit your options. Let these recipes help you think beyond the bread. Look here for made-from-scratch pizzas, inventive sandwich wraps, and tempting tacos—all deliciously gluten-free.

Homemade Gluten-Free Pizza

PREP: 20 minutes   **RISE:** 20 minutes   **BAKE:** 15 minutes per pizza at 400°F   **MAKES:** 6 servings

2 cups Gluten-Free Flour Mix or purchased gluten-free all-purpose flour
1 teaspoon kosher salt
½ cup milk
¼ cup water
1 package active dry yeast
2 teaspoons sugar
2 egg whites
2 tablespoons olive oil
 Olive oil
 Gluten-free pizza toppings

1. In a large mixing bowl stir together the 2 cups Gluten-Free Flour Mix and salt; set aside. In a small saucepan combine milk and the water. Heat and stir over medium-low heat just until warm (105°F to 115°F). Remove from heat. Stir in yeast and sugar. Add yeast mixture to flour mixture; add egg whites and the 2 tablespoons oil. Beat with an electric mixer for 1 to 2 minutes or until smooth, scraping sides of bowl occasionally.

2. Line two flat baking sheets with parchment paper. Divide dough in half (dough will be soft); place each dough portion on a prepared baking sheet. Drizzle each portion with ½ teaspoon additional oil. Using oiled hands, press each portion into a 9-inch circle, building up edges slightly. Let rise at room temperature for 20 minutes.

3. Meanwhile, place a cold pizza stone or flat baking sheet in a cold oven. Preheat oven to 400°F. Gently slide one parchment sheet with pizza crust onto the hot baking stone or baking sheet. Bake for 5 to 8 minutes or until bottom of crust is browned and top appears set. Return crust to cold baking sheet and remove from oven; slide onto a wire rack. Repeat with the remaining crust.

4. Top crusts with gluten-free pizza toppings. Return pizzas, one at a time, to hot pizza stone or baking sheet. Bake about 10 minutes more or until bottom is browned and toppings are heated through.

PER SERVING: 313 cal., 10 g fat (3 g sat. fat), 9 mg chol., 481 mg sodium, 48 g carb., 2 g fiber, 8 g pro.

Gluten-Free Flour Mix: In a large airtight container whisk together 3 cups white rice flour, 3 cups potato starch, 2 cups sorghum flour, and 4 teaspoons xanthan gum. Cover and store at room temperature for up to 3 months.

Swiss Chard and Asparagus Pizza

PREP: 40 minutes
BAKE: 10 minutes at 400°F
BROIL: 3 minutes
STAND: 3 minutes
MAKES: 4 servings

Nonstick cooking spray*
10 ounces fresh Swiss chard
1 tablespoon olive oil
¾ cup finely chopped red onion
4 cloves garlic, minced
⅛ teaspoon salt
6 ounces fresh asparagus spears, trimmed and cut into ¼-inch pieces
2 eggs, lightly beaten
1 egg white
¼ teaspoon dried oregano, crushed
¼ teaspoon black pepper
⅛ teaspoon ground nutmeg
1½ cups cooked brown rice, cooled to room temperature
3 tablespoons grated Parmesan cheese*
4 ounces Havarti cheese, shredded (1 cup)
⅔ cup grape tomatoes, quartered or halved
½ cup thinly sliced sweet pepper
2 tablespoons thinly sliced pepperoncini salad peppers
1 tablespoon snipped fresh Italian parsley
1 tablespoon red wine vinegar
⅛ teaspoon black pepper

1. Preheat oven to 400°F. Line a baking sheet with foil. Coat foil with cooking spray; set baking sheet aside. Separate chard stems from leaves; cut into bite-size pieces, keeping stems and leaves separate.

2. In a large nonstick skillet heat 2 teaspoons of the oil over medium-high heat. Add ⅔ cup of the red onion, the garlic, and salt; cook for 2 minutes. Add chard stems and cook for 5 minutes, stirring frequently. Add chard leaves; cook about 5 minutes or until wilted and moisture evaporates, stirring occasionally. Add asparagus; cook and stir about 3 minutes more or until asparagus is crisp-tender. Spread vegetables on a plate to cool.

2. For crust, in a medium bowl combine eggs, egg white, oregano, the ¼ teaspoon pepper, and the nutmeg. Stir in cooked rice, Parmesan cheese, and the cooked vegetables. Spoon onto the prepared baking sheet. Press into a 12-inch circle. Bake for 10 minutes. Remove from oven.

4. Preheat broiler. Broil crust 4 to 5 inches from the heat for 2 minutes or just until golden. Sprinkle with Havarti cheese. Broil for 1 minute more. Let stand for 2 minutes. Lift foil and carefully slide a cutting board under crust; let stand 1 minute.

5. In a medium bowl combine the remaining 1 teaspoon oil, the remaining red onion, grape tomatoes, sweet pepper, pepperoncini peppers, parsley, vinegar, and the ⅛ teaspoon black pepper. To serve, cut crust into wedges; top with tomato mixture.

PER SERVING: 298 cal., 15 g fat (7 g sat. fat), 117 mg chol., 515 mg sodium, 27 g carb., 4 g fiber, 15 g pro.

***Tip:** Check the labels of these products carefully to be sure they do not contain added gluten.

Zucchini-and-Sage-Crusted Pizza

PREP: 25 minutes
BAKE: 33 minutes at 400°F
MAKES: 6 servings

1 tablespoon gluten-free stone-ground cornmeal

2½ cups packed shredded zucchini

1 egg, lightly beaten

6 ounces cheddar cheese, shredded (1½ cups)

¼ cup Gluten-Free Flour Mix (recipe, page 162) or purchased gluten-free all-purpose flour

¼ cup gluten-free stone-ground cornmeal

1 tablespoon snipped fresh sage

6 cloves garlic, minced

2 tablespoons olive oil
Gluten-free pizza toppings, such as All-Purpose Pizza Sauce (recipe, page 285), 20-Minute Marinara Sauce (recipe, page 287), or purchased gluten-free pizza sauce; sliced gluten-free pepperoni; and/or sliced or chopped vegetables

1. Preheat oven to 400°F. Line a 12-inch pizza pan with parchment paper. Sprinkle with the 1 tablespoon cornmeal; set aside.

2. Place shredded zucchini in a colander set in the sink; press several times with paper towels to remove excess moisture (you should have 2 cups packed zucchini after draining).

3. For crust, in a large bowl combine egg, 1 cup of the cheese, the flour, the ¼ cup cornmeal, the sage, and garlic. Stir in the drained zucchini. Spoon onto the prepared pizza pan. Using your hands, press into an even layer. Drizzle with oil.

4. Bake for 25 to 30 minutes or until golden. Remove from oven; cool slightly. Using a spatula, loosen crust but do not remove from pan (this keeps the crust from sticking after the final baking).

5. Top with pizza toppings and the remaining ½ cup cheese. Bake about 8 minutes more or until toppings are heated through and cheese is melted.

PER SERVING: 262 cal., 17 g fat (8 g sat. fat), 67 mg chol., 292 mg sodium, 15 g carb., 1 g fiber, 13 g pro.

Mini Pizzas with Spaghetti Squash Crusts

PREP: 20 minutes   **ROAST:** 50 minutes at 400°F   **BROIL:** 7 minutes per batch at 400°F   **MAKES:** 6 servings

1   3½- to 3¾-pound spaghetti squash
1   tablespoon olive oil
    Nonstick cooking spray*
1   egg, lightly beaten
1   tablespoon snipped fresh basil or 1 teaspoon dried basil, crushed
½   teaspoon salt
    Pizza toppings, such as All-Purpose Pizza Sauce (recipe, page 285), 20-Minute Marinara Sauce (recipe, page 287), or purchased gluten-free pizza sauce; sliced gluten-free pepperoni; crisp-cooked gluten-free bacon; sliced or chopped vegetables; shredded mozzarella cheese;* and/or grated Parmesan cheese*

1. Preheat oven to 400°F. Cut squash in half lengthwise; remove and discard seeds. Brush the insides of squash halves with oil. Place squash halves, cut sides down, in a 15×10×1-inch baking pan. Roast for 50 to 60 minutes or until squash is tender. Remove from oven; cool slightly.

2. Preheat broiler. Using a fork, remove squash pulp from shells. Place squash pulp in a colander set in the sink and press with a spatula to remove any excess moisture.

3. For crusts, line two large baking sheets with foil; coat foil with cooking spray. In a medium bowl combine egg, basil, and salt. Stir in drained squash. Spoon squash mixture into six mounds (about ½ cup each) onto the prepared baking sheets. Spread each mound into a 6-inch circle; lightly coat with cooking spray.

4. Broil crusts, one baking sheet at a time, 4 inches from the heat about 5 minutes or until lightly browned. Top with pizza toppings. Broil about 2 minutes more or until toppings are heated through and cheese(s) (if using) are melted.**

PER SERVING: 91 cal., 4 g fat (1 g sat. fat), 31 mg chol., 238 mg sodium, 13 g carb., 3 g fiber, 2 g pro.

*Tip: Check the label of this product carefully to be sure it does not contain added gluten.

**Tip: After broiling one pan of mini pizzas, place them on the bottom oven rack to keep warm while broiling the second pan of mini pizzas.

Grilled Strawberry, Tomato, and Chicken Wraps

PREP: 30 minutes
GRILL: 8 minutes
MAKES: 4 servings

12 ounces skinless, boneless chicken breast halves
  Salt and black pepper
1 small red onion, cut into thin wedges
2 cups fresh strawberries, hulled
2 cups grape or cherry tomatoes
2 tablespoons white balsamic vinegar
2 tablespoons olive oil
1 tablespoon snipped fresh mint
1 teaspoon honey
1 clove garlic, minced
  Salt and black pepper
12 butterhead (Boston or Bibb) lettuce leaves
1 ounce feta cheese, crumbled (¼ cup)
¼ cup sliced almonds, toasted

1. Cut chicken into 1½-inch pieces; sprinkle with salt and pepper. Alternately thread chicken and onion wedges onto skewers,* leaving ¼ inch between pieces. Alternately thread strawberries and tomatoes onto separate skewers, leaving ¼ inch between pieces.

2. For a charcoal or gas grill, place chicken kabobs on the rack of a covered grill directly over medium heat. Grill for 8 to 10 minutes or until chicken is no longer pink, turning once halfway through grilling. Add strawberry kabobs to grill for the last 3 to 5 minutes of grilling or until strawberries and tomatoes are softened and heated through, turning once halfway through grilling.

3. For vinaigrette, in a screw-top jar combine vinegar, oil, mint, honey, and garlic. Cover and shake well. Season to taste with salt and pepper.

4. Remove chicken, onion, strawberries, and tomatoes from skewers and place in a large bowl. Drizzle with vinaigrette; toss gently to coat. Serve in lettuce leaves and top with cheese and almonds.

PER SERVING: 284 cal., 14 g fat (3 g sat. fat), 63 mg chol., 356 mg sodium, 18 g carb., 4 g fiber, 22 g pro.

***Tip:** If using wooden skewers, soak them in enough water to cover for at least 30 minutes before using.

Turkey Lettuce Wraps with Spicy Peanut Sauce

PREP: 15 minutes
COOK: 20 minutes
MAKES: 8 servings

- 1 **pound ground uncooked turkey**
- 3 **cloves garlic, minced**
- 1 **tablespoon grated fresh ginger**
- 1 **teaspoon Chinese five-spice powder* or curry powder***
- 2 **cups shredded broccoli**
- 1 **small red onion, thinly sliced Salt and black pepper**
- 1 **recipe Spicy Peanut Sauce or ½ cup purchased gluten-free hoisin sauce**
- 8 **large Boston or Bibb lettuce leaves (about 2 heads)**
- 8 **lime wedges Snipped fresh cilantro (optional)**

1. In a large nonstick skillet cook turkey over medium-high heat for 5 minutes, breaking up turkey with a wooden spoon as it cooks. Stir in garlic, ginger, and ½ teaspoon of the five-spice powder; cook about 5 minutes more or until turkey is no longer pink. Using a slotted spoon transfer turkey mixture to a bowl; set aside.

2. In the same skillet cook broccoli, onion, and the remaining ½ teaspoon five-spice powder about 4 minutes or just until broccoli and onion are tender. Stir in the turkey mixture; heat through. Season to taste with salt and pepper.

3. To serve, spoon about 1 tablespoon Spicy Peanut Sauce on each lettuce leaf. Divide turkey-broccoli filling among lettuce leaves. Squeeze a lime wedge over each. If desired, top with cilantro. Serve immediately.

Spicy Peanut Sauce: In a small saucepan combine ¼ cup sugar, ¼ cup gluten-free crunchy peanut butter, 2 tablespoons water, and 1 tablespoon vegetable oil. Heat over medium-low heat just until bubbly and smooth (it will look a little curdled before this stage), stirring frequently. Season to taste with Sriracha sauce.

PER SERVING: 210 cal., 13 g fat (3 g sat. fat), 44 mg chol., 160 mg sodium, 12 g carb., 2 g fiber, 13 g pro.

*Tip: Check the labels of these products carefully to be sure they do not contain added gluten.

Vietnamese Beef Lettuce Wraps

PREP: 30 minutes **MARINATE:** 2 hours **GRILL:** 10 minutes **MAKES:** 4 servings

1   **pound boneless beef top sirloin steak, cut 1 inch thick**
¼   **cup chopped green onions**
2   **tablespoons sugar**
2   **tablespoons lime juice**
2   **tablespoons fish sauce**
1   **tablespoon chopped fresh lemongrass or ½ teaspoon finely shredded lemon peel**
3   **cloves garlic, minced**
8   **large lettuce leaves Assorted toppings (such as shredded carrot, fresh cilantro leaves, fresh mint leaves, and/or chopped unsalted peanuts)**
1   **recipe Rice Vinegar Sauce**

1. Trim fat from steak. Place steak in a large resealable plastic bag set in a shallow dish. For marinade, in a small bowl stir together green onions, sugar, lime juice, fish sauce, lemongrass, and garlic. Pour marinade over steak in bag; seal bag. Turn to coat steak. Marinate in the refrigerator for 2 to 24 hours, turning bag occasionally. Drain steak, discarding marinade.

2. For a charcoal or gas grill, place steak on the rack of an uncovered grill directly over medium heat. Grill to desired doneness, turning once halfway through grilling. Allow 10 to 12 minutes for medium rare (145°F) or 12 to 15 minutes for medium (160°F).

3. Thinly slice steak. Arrange steak slices in lettuce leaves. Add assorted toppings; drizzle with Rice Vinegar Sauce.

Rice Vinegar Sauce: In a small bowl stir together ¼ cup sugar; ¼ cup rice vinegar; 2 tablespoons lime juice; 2 tablespoons fish sauce; 2 cloves garlic, minced; and dash cayenne pepper.

PER SERVING: 348 cal., 13 g fat (5 g sat. fat), 76 mg chol., 671 mg sodium, 30 g carb., 1 g fiber, 29 g pro.

Pho-Flavor Flank Steak Lettuce Wraps

PREP: 30 minutes
SLOW COOK: 5 hours (low) or 2½ hours (high)
MAKES: 6 servings

2 pounds beef flank steak
2 cups coarsely chopped yellow onions
2 cups water
¼ cup fish sauce
2 tablespoons sugar
2 tablespoons rice vinegar
2 fresh jalapeño chile peppers, finely chopped (see tip, page 21)
4 teaspoons Chinese five-spice powder*
12 large Boston lettuce, Swiss chard, or napa cabbage leaves
4 ounces radishes, cut into thin strips (1 cup)
¾ cup fresh Thai basil leaves
3 green onions, thinly sliced diagonally
2 tablespoons lime juice
Sriracha sauce* (optional)
Lime wedges (optional)

1. Cut meat into 2-inch pieces. Place meat in a 3½- or 4-quart slow cooker. Top with yellow onions. For pho sauce, in a medium bowl combine the water, fish sauce, sugar, vinegar, half of the jalapeño peppers, and the five-spice powder. Pour pho sauce over meat and onions in cooker.

2. Cover and cook on low-heat setting for 5 to 6 hours or on high-heat setting for 2½ to 3 hours.

3. Remove meat from cooker, reserving cooking liquid. Transfer half of the meat to an airtight container or freezer container; cover and chill or freeze for another use. Shred or chop the remaining meat; transfer to a medium bowl. Strain cooking liquid. Stir enough of the strained liquid (about ¼ cup) into shredded meat to moisten.

4. To serve, divide shredded meat among lettuce leaves. Top with radishes, basil leaves, green onions, and the remaining jalapeño pepper. Sprinkle with lime juice. If desired, serve with sriracha sauce and lime wedges.

PER SERVING: 137 cal., 6 g fat (2 g sat. fat), 33 mg chol., 257 mg sodium, 4 g carb., 1 g fiber, 17 g pro.

*Tip: Check the labels of these products carefully to be sure they do not contain added gluten.

Pizza Lettuce Wraps

START TO FINISH: 20 minutes
MAKES: 4 servings

1 cup cherry or grape tomatoes, quartered
1 cup canned cannellini beans (white kidney beans),* rinsed and drained
3 ounces reduced-fat mozzarella cheese, shredded (¾ cup)
1 ounce gluten-free sliced cooked turkey pepperoni, chopped (¼ cup)
¼ cup snipped fresh basil
1 tablespoon snipped fresh oregano
8 large Bibb lettuce leaves

1. In a medium bowl combine tomatoes, beans, cheese, pepperoni, basil, and oregano.

2. Divide tomato mixture among lettuce leaves. Roll lettuce leaves around filling or leave open as cups.

PER SERVING: 144 cal., 5 g fat (2 g sat. fat), 16 mg chol., 435 mg sodium, 12 g carb., 4 g fiber, 12 g pro.

***Tip:** Check the label of this product carefully to be sure it does not contain added gluten.

Crunchy Peanut Pork Lettuce Wraps

START TO FINISH: 25 minutes   MAKES: 4 servings

Nonstick cooking spray*
- 1 teaspoon canola oil
- 1 clove garlic, minced
- 1 pound natural pork loin, trimmed of fat and cut into thin strips
- ⅛ teaspoon black pepper
- 2 tablespoons gluten-free peanut butter
- 2 tablespoons gluten-free, reduced-sodium soy sauce or gluten-free tamari
- 2 tablespoons water
- 1½ teaspoons grated fresh ginger
- 1 teaspoon sriracha sauce*
- ½ teaspoon apple cider vinegar
- 1 8-ounce can sliced water chestnuts, drained, rinsed, and chopped
- ¼ cup shredded carrot
- ¼ cup thinly sliced green onions
- 3 tablespoons gluten-free roasted and salted peanuts, chopped
- 12 large butterhead (Boston or Bibb) lettuce leaves

1. Coat a large nonstick skillet with cooking spray. Add the oil to the skillet and heat over medium-high heat.

2. Cook garlic in the hot oil for 30 seconds. Add pork to the skillet and sprinkle with the pepper. Cook about 5 minutes or until pork is no longer pink, turning once.

3. In a small bowl whisk together peanut butter, soy sauce, the water, ginger, sriracha sauce, and vinegar; pour over the pork in the hot skillet. Stir in the water chestnuts, carrot, onions, and peanuts. Heat through.

4. Spoon ¼ cup of pork mixture onto each lettuce leaf.

PER SERVING: 274 cal., 14 g fat (3 g sat. fat), 63 mg chol., 391 mg sodium, 7 g carb., 2 g fiber, 30 g pro.

*Tip: Check the labels of these products carefully to be sure they do not contain added gluten.

Thai Halibut Lettuce Wraps

PREP: 30 minutes
COOK: 11 minutes
MAKES: 4 servings

1 pound fresh or frozen halibut steaks, cut 1 inch thick
2 ounces thin rice noodles or rice sticks
¼ teaspoon salt
¼ teaspoon black pepper
1 tablespoon sesame oil
2 tablespoons rice vinegar
1 tablespoon fish sauce
1 tablespoon lime juice
1 tablespoon packed brown sugar
½ to 1 teaspoon crushed red pepper
1 medium carrot, cut into matchstick size pieces
1 cup snow peas, trimmed and very thinly sliced
¼ cup thinly sliced green onions
¼ cup canned bean sprouts, drained
¼ cup snipped fresh cilantro
¼ cup snipped fresh mint
8 to 12 leaves butterhead (Boston or Bibb) or romaine lettuce
4 teaspoons chopped unsalted peanuts

1. Thaw fish, if frozen. Rinse fish; pat dry with paper towels. Cut fish into 1-inch pieces; set aside. Fill a large saucepan with water and bring to boiling. Add rice noodles or rice sticks; cook about 3 minutes or just until tender. Drain and rinse with cold water. Gently squeeze noodles to remove most of the water. If desired, snip noodles into 2- to 3-inch pieces.

2. Meanwhile, sprinkle fish with the salt and black pepper. In a large skillet heat sesame oil over medium heat. Add fish to skillet. Cook for 8 to 12 minutes or until fish flakes when tested with a fork, turning frequently to brown all sides.

3. For dressing, in a small bowl combine rice vinegar, fish sauce, lime juice, brown sugar, and crushed red pepper.

4. Place 2 to 3 lettuce leaves on each of four plates. Spoon fish, noodles, vegetables, cilantro, and mint into lettuce leaves. Drizzle with dressing and sprinkle with peanuts.

PER SERVING: 244 cal., 7 g fat (1 g sat. fat), 56 mg chol., 634 mg sodium, 21 g carb., 2 g fiber, 24 g pro.

Steak and Herb Tacos

PREP: 25 minutes
MARINATE: 2 hours
GRILL: 14 minutes
MAKES: 6 servings

- 1 to 1½ pounds boneless beef top sirloin steak, cut 1 inch thick
- 2 tablespoons snipped fresh marjoram or oregano or 2 teaspoon dried marjoram or oregano, crushed
- 1 tablespoon chili powder*
- 2 teaspoons garlic powder
- ¼ teaspoon salt
- ¼ teaspoon cayenne pepper
- 1 tablespoon olive oil or vegetable oil
- 12 6- to 8-inch corn tortillas*
- 1 cup chopped tomatoes
- 4 to 6 radishes, sliced
- ½ cup snipped fresh cilantro
- ⅓ cup chopped onion
- 6 ounces queso fresco, crumbled, or Monterey Jack cheese, shredded (1½ cups)
  Lime wedges (optional)

1. Trim fat from meat. Place meat in a shallow dish. For marinade, in a small bowl combine marjoram, chili powder, garlic powder, salt, and cayenne pepper; stir in oil. Spread marinade evenly over both sides of meat. Cover and marinate in the refrigerator for 2 to 4 hours.

2. For a charcoal or gas grill, place meat on the grill rack directly over medium heat. Cover and grill for 14 to 18 minutes for medium rare (145°F) or 18 to 22 minutes for medium (160°F), turning once halfway through grilling.

3. Meanwhile, stack tortillas and wrap in foil. Add packet to grill for the last 10 minutes of grilling or until heated through, turning occasionally.

4. Slice or coarsely chop meat. Serve in warm tortillas with tomatoes, radishes, cilantro, and onion. Sprinkle with cheese. If desired, serve with lime wedges.

PER SERVING: 326 cal., 14 g fat (5 g sat. fat), 65 mg chol., 400 mg sodium, 26 g carb., 4 g fiber, 25 g pro.

*Tip: Check the labels of these products carefully to be sure they do not contain added gluten.

Fajita-Style Beef Tacos

PREP: 15 minutes   BROIL: 8 minutes   COOK: 12 minutes   STAND: 5 minutes   MAKES: 4 servings

12 ounces boneless beef sirloin steak, cut ¾ inch thick
⅛ teaspoon salt
⅛ teaspoon black pepper
⅛ teaspoon cayenne pepper
1 tablespoon canola oil
2 cups halved and thinly sliced sweet onions, such as Vidalia or Maui
1 mango, seeded, peeled, and chopped
8 6-inch corn tortillas,* warmed
¼ cup snipped fresh cilantro
Lime wedges
Fresh jalapeño chile peppers, sliced (see tip, page 21) (optional)

1. Preheat broiler. Trim fat from steak. In a small bowl combine salt, black pepper, and cayenne pepper; sprinkle evenly over steak. Place steak on the unheated rack of a broiler pan. Broil 3 to 4 inches from heat for 8 to 12 minutes or until desired doneness, turning once. Cover with foil; let stand for 5 minutes.

2. Meanwhile, in a large skillet heat oil over medium heat. Add onions; cover and cook about 12 minutes or until very tender and browned, stirring occasionally. Reduce heat if onions brown too quickly.

3. Thinly slice steak across the grain. Divide steak, onions, and mango among tortillas. Sprinkle with cilantro and serve with lime wedges and, if desired, jalapeños. Serve immediately.

PER SERVING: 377 cal., 15 g fat (5 g sat. fat), 39 mg chol., 140 mg sodium, 41 g carb., 6 g fiber, 22 g pro.

*Tip: Check the label of this product carefully to be sure it does not contain added gluten.

Pork Tacos with Spicy Watermelon Salsa

PREP: 10 minutes
GRILL: 10 minutes
MAKES: 6 servings

1½ cups chopped seeded watermelon
1 to 2 fresh banana or Anaheim chile peppers, finely chopped (see tip, page 21)
¼ cup snipped fresh cilantro
1 recipe Homemade Southwestern Seasoning or 2 teaspoons purchased Southwestern seasoning*
4 boneless pork country-style ribs (about 1¼ pounds total)
12 corn tortillas*

1. For watermelon salsa, in a medium bowl combine watermelon, banana pepper, and cilantro; set aside.

2. Rub Homemade Southwestern Seasoning onto ribs to coat. Set ribs aside. Wrap tortillas in foil.

3. For a charcoal or gas grill, place ribs on the rack of a covered grill directly over medium heat. Grill for 10 to 12 minutes or until an instant-read thermometer inserted in meat registers 145°F, turning once halfway through grilling. Place foil-wrapped tortillas on grill rack for the last 5 minutes of grilling; turn once.

4. Transfer ribs to a cutting board; let rest for 2 minutes. Thinly slice meat. Serve with tortillas and watermelon salsa.

Homemade Southwestern Seasoning: In a small bowl combine ½ teaspoon salt, ½ teaspoon sugar, ½ teaspoon garlic powder, and ½ teaspoon ground chipotle chile pepper or chili powder.*

PER SERVING: 294 cal., 12 g fat (2 g sat. fat), 69 mg chol., 265 mg sodium, 25 g carb., 4 g fiber, 21 g pro.

*Tip: Check the labels of these products carefully to be sure they do not contain added gluten.

Pork-Chile Verde Tacos

PREP: 40 minutes
COOK: 15 minutes
SLOW COOK: 6 hours (low) or
3 hours (high) + 15 minutes (high)
MAKES: 6 servings

1 teaspoon ground cumin
½ teaspoon salt
¼ teaspoon black pepper
1½ pounds boneless pork
   shoulder
   Nonstick cooking spray*
1 tablespoon olive oil
1 pound fresh tomatillos, husks
   removed and chopped (about
   4 cups)
1 cup chopped onion
3 teaspoons finely shredded
   lime peel
2 tablespoons lime juice
4 cloves garlic, minced
¾ cup chopped yellow or red
   sweet pepper
12 6-inch corn tortillas*
2 tablespoons snipped fresh
   cilantro
   Salsa Verde (recipe,
   page 289) or purchased
   gluten-free salsa verde
   (optional)

1. In a small bowl combine cumin, salt, and black pepper; set aside. Trim fat from meat. Cut meat into 1-inch pieces. Sprinkle cumin mixture over meat. Coat a large skillet with cooking spray. Cook half of the meat in hot skillet over medium heat until browned. Remove meat from skillet. Add oil to skillet. Brown remaining meat in hot oil. Drain off fat. Place meat in a 3½- or 4-quart slow cooker. Add tomatillos, onion, 1 teaspoon of the lime peel, the lime juice, and garlic. Stir to combine.

2. Cover and cook on low-heat setting for 6 to 8 hours or on high-heat setting for 3 to 4 hours.

3. If using low-heat setting, turn to high-heat setting. Add sweet pepper to cooker. Cover and cook for 15 minutes more. Fill corn tortillas with pork-chile verde; sprinkle with cilantro and the remaining lime peel. If desired, serve with Salsa Verde.

PER SERVING: 333 cal., 11 g fat (3 g sat. fat), 73 mg chol., 314 mg sodium, 32 g carb., 4 g fiber, 27 g pro.

***Tip:** Check the labels of these products carefully to be sure they do not contain added gluten.

Fish Tacos with Cabbage and Chile Pepper Slaw

PREP: 40 minutes   **BAKE:** 10 minutes at 400°F   **MAKES:** 6 servings

1½ **pounds fresh or frozen cod or halibut fillets**
 2 **fresh tomatillos, husked and cut into ½-inch pieces**
 2 **teaspoons olive oil**
 1 **clove garlic, minced**
 ½ **teaspoon finely shredded orange peel**
 ½ **teaspoon finely shredded lime peel**
   Salt and black pepper
12 **6-inch corn tortillas***
 1 **recipe Cabbage and Chile Pepper Slaw**

1. Thaw fish, if frozen. Preheat oven to 400°F. Rinse fish; pat dry with paper towels. Cut fish into 1-inch pieces. In a large bowl toss together fish, tomatillos, oil, garlic, orange peel, and lime peel. Season with salt and pepper; set aside.

2. Cut six 12-inch-squares of foil. Place about ⅔ cup of the fish mixture in the center of each foil square. Fold foil in half diagonally to form a triangle. Fold edges together two or three times to seal, leaving space for steam to build. Place packets in a single layer on a large baking sheet.

3. Bake for 10 to 12 minutes or until fish flakes when tested with a fork (carefully open a packet to check doneness).

4. Meanwhile, in a dry skillet heat each tortilla over medium-high heat about 30 seconds or until softened, turning once.

5. To serve, carefully open packets. Divide fish mixture among tortillas. Top tacos with Cabbage and Chile Pepper Slaw.

Cabbage and Chile Pepper Slaw: In a medium bowl combine 1¼ cups finely shredded green cabbage; ½ cup thinly sliced red onion; ½ cup shredded carrot; 1 medium poblano or pasilla chile pepper, halved crosswise, seeded, and thinly sliced (see tip, page 21); and ¼ cup snipped fresh cilantro. For dressing, in a small bowl combine 3 tablespoons olive oil, 2 tablespoons lime juice, and 1 tablespoon orange juice. Season to taste with salt. Pour dressing over cabbage mixture; toss to coat.

PER SERVING: 341 cal., 13 g fat (2 g sat. fat), 36 mg chol., 293 mg sodium, 30 g carb., 5 g fiber, 28 g pro.

***Tip:** Check the label of this product carefully to be sure it does not contain added gluten.

Tamarind Shrimp Tacos with Roasted Corn Slaw

PREP: 30 minutes   MARINATE: 30 minutes   BAKE: 10 minutes at 350°F   MAKES: 6 servings

1 pound fresh or frozen medium shrimp
2 tablespoons canola oil or vegetable oil
2 tablespoons tamarind concentrate*
6 cloves garlic, minced
1 tablespoon packed brown sugar
1 to 2 teaspoons adobo sauce from canned gluten-free chipotle chile peppers in adobo sauce
  Dash salt
2 tablespoons hot water
12 6-inch corn tortillas**
  Nonstick cooking spray**
1 cup frozen whole kernel corn
2 tablespoons mayonnaise**
1 tablespoon lime juice
¼ teaspoon salt
2 cups finely shredded cabbage
½ cup finely chopped red onion
½ cup snipped fresh parsley
  Salsa Verde (recipe, page 289) or purchased gluten-free salsa verde (optional)

1. Thaw shrimp, if frozen. Peel and devein shrimp. Rinse shrimp; pat dry with paper towels. Set aside.

2. For marinade, in a medium bowl combine oil, tamarind concentrate, garlic, brown sugar, adobo sauce, and the dash salt. Add the hot water, whisking until smooth. Coarsely chop the shrimp; add to marinade, tossing to coat. Cover and marinate in the refrigerator for 30 minutes.

3. Preheat oven to 350°F. Stack tortillas and wrap tightly in foil. Bake about 10 minutes or until heated through.

4. For roasted corn slaw, coat a large skillet with cooking spray; heat over medium-high heat. Add frozen corn all at once to hot skillet and spread in a single layer. Cook, without stirring, for 3 minutes; then stir. Cook, without stirring, for 3 minutes more or until corn is light golden brown. Transfer to a medium bowl. Cool completely. Set skillet aside. When corn is cool, stir in mayonnaise, lime juice, and the ¼ teaspoon salt. Add cabbage, onion, and parsley; stir to coat. Set corn slaw aside.

5. Return skillet to medium-high heat. Add shrimp with the marinade; cook and stir for 3 to 4 minutes or until the shrimp are opaque.

6. To assemble tacos, use a slotted spoon to spoon cooked shrimp onto warm tortillas, reserving cooking juices in skillet. Top shrimp with roasted corn slaw. Drizzle with reserved cooking juices. Fold tortillas around filling. If desired, serve with Salsa Verde.

PER SERVING: 303 cal., 11 g fat (1 g sat. fat), 97 mg chol., 1,020 mg sodium, 38 g carb., 4 g fiber, 14 g pro.

*Tip: Tamarind concentrate can be found in Asian and Mexican sections of large grocery stores. If you can't find it, simmer 1 cup tamarind juice until it is reduced to a syrupy consistency.

**Tip: Check the labels of these products carefully to be sure they do not contain added gluten.

Skillets & Stir-Fries

When you use a hot skillet or wok to sear and caramelize meats, vegetables, and gluten-free grains, you'll enhance their natural flavors with little effort. These recipes show you how to use this quick cooking method to make weeknight-friendly stove-top meals.

Jerk Braised Chicken Thighs with Sweet Potatoes

PREP: 25 minutes   COOK: 35 minutes   MAKES: 4 servings

8 bone-in chicken thighs, skinned
¼ teaspoon salt
¼ teaspoon black pepper
1 tablespoon olive oil
1 medium onion, halved and thinly sliced
1 tablespoon grated fresh ginger
2 cloves garlic, minced
1 cup gluten-free, reduced-sodium chicken broth
2 teaspoons Jamaican Jerk Rub (recipe, page 303) or purchased gluten-free Jamaican jerk seasoning
2 small sweet potatoes, peeled, halved lengthwise, and sliced ½ inch thick (about 1 pound)
Snipped fresh cilantro

1. Sprinkle chicken thighs with the salt and pepper. In an extra-large skillet heat oil over medium-high heat. Add chicken; cook until browned on both sides. Remove chicken from skillet. Drain skillet, reserving 1 tablespoon drippings.

2. In the same skillet cook and stir onion, ginger, and garlic in the 1 tablespoon drippings about 4 minutes or until tender. Add broth, stirring to scrape up any browned bits from the bottom of the skillet. Bring to boiling.

3. Return chicken to skillet. Sprinkle chicken with jerk rub. Return to boiling; reduce heat. Simmer, covered, for 20 minutes. Add sweet potatoes to skillet. Simmer, covered, about 15 minutes more or until chicken is done (180°F) and sweet potatoes are tender. Sprinkle with cilantro.

PER SERVING: 283 cal., 9 g fat (2 g sat. fat), 115 mg chol., 604 mg sodium, 20 g carb., 3 g fiber, 30 g pro.

Cilantro Chicken with Peanuts

START TO FINISH: 25 minutes
MAKES: 4 servings

2 teaspoons peanut oil
1 pound skinless, boneless chicken breast halves, cut into 1-inch pieces
¼ cup honey-roasted peanuts*
4 cloves garlic, minced
2 teaspoons minced fresh ginger
¼ cup sliced green onions
1 tablespoon gluten-free soy sauce or gluten-free tamari
2 teaspoons rice vinegar
1 teaspoon toasted sesame oil
1 cup fresh cilantro leaves
4 cups finely shredded napa cabbage or 2 cups hot cooked brown rice
Fresh cilantro (optional)
Lime wedges (optional)

1. In a large heavy skillet heat peanut oil over medium-high heat. Add chicken; cook and stir for 2 minutes. Add peanuts, garlic, and ginger; cook and stir about 3 minutes or until chicken is no longer pink.

2. Add green onions, soy sauce, rice vinegar, and sesame oil to skillet. Cook and stir for 2 minutes more. Remove from heat. Stir in the 1 cup cilantro.

3. Serve chicken stir-fry over cabbage. If desired, garnish with additional cilantro and/or serve with lime wedges.

PER SERVING: 222 cal., 9 g fat (2 g sat. fat), 66 mg chol., 362 mg sodium, 7 g carb., 2 g fiber, 30 g pro.

*Tip: Check the label of this product carefully to be sure it does not contain added gluten.

Triple-Mango Chicken

START TO FINISH: 20 minutes
MAKES: 4 servings

- 1 tablespoon olive oil
- 4 small skinless, boneless chicken breast halves
- 1 mango, seeded, peeled, and cubed
- ½ cup mango-blend fruit drink*
- ¼ cup gluten-free mango chutney
- 2 medium zucchini, thinly sliced lengthwise
- ¼ cup water
  Salt
  Crushed red pepper

1. In an extra-large skillet heat oil over medium-high heat; reduce heat to medium. Add chicken. Cook for 6 minutes; turn chicken over. Add mango cubes, mango drink, and chutney. Cook for 4 to 6 minutes or until chicken is done (165°F), stirring occasionally.

2. Meanwhile, in a 2-quart square microwave-safe dish place zucchini and the water. Cover with vented plastic wrap. Microwave for 2 to 3 minutes or until crisp-tender, stirring once; drain. Place chicken on top of zucchini. Season to taste with salt and crushed red pepper.

PER SERVING: 274 cal., 9 g fat (1 g sat. fat), 66 mg chol., 277 mg sodium, 22 g carb., 2 g fiber, 28 g pro.

*Tip: If you like, substitute mango nectar, carrot juice, or orange juice for the mango-blend fruit drink.

Orange-Ginger Chicken Stir-Fry

START TO FINISH: 45 minutes   **MAKES:** 6 servings

- 3 tablespoons olive oil
- 1 pound carrots, cut into thin strips
- 1 medium red sweet pepper, seeded and cut into thin bite-size strips
- 1 pound skinless, boneless chicken breast halves, cut into 1-inch pieces
- 1 cup frozen shelled sweet soybeans (edamame), thawed
- 1 tablespoon grated fresh ginger
- 3 cloves garlic, minced
- ½ teaspoon crushed red pepper (optional)
- 1½ cups gluten-free, reduced-sodium chicken broth
- ¼ cup frozen orange juice concentrate, thawed
- 2 tablespoons gluten-free, reduced-sodium soy sauce or gluten-free tamari
- 2 tablespoons cornstarch*
- 2 tablespoons water
- 3 cups hot cooked quinoa
- 1 tablespoon toasted sesame seeds

1. In a large skillet heat 1 tablespoon of the oil over medium heat. Add carrots; cook and stir for 5 minutes. Add sweet pepper; cook and stir about 3 minutes more or until carrots are tender. Transfer to a medium bowl. In the same skillet heat 1 tablespoon of the oil over medium-high heat. Add chicken; cook and stir for 4 to 5 minutes or until chicken is no longer pink. Transfer chicken to the bowl with vegetables; stir in edamame.

2. In the same skillet heat the remaining 1 tablespoon oil over medium heat. Add ginger, garlic, and, if desired, crushed red pepper; cook and stir for 30 seconds. Stir in broth, orange juice concentrate, and soy sauce. Bring to boiling.

3. In a small bowl combine cornstarch and the water; stir into broth mixture. Simmer, uncovered, for 2 minutes. Stir in chicken and vegetables. Cook and stir until heated through. Serve over quinoa and sprinkle with sesame seeds.

PER SERVING: 373 cal., 13 g fat (2 g sat. fat), 48 mg chol., 481 mg sodium, 39 g carb., 7 g fiber, 26 g pro.

*Tip: Check the label of this product carefully to be sure it does not contain added gluten.

Parmesan-Stuffed Chicken and Melted Strawberries

PREP: 30 minutes
BAKE: 15 minutes at 400°F
MAKES: 6 servings

- 3 **cups fresh strawberries (halve or quarter large berries)**
- ¼ **cup low-sugar strawberry preserves***
- 2 **tablespoons white balsamic vinegar or white wine vinegar**
- ½ **teaspoon sea salt or regular salt**
- ¼ **teaspoon black pepper**
- 6 **skinless, boneless chicken breast halves (1½ to 2 pounds total)**
- 2 **ounces Parmesan cheese or white cheddar cheese**
- 6 **large fresh basil leaves**
- 2 **cloves garlic, minced**
- 1 **tablespoon olive oil Coarsely ground black pepper (optional)**

1. Preheat oven to 400°F. In a 3-quart rectangular baking dish combine strawberries, preserves, and vinegar. Sprinkle with ¼ teaspoon of the salt and ⅛ teaspoon of the black pepper; set aside.

2. Cut a horizontal pocket in each chicken breast half by cutting from one side almost to, but not through, the opposite side. Cut cheese into six 3×½-inch pieces. Wrap a basil leaf around each piece of cheese; stuff into chicken breast pockets. Use wooden toothpicks or skewers to close and secure pockets. Sprinkle with the remaining ¼ teaspoon salt and ⅛ teaspoon pepper.

3. In an extra-large oven-going skillet cook garlic in hot oil over medium heat for 30 seconds. Add chicken; cook about 5 minutes or until golden brown, turning once.

4. Place skillet in oven. Bake, uncovered, for 5 minutes. Add baking dish with the strawberry mixture to oven. Bake for 10 to 13 minutes or until chicken is done (170°F), the berries are softened, and the jam mixture has thickened. Serve chicken with melted strawberries. If desired, sprinkle with coarsely ground pepper.

PER SERVING: 229 cal., 6 g fat (2 g sat. fat), 72 mg chol., 355 mg sodium, 11 g carb., 2 g fiber, 30 g pro.

*Tip: Check the label of this product carefully to be sure it does not contain added gluten.

Lemon–Braised Chicken Tenders and Cauliflower

START TO FINISH: 30 minutes
MAKES: 4 servings

- 2 **tablespoons olive oil**
- 1 **pound chicken breast tenderloins**
- 2 **cups cauliflower florets**
- ⅓ **cup chopped onion**
- 5 **cloves garlic, slivered**
- 1 **teaspoon snipped fresh thyme**
- ¼ **teaspoon salt**
- ¼ **teaspoon coarsely ground black pepper**
- 1 **teaspoon finely shredded lemon peel**
- ¼ **cup lemon juice**
- ¾ **cup gluten-free, reduced-sodium chicken broth**
- 4 **cups packaged fresh baby spinach**
- ¼ **cup bias-sliced green onions**
- 2 **cups hot cooked brown rice (optional)**
  Finely shredded lemon peel and/or fresh thyme (optional)

1. In an extra-large skillet heat oil over medium-high heat. Add chicken; cook for 6 to 8 minutes or until chicken is done (165°F), turning once halfway through cooking. Remove from skillet; cover and keep warm.

2. Add cauliflower and chopped onion to skillet; cook about 2 minutes or until lightly browned, stirring frequently. Add garlic, snipped thyme, salt, and pepper; cook and stir for 30 seconds more. Add lemon juice, stirring to scrape up any crusty browned bits from bottom of skillet. Add the 1 teaspoon lemon peel and the broth. Bring to boiling; reduce heat. Simmer, covered, for 6 to 8 minutes or until cauliflower is tender. Remove from heat.

3. Stir in chicken, spinach, and green onions. Cover and let stand about 2 minutes or until spinach is slightly wilted.

4. If desired, serve lemon-braised chicken over brown rice and sprinkle with additional lemon peel and/or thyme.

PER SERVING: 235 cal., 10 g fat (2 g sat. fat), 73 mg chol., 442 mg sodium, 9 g carb., 3 g fiber, 28 g pro.

Curried Chicken with Cabbage, Apple, and Onion

PREP: 15 minutes   **COOK:** 16 minutes   **MAKES:** 4 servings

1 teaspoon curry powder*
¼ teaspoon salt
¼ teaspoon black pepper
4 small skinless, boneless chicken breast halves (1 to 1¼ pounds total)
2 teaspoons olive oil
2 teaspoons butter
1 medium onion, sliced and separated into rings
3 cups shredded cabbage
2 red-skin cooking apples (such as Rome or Jonathan), cored and thinly sliced
½ cup apple juice

1. In a small bowl combine ½ teaspoon of the curry powder, the salt, and pepper. Sprinkle spice mixture evenly over chicken; rub in with your fingers.

2. In a large nonstick skillet heat oil over medium-high heat. Add chicken. Cook for 8 to 12 minutes or until chicken is done (165°F), turning once halfway through cooking. Transfer chicken to a platter. Cover to keep warm.

3. Melt butter in the hot skillet. Add onion. Cook about 5 minutes or until tender, stirring occasionally. Stir in cabbage, apple slices, and apple juice. Sprinkle with the remaining ½ teaspoon curry powder. Cook for 3 to 4 minutes or just until apples and vegetables are tender, stirring occasionally. Return chicken to skillet; heat through.

PER SERVING: 237 cal., 6 g fat (2 g sat. fat), 71 mg chol., 231 mg sodium, 19 g carb., 4 g fiber, 27 g pro.

***Tip:** Check the label of this product carefully to be sure it does not contain added gluten.

Chicken and Lentils in Apple-Curry Sauce

PREP: 25 minutes
COOK: 40 minutes
MAKES: 6 servings

2 tablespoons olive oil
6 skinless, boneless chicken thighs
1 large yellow onion, halved and thinly sliced
1 tablespoon grated fresh ginger
4 cloves garlic, minced
2 tablespoons tomato paste
1 tablespoon mild curry powder*
1 teaspoon salt
1 teaspoon garam masala*
3 cups gluten-free, reduced-sodium chicken broth
1½ cups lentils, rinsed and drained
3 medium red and/or green cooking apples, cored and cut into 1-inch pieces
2 5-ounce packages fresh baby spinach
 Plain yogurt* (optional)
 Sliced green onions (optional)

1. In an extra-large skillet heat oil over medium-high heat. Add chicken; cook for 4 to 6 minutes or until browned, turning once. Remove chicken from skillet; set aside.

2. Add yellow onion to skillet; cook over medium heat for 3 minutes, stirring occasionally. Add ginger and garlic; cook and stir for 1 minute more. Stir in tomato paste, curry powder, salt, and garam masala. Add broth and lentils; return chicken to skillet. Bring to boiling; reduce heat. Simmer, covered, for 30 minutes.

3. Add apples to skillet. Simmer, covered, about 10 minutes more or until lentils are tender. Gradually stir in about 3 cups of the spinach.

4. To serve, divide the remaining spinach among shallow bowls. Add chicken and lentils in sauce. If desired, top with yogurt and sprinkle with green onions.

PER SERVING: 383 cal., 8 g fat (1 g sat. fat), 66 mg chol., 812 mg sodium, 49 g carb., 19 g fiber, 30 g pro.

*Tip: Check the labels of these products carefully to be sure they do not contain added gluten.

Asian Orange Chicken Thighs with Cauliflower Rice

PREP: 25 minutes
COOK: 18 minutes
BAKE: 30 minutes at 375°F
MAKES: 4 servings

Nonstick cooking spray*
2 tablespoons sesame oil (not toasted)
4 large bone-in chicken thighs (about 2¼ pounds total), skin removed
1 tablespoon gluten-free, reduced-sodium soy sauce or gluten-free tamari
1 teaspoon finely shredded orange peel
1 tablespoon orange juice
1 tablespoon rice vinegar
1 tablespoon packed brown sugar
¼ teaspoon crushed red pepper
2 tablespoons cold water
1 teaspoon cornstarch*
4 cups coarsely chopped purple or white cauliflower florets
½ teaspoon kosher salt
⅛ teaspoon black pepper
Snipped fresh cilantro (optional)

1. Preheat oven to 375°F. Coat a 2-quart square baking dish with cooking spray. In an extra-large nonstick skillet heat 1 tablespoon of the sesame oil over medium-high heat. Add chicken to hot oil; cook about 10 minutes, turning to brown evenly. Transfer chicken to prepared dish, arranging in a single layer. Drain and discard drippings from the skillet.

2. For sauce, in a small bowl whisk together soy sauce, orange peel, orange juice, vinegar, brown sugar, and the crushed red pepper. Whisk together the cold water and cornstarch; whisk into sauce. Add sauce to the skillet. Cook and stir until thickened and bubbly; pour sauce over chicken thighs in dish.

3. Bake, uncovered, about 30 minutes or until chicken is done (180°F).

4. Meanwhile, place cauliflower in a large food processor. Cover and pulse several times until evenly chopped into rice-size pieces.

5. Wipe out the skillet. Heat the remaining 1 tablespoon oil in the skillet over medium-high heat; add the cauliflower rice, salt, and pepper. Cook the cauliflower for 8 to 10 minutes or until it begins to brown, stirring occasionally. If desired, sprinkle chicken and cauliflower rice with cilantro and additional orange peel.

PER SERVING: 285 cal., 13 g fat (3 g sat. fat), 145 mg chol., 526 mg sodium, 9 g carb., 2 g fiber, 32 g pro.

*Tip: Check the labels of these products carefully to be sure they do not contain added gluten.

Sloppy Joe Tostadas with Yams and Black Beans

START TO FINISH: 35 minutes   MAKES: 6 servings

- 8 ounces lean ground beef
- 8 ounces lean uncooked ground turkey
- 1 cup chopped, peeled sweet potato
- 1 14.5-ounce can no-salt-added diced fire-roasted tomatoes, undrained
- ½ cup water
- ½ of a 6-ounce can (⅓ cup) tomato paste
- 2 teaspoons hot chili powder
- 1 teaspoon cider vinegar
- ¼ teaspoon salt
- 6 6-inch corn tortillas* Nonstick cooking spray*
- 1 15-ounce can black beans,* rinsed and drained
- 1 to 2 tablespoons water (optional)
- 1 ounce queso fresco, crumbled (¼ cup)
- 2 tablespoons snipped fresh cilantro (optional)

1. Preheat oven to 425°F. In a large skillet cook ground beef, ground turkey, and sweet potato over medium heat until meat is browned, using a wooden spoon to break up meat as it cooks. Drain off fat. Stir in tomatoes, the water, tomato paste, chili powder, vinegar, and salt. Bring to boiling; reduce heat. Simmer, uncovered, about 10 minutes or until sweet potato is tender and mixture is desired consistency, stirring occasionally.

2. Meanwhile, place tortillas on a baking sheet. Coat both sides of tortillas with cooking spray. Bake about 7 minutes or until tortillas are crisp and starting to brown.

3. In a medium microwave-safe bowl coarsely mash beans with a fork or potato masher just until they cling together. If needed, add 1 to 2 tablespoons of water to the beans to help mash. Microwave for 1 to 2 minutes or until heated through.

4. To serve, spread mashed beans on tortillas. Spoon meat mixture on beans. Sprinkle with queso fresco and, if desired, cilantro.

PER SERVING: 255 cal., 6 g fat (2 g sat. fat), 46 mg chol., 557 mg sodium, 28 g carb., 6 g fiber, 24 g pro.

*Tip: Check the labels of these products carefully to be sure they do not contain added gluten.

Beef Medallions with Kasha Pilaf

START TO FINISH: 35 minutes
MAKES: 4 servings

1½ cups water
⅔ cup gluten-free toasted buckwheat groats (kasha)
5 teaspoons olive oil
½ cup chopped red onion
2 large cloves garlic, minced
¼ cup dried cherries
¼ cup coarsely snipped fresh basil
1 tablespoon balsamic vinegar
½ teaspoon salt
1 pound beef shoulder petite tenders
¼ teaspoon Montreal steak seasoning*
2 tablespoons sliced almonds, toasted
Snipped fresh basil (optional)

1. In a medium saucepan bring the water to boiling. Stir in buckwheat groats; reduce heat. Simmer, covered, for 5 to 7 minutes or until the water is absorbed (you should have about 2 cups cooked groats). Set aside.

2. In a large nonstick skillet heat 1 teaspoon of the oil over medium-high heat. Add onion and garlic; cook and stir for 2 to 3 minutes or just until onion begins to soften.

3. Drain cooked groats if necessary. Add onion mixture to the groats. Stir in 3 teaspoons of the remaining oil, the cherries, the ¼ cup basil, the vinegar, and salt. Let stand at room temperature while preparing the beef.

4. Cut beef crosswise into twelve 1-inch slices. Add the remaining 1 teaspoon oil to the same skillet; heat over medium heat. Evenly sprinkle beef pieces with Montreal seasoning. Cook beef pieces in hot oil about 6 minutes or until medium (145°F), turning once halfway through cooking. Serve beef over groats. Sprinkle with almonds and, if desired, additional snipped fresh basil.

PER SERVING: 314 cal., 15 g fat (4 g sat. fat), 65 mg chol., 407 mg sodium, 31 g carb., 4 g fiber, 27 g pro.

*Tip: Check the label of this product carefully to be sure it does not contain added gluten.

Pork Stir–Fry with Crispy Rice Noodles

START TO FINISH: 30 minutes
MAKES: 4 servings

½ cup gluten-free, reduced-sodium chicken broth
¼ cup sweet rice wine (mirin)
¼ cup gluten-free, reduced-sodium soy sauce or gluten-free tamari
2 tablespoons water
4 teaspoons fish sauce
1 tablespoon cornstarch*
½ to 1 teaspoon crushed red pepper
1 tablespoon vegetable oil
1 teaspoon grated fresh ginger
2 cloves garlic, minced
2 heads baby bok choy, halved or quartered (8 ounces)
1½ cups thinly sliced carrots
1½ cups fresh pea pods, tips and strings removed
1 large red sweet pepper, seeded and cut into strips
4 green onions, bias-sliced
1 pound boneless pork loin, trimmed of fat and cut into thin bite-size strips
Crispy rice noodles** or hot cooked rice

1. For sauce, in a small bowl stir together broth, mirin, soy sauce, the water, the fish sauce, cornstarch, and crushed red pepper; set aside.

2. In a wok or extra-large skillet heat oil over medium-high heat. Add ginger and garlic to skillet; cook and stir for 15 seconds. Add bok choy; cook and stir for 2 minutes, turning frequently. Add carrots; cook and stir for 2 minutes. Add pea pods, sweet pepper, and green onions; cook and stir for 3 to 4 minutes or until vegetables are crisp-tender. Remove vegetables from the wok.

3. Add half of the pork to hot wok. (If necessary, add more oil during cooking.) Cook and stir for 2 to 3 minutes or until pork is no longer pink. Remove from wok. Repeat with the remaining pork. Return all of the pork to the wok. Push pork from center of wok. Stir sauce; add to the center of the wok. Cook and stir until thickened and bubbly. Return vegetables to wok. Cook and stir until heated through. Serve with crispy rice noodles.

PER SERVING: 349 cal., 8 g fat (2 g sat. fat), 78 mg chol., 1,561 mg sodium, 37 g carb., 4 g fiber, 31 g pro.

*Tip: Check the label of this product carefully to be sure it does not contain added gluten.

**Tip: To make crispy rice noodles, use rice sticks (rice vermicelli). Separate the bundle of noodles into smaller portions. If desired, cut into 4- to 5-inch lengths. Add vegetable oil to a large skillet to a depth of 1 inch. Heat oil over medium heat. (Oil is hot enough when a few noodles puff within seconds of being placed in the skillet.) Cook noodles in batches in the hot oil just until puffed. Remove noodles immediately and drain well on paper towels.

Skillet Pork Chops with Butter Beans, Peas, and Charred Green Onions

PREP: 25 minutes   **ROAST:** 10 minutes at 400°F   **MAKES:** 4 servings

4   pork loin rib chops, cut 1¼ inches thick
2   tablespoons snipped fresh Italian parsley
2   tablespoons snipped fresh tarragon
2   teaspoons finely shredded lemon peel
¼   teaspoon salt
¼   teaspoon black pepper
1   tablespoon olive oil
6   green onions, cut into 2-inch pieces
1   15.5- to 16-ounce can butter beans,* rinsed and drained
1   5-ounce package fresh baby spinach
1   cup shelled fresh English peas or frozen peas, thawed
1   tablespoon lemon juice
1   lemon, cut into wedges

1. Preheat oven to 400°F. Trim fat from chops. In a small bowl combine parsley, tarragon, lemon peel, salt, and pepper. Sprinkle herb mixture evenly over chops; rub in with your fingers.

2. In an extra-large oven-going skillet heat oil over medium-high heat. Add chops to skillet; cook about 6 minutes or until browned, turning once. Add green onions to skillet around chops. Transfer skillet to the oven. Roast for 10 to 12 minutes or until an instant-read thermometer inserted into chops registers 150°F. Remove chops from skillet; cover and keep warm.

3. Stir beans, spinach, peas, and lemon juice into green onions in skillet. Cook and stir over medium heat until beans are heated through and peas are tender. Serve chops with vegetables and lemon wedges.

PER SERVING: 467 cal., 22 g fat (5 g sat. fat), 99 mg chol., 603 mg sodium, 27 g carb., 8 g fiber, 43 g pro.

*Tip: Check the label of this product carefully to be sure it does not contain added gluten.

Jamaican Pork Stir-Fry

START TO FINISH: 20 minutes
MAKES: 4 servings

1 tablespoon vegetable oil
1 16-ounce package frozen sweet pepper and onion stir-fry vegetables
12 ounces pork strips for stir-frying*
2 to 3 teaspoons Jamaican Jerk Rub (recipe, page 303) or purchased gluten-free Jamaican jerk seasoning
½ cup gluten-free plum sauce
2 cups hot cooked rice

1. In a large skillet or wok heat oil over medium-high heat. (Add more oil as necessary during cooking.) Add frozen vegetables; cook and stir for 5 to 7 minutes or until vegetables are crisp-tender. Remove from skillet.

2. Toss meat with jerk rub; add to hot skillet. Cook and stir for 2 to 4 minutes or until meat is slightly pink in center.

3. Add plum sauce to skillet; return vegetables to skillet. Gently stir all ingredients together to coat with sauce; heat through. Serve over hot cooked rice.

PER SERVING: 357 cal., 9 g fat (2 g sat. fat), 54 mg chol., 405 mg sodium, 45 g carb., 2 g fiber, 22 g pro.

*Tip: If the supermarket doesn't sell pork strips, cut strips from boneless pork loin.

Caramelized Pork with Melon

START TO FINISH: 25 minutes
MAKES: 4 servings

- 1 **small cantaloupe**
- ¼ **cup orange juice**
- 3 **tablespoons gluten-free hoisin sauce**
- 4 **pork loin rib chops, cut ½ inch thick**
  Salt and black pepper
- 1 **tablespoon vegetable oil**
- 3 **green onions, thinly sliced**
  Shredded napa cabbage (optional)

1. Remove rind and seeds from cantaloupe; chop melon. In a food processor or blender combine 2 cups of the chopped melon and the orange juice. Cover and process or blend until smooth.

2. For sauce, transfer ½ cup of the pureed melon to a small bowl; stir in hoisin sauce. Set sauce aside. Press the remaining melon puree through a fine-mesh sieve placed over a bowl. Discard solids left in sieve. Set melon juice aside.

3. Sprinkle chops lightly with salt and pepper; brush generously with some of the sauce. In an extra-large skillet heat oil over medium-high heat. Add chops to skillet; cook for 6 to 8 minutes or until chops are well browned and slightly pink inside (145°F), turning once. Remove chops from skillet; let stand for 3 minutes.

4. Meanwhile, in a large bowl combine the remaining chopped melon, the melon juice, and the green onions; set aside.

5. Add the remaining sauce to the skillet; cook and stir until heated through. Spoon sauce onto plates. Top with chops. Add chopped melon mixture to skillet to warm slightly; spoon over chops. If desired, serve with shredded napa cabbage.

PER SERVING: 327 cal., 10 g fat (2 g sat. fat), 117 mg chol., 452 mg sodium, 19 g carb., 2 g fiber, 39 g pro.

Pork Medallions with Cherry Sauce

START TO FINISH: 25 minutes   MAKES: 4 servings

1 pound pork tenderloin
¼ teaspoon salt
¼ teaspoon black pepper
  Nonstick cooking spray*
¾ cup cranberry juice, cherry juice, or apple juice
2 teaspoons gluten-free spicy brown mustard
1 teaspoon cornstarch*
1 cup fresh sweet cherries, halved and pitted, or 1 cup frozen unsweetened pitted dark sweet cherries, thawed
  Snipped fresh parsley (optional)

1. Cut pork crosswise into 1-inch slices. Place each slice between two pieces of plastic wrap. Using the flat side of a meat mallet, lightly pound each slice into a ½-inch-thick medallion. Discard plastic wrap. Sprinkle pork evenly with the salt and pepper.

2. Coat an large unheated nonstick skillet with cooking spray. Heat skillet over medium-high heat. Add pork medallions and cook about 6 minutes or until pork is slightly pink in center and juices run clear, turning once. Transfer to a serving platter; cover with foil to keep warm.

3. For cherry sauce, in a small bowl stir together cranberry juice, mustard, and cornstarch; add to skillet. Cook and stir until thickened and bubbly. Cook and stir for 2 minutes more. Stir in cherries. Serve cherry sauce over pork. If desired, top with fresh parsley.

PER SERVING: 178 cal., 2 g fat (1 g sat. fat), 74 mg chol., 247 mg sodium, 13 g carb., 1 g fiber, 24 g pro.

*Tip: Check the labels of these products carefully to be sure they do not contain added gluten.

Sweet-and-Sour Pork

START TO FINISH: 30 minutes
MAKES: 6 servings

¾ cup gluten-free, reduced-sodium chicken broth
3 tablespoons red wine vinegar
2 tablespoons gluten-free, reduced-sodium soy sauce
4 teaspoons sugar
1 tablespoon cornstarch*
1 clove garlic, minced
4 teaspoons vegetable oil
1 cup thinly sliced carrots
1 cup bite-size strips red sweet pepper
1 cup fresh pea pods, trimmed
12 ounces boneless pork loin, trimmed of fat and cut into 1-inch pieces
1 8-ounce can pineapple chunks (juice pack), drained
2 cups hot cooked brown rice

1. For sauce, in a small bowl stir together broth, vinegar, soy sauce, sugar, cornstarch, and garlic; set aside.

2. In a large nonstick skillet heat 3 teaspoons of the oil over medium-high heat. Add carrots and sweet pepper; cook and stir for 3 minutes. Add pea pods. Cook and stir about 1 minute more or until vegetables are crisp-tender. Remove from skillet; set aside.

3. Add the remaining 1 teaspoon oil to the skillet. Add pork; cook and stir for 4 to 6 minutes or until pork is slightly pink in the center. Push pork from center of skillet. Stir sauce; add to center of skillet. Cook and stir until thickened and bubbly. Add the vegetables and pineapple chunks; heat through. Serve with hot cooked rice.

PER SERVING: 250 cal., 7 g fat (2 g sat. fat), 31 mg chol., 306 mg sodium, 29 g carb., 3 g fiber, 16 g pro.

*Tip: Check the label of this product carefully to be sure it does not contain added gluten.

Cajun Tri-Pepper Sausage Skillet

PREP: 30 minutes
COOK: 10 minutes
MAKES: 4 servings

1 tablespoon vegetable oil
1 pound gluten-free cooked andouille sausage or gluten-free spicy cooked smoked sausage, cut into ½-inch slices
1 large onion, cut into thin wedges
2 stalks celery, thinly bias-sliced
3 cloves garlic, minced
1 large green sweet pepper, seeded and thinly sliced
1 large red sweet pepper, seeded and thinly sliced
1 large yellow sweet pepper, seeded and thinly sliced
2 cups gluten-free chicken broth
2 tablespoons cornstarch*
2 teaspoons brown sugar
2 teaspoons paprika
1 teaspoon snipped fresh thyme
½ teaspoon salt
¼ teaspoon cayenne pepper
2 to 3 cups hot cooked rice
Fresh thyme sprigs (optional)

1. In an extra-large skillet heat oil over medium-high heat. Add sausage; cook and stir about 3 minutes or until browned.

2. Add onion, celery, and garlic to skillet. Cook and stir for 2 to 3 minutes or until tender. Add sweet peppers to skillet. Cook and stir for 3 to 4 minutes or until crisp-tender.

3. For sauce, in a small bowl combine broth, cornstarch, brown sugar, paprika, snipped thyme, salt, and cayenne pepper. Add sauce to skillet; cook and stir until thickened and bubbly. Serve over hot cooked rice. If desired, garnish with fresh thyme sprigs.

PER SERVING: 373 cal., 9 g fat (2 g sat. fat), 95 mg chol., 1,622 mg sodium, 45 g carb., 4 g fiber, 28 g pro.

*__Tip:__ Check the label of this product carefully to be sure it does not contain added gluten.

Cod and Potatoes Puttanesca

PREP: 25 minutes
COOK: 20 minutes
MAKES: 4 servings

1   **pound fresh or frozen cod fillets**

2   **teaspoons olive oil**

3   **cloves garlic, minced**

2   **to 3 anchovy fillets, drained well and chopped**

2   **14.5-ounce cans no-salt-added diced tomatoes, undrained**

1¼ **pounds yellow potatoes, unpeeled and cut into ¾- to 1-inch pieces**

2   **teaspoons dried oregano, crushed**

¼ **teaspoon black pepper**

¼ **teaspoon crushed red pepper**

¼ **teaspoon salt**

¼ **cup pitted Kalamata olives, quartered lengthwise**

1   **tablespoon capers, rinsed and drained**

2   **tablespoons snipped fresh parsley**

2   **tablespoons finely shredded Parmesan cheese***

1. Thaw fish, if frozen. Rinse fish; pat dry with paper towels. Cut fish into 1½-inch cubes. Set fish aside.

2. In a large skillet heat oil over medium-high heat. Add garlic and anchovy fillets; cook and stir for 30 seconds. Add tomatoes, potatoes, oregano, black pepper, crushed red pepper, and salt. Bring mixture to boiling; reduce heat. Simmer, covered, for 10 minutes, stirring once.

3. Stir in olives and capers. Place the cod on the potato mixture. Simmer, covered, about 10 minutes or until potatoes are tender and fish flakes when tested with a fork. In a small bowl stir together parsley and Parmesan cheese; sprinkle over cod and potatoes.

PER SERVING: 286 cal., 5 g fat (1 g sat. fat), 52 mg chol., 582 mg sodium, 35 g carb., 8 g fiber, 26 g pro.

***Tip:** Check the label of this product carefully to be sure it does not contain added gluten.

Coconut Salmon Curry

START TO FINISH: 40 minutes
MAKES: 4 servings

1   1-pound fresh or frozen skinless salmon fillet
1   tablespoon cornstarch*
1   teaspoon salt
½   teaspoon black pepper
    Nonstick cooking spray*
1   large onion, cut into 1-inch pieces
1   cup red sweet pepper strips
1   cup packaged julienned fresh carrots
1   tablespoon grated fresh ginger
1   to 2 teaspoons curry powder*
1   clove garlic, minced
¼   teaspoon crushed red pepper (optional)
1   tablespoon canola oil
1   8-ounce can pineapple chunks (juice pack), undrained
⅓   cup unsweetened light coconut milk*
2   cups hot cooked brown rice

1. Thaw salmon if frozen. Rinse salmon; pat dry with paper towels. Cut salmon into 1-inch pieces. In a medium bowl toss together salmon, cornstarch, salt, and black pepper; set aside.

2. Coat a large nonstick skillet with cooking spray; heat skillet over medium-high heat. Add onion, sweet pepper, carrots, ginger, curry powder, garlic, and, if desired, crushed red pepper; cook and stir for 5 to 6 minutes or until vegetables are crisp-tender. Remove from skillet.

3. Add oil to hot skillet. Add seasoned salmon; cook about 4 minutes or until fish flakes when tested with a fork, gently stirring occasionally. Stir in pineapple and coconut milk; reduce heat. Cook about 1 minute or until sauce is thickened, stirring gently. Stir in cooked vegetables; heat through. Serve with hot cooked rice.

PER SERVING: 436 cal., 18 g fat (4 g sat. fat), 67 mg chol., 686 mg sodium, 42 g carb., 5 g fiber, 26 g pro.

*Tip: Check the labels of these products carefully to be sure they do not contain added gluten.

Pepper Poached Salmon and Herbed Beets

PREP: 45 minutes COOK: 20 minutes STAND: 10 minutes MAKES: 4 servings

- 1 to 1½ pounds fresh or frozen salmon fillets
- ½ teaspoon salt
- 1 cup loosely packed fresh watercress
- 2 tablespoons snipped fresh tarragon
- ½ of a lemon, cut into thick slices
- 2 teaspoons whole peppercorns
- 3 bay leaves
- ½ cup light sour cream*
- 1 tablespoon snipped fresh chives
- 1 teaspoon snipped fresh tarragon
- ½ teaspoon black pepper
- ¼ teaspoon salt
- 1 recipe Herbed Beets Watercress and fresh tarragon sprigs (optional)

1. Thaw fish, if frozen. Rinse fish and pat dry with paper towels. Cut salmon into four equal pieces. Measure thickness of fish; set aside. In a large skillet combine 1 cup water and the ½ teaspoon salt.

2. For a bouquet garni, place ½ cup of the watercress, the 2 tablespoons tarragon, the lemon slices, peppercorns, and bay leaves in the center of a double-thick 9-inch square of 100%-cotton cheesecloth. Bring the corners of the cheesecloth together and tie with 100%-cotton kitchen string.

3. Place the bouquet garni in the skillet. Bring water to boiling; reduce heat. With a spatula, lower the fish into the water. Simmer, covered, until fish flakes when tested with a fork, allowing 4 to 6 minutes for each ½-inch thickness of fish. Carefully transfer salmon to a platter; cover and keep warm.

4. For sauce, in a small bowl combine the remaining ½ cup watercress, the sour cream, chives, 1 teaspoon tarragon, pepper, and salt. Spoon sauce onto plates and top with fish. Serve with Herbed Beets. If desired, garnish with additional watercress and tarragon.

Herbed Beets: Cut green tops off 1 pound fresh baby beets (about 12) or small beets, quartered; discard tops. Wash beets; do not peel. In a medium saucepan bring a small amount of lightly salted water to boiling. Add beets. Cook, covered, over medium heat about 20 minutes or until crisp-tender; drain. Let beets stand at room temperature about 10 minutes or until cool enough to handle. Holding beets under running water, slip skins off beets. Place beets in a serving bowl. Add 1 tablespoon olive oil, 1 tablespoon red wine vinegar, and ⅛ teaspoon salt. Toss to coat. Sprinkle with 2 tablespoons snipped fresh watercress and 1 tablespoon snipped fresh tarragon.

PER SERVING: 259 cal., 13 g fat (3 g sat. fat), 71 mg chol., 563 mg sodium, 9 g carb., 2 g fiber, 25 g pro.

*Tip: Check the label of this product carefully to be sure it does not contain added gluten.

Pacific Salmon Paella

START TO FINISH: 45 minutes
MAKES: 6 servings

1¼ pounds fresh or frozen skinless salmon fillets, about 1 inch thick
4 slices gluten-free applewood-smoked bacon
3 cups sliced fresh cremini or button mushrooms (8 ounces)
1 cup chopped onion
2 cloves garlic, minced
2½ cups gluten-free chicken broth
1 cup uncooked long grain white rice
2 teaspoons snipped fresh thyme or ½ teaspoon dried thyme, crushed
¼ teaspoon coarsely ground black pepper
1 pound fresh asparagus, trimmed and cut into 1-inch pieces, or one 10-ounce package frozen cut asparagus, thawed
⅓ cup chopped roma tomato

1. Thaw fish, if frozen. Rinse fish and pat dry with paper towels. Cut fish into 1-inch pieces; set aside. In a large deep skillet or paella pan cook bacon over medium heat until crisp. Drain bacon on paper towels, reserving drippings in skillet. Crumble bacon; set aside.

2. Add mushrooms, onion, and garlic to the reserved drippings in skillet. Cook about 5 minutes or until onion is tender. Stir in broth, rice, and thyme. Bring to boiling; reduce heat. Simmer, covered, for 10 minutes.

3. Sprinkle salmon with pepper; toss gently to coat. Place fish and asparagus on top of rice mixture. Simmer, covered, for 10 to 12 minutes or until salmon flakes when tested with a fork and asparagus is crisp-tender. Sprinkle with tomato and crumbled bacon.

PER SERVING: 313 cal., 9 g fat (2 g sat. fat), 60 mg chol., 498 mg sodium, 32 g carb., 2 g fiber, 26 g pro.

Creole–Style Shrimp and Grits

START TO FINISH: 35 minutes
MAKES: 4 servings

1 pound fresh or frozen medium shrimp in shells
1 cup gluten-free yellow grits
1 tablespoon olive oil
12 ounces fresh asparagus spears, trimmed and cut diagonally into 2-inch pieces
1 medium red sweet pepper, seeded and cut into ½-inch pieces
½ cup chopped onion
2 cloves garlic, minced
2 tablespoons Gluten-Free Flour Mix (recipe, page 312) or purchased gluten-free all-purpose flour
2 teaspoons salt-free Creole seasoning*
¼ teaspoon salt
¼ teaspoon black pepper
¾ cup gluten-free, reduced-sodium chicken broth

1. Thaw shrimp, if frozen. Peel and devein shrimp, leaving tails intact if desired. Rinse shrimp; pat dry with paper towels. Prepare grits according to package directions. Cover and keep warm.

2. Meanwhile, in a large skillet heat oil over medium heat. Add asparagus, sweet pepper, onion, and garlic; cook for 4 to 5 minutes or just until vegetables are tender, stirring occasionally.

3. Stir flour, Creole seasoning, salt, and black pepper into vegetables in skillet. Gradually stir in broth. Cook and stir over medium heat just until thickened and bubbly; reduce heat. Stir in shrimp. Simmer, covered, for 1 to 3 minutes or until shrimp are opaque, stirring once. Serve over cooked grits.

PER SERVING: 308 cal., 5 g fat (1 g sat. fat), 143 mg chol., 899 mg sodium, 43 g carb., 4 g fiber, 21 g pro.

*Tip: Check the label of this product carefully to be sure it does not contain added gluten.

Spanish Shrimp Stir-Fry

START TO FINISH: 35 minutes **MAKES:** 4 servings

12 **ounces fresh or frozen peeled and deveined medium shrimp**
2 **tablespoons vegetable oil or canola oil**
8 **ounces small red-skin or fingerling potatoes, cut into bite-size chunks**
½ **cup chicken broth**
1 **cup gluten-free chunky salsa**
4 **ounces oil-cured black olives, pitted and sliced**
½ **teaspoon smoked paprika or chili powder***
4 **cups hot cooked rice**
Snipped fresh Italian parsley (optional)

1. Thaw shrimp, if frozen. Rinse shrimp; pat dry with paper towels. Set aside.

2. In a large skillet or wok heat oil over medium-high heat. Add potatoes; stir to coat with oil. Cook for 3 to 4 minutes or until browned, stirring frequently. Carefully add broth. Cook, covered, for 8 to 10 minutes or just until potatoes are tender.

3. Add shrimp to skillet. Cook and stir for 3 to 4 minutes or until shrimp are opaque. Stir in salsa, olives, and paprika; heat through. Serve over hot cooked rice. If desired, sprinkle with parsley.

PER SERVING: 429 cal., 11 g fat (1 g sat. fat), 138 mg chol., 744 mg sodium, 58 g carb., 3 g fiber, 23 g pro.

*Tip: Check the label of this product carefully to be sure it does not contain added gluten.

Spicy Vegetable Fried Rice

START TO FINISH: 30 minutes
MAKES: 4 servings

4 eggs
2 tablespoons water
  Nonstick cooking spray*
1 tablespoon finely chopped, peeled fresh ginger
2 cloves garlic, minced
1 tablespoon olive oil
2 cups chopped napa cabbage
1 cup coarsely shredded carrots
1 cup fresh pea pods, trimmed
2 cups cooked brown rice
⅓ cup sliced green onions
2 tablespoons gluten-free, reduced-sodium soy sauce or gluten-free tamari
1 to 2 teaspoons sriracha sauce*
2 tablespoons snipped fresh cilantro
  Lime slices or wedges

1. In a small bowl whisk together eggs and the water. Coat an extra-large nonstick skillet with cooking spray. Heat skillet over medium heat. Pour in egg mixture. Cook, without stirring, until eggs begin to set on the bottom and around the edges. Using a spatula or large spoon, lift and fold the partially cooked eggs so the uncooked portion flows underneath. Continue cooking over medium heat for 2 to 3 minutes or until eggs are cooked through but still glossy and moist, keeping eggs in large pieces. Carefully transfer eggs to a medium bowl; set aside.

2. In the same skillet cook and stir ginger and garlic in hot oil over medium-high heat for 30 seconds. Add cabbage, carrots, and pea pods; cook and stir for 2 minutes. Stir in cooked eggs, cooked rice, green onions, soy sauce, and sriracha sauce; cook and stir about 2 minutes or until heated through. Top with fresh cilantro. Serve with lime slices.

PER SERVING: 250 cal., 9 g fat (2 g sat. fat), 212 mg chol., 367 mg sodium, 31 g carb., 4 g fiber, 11 g pro.

***Tip:** Check the labels of these products carefully to be sure they do not contain added gluten.

Tomato, Greens, and Chickpea Skillet

START TO FINISH: 25 minutes
MAKES: 4 servings

- 3 tablespoons olive oil
- ½ cup chopped onion
- 1 clove garlic, minced
- 1 tablespoon curry powder*
- 1 14.5-ounce can diced tomatoes, undrained
- ¼ teaspoon salt
- 1 15-ounce can garbanzo beans (chickpeas),* rinsed and drained
- 2 cups torn fresh Swiss chard or spinach
- 4 eggs
  Salt and black pepper
  Fresh cilantro sprigs (optional)

1. In a large skillet heat 2 tablespoons of the oil over medium heat. Add onion and garlic; cook and stir for 5 minutes. Add curry powder; cook and stir for 1 minute. Add tomatoes and salt; cook for 3 minutes, stirring occasionally. Add chickpeas; cook and stir about 3 minutes or until heated through. Add Swiss chard; cook and stir about 3 minutes or until slightly wilted.

2. In another large skillet heat the remaining 1 tablespoon oil over medium heat. Break eggs into skillet. Sprinkle with salt and pepper. Cook, covered, until eggs reach desired doneness.

3. Serve cooked eggs with tomato mixture. If desired, garnish with fresh cilantro.

PER SERVING: 279 cal., 17 g fat (3 g sat. fat), 186 mg chol., 675 mg sodium, 21 g carb., 2 g fiber, 12 g pro.

*Tip: Check the labels of these products carefully to be sure they do not contain added gluten.

Soups & Stews

With just a soup pot and a stovetop, it's easy to make a one-dish meal that's warming, comforting, and satisfying. This assortment of soup and stew recipes—each deliciously nutritious and naturally gluten-free—show how simple it can be to make these savory bowlfuls from scratch.

White Chicken Chili

PREP: 40 minutes   COOK: 20 minutes   MAKES: 5 servings

¾ cup chopped red sweet
   pepper
½ cup chopped onion
2 cloves garlic, minced
1 tablespoon vegetable oil
1 pound skinless, boneless
   chicken thighs, cut into
   1-inch pieces
2 14.5-ounce cans gluten-free,
   reduced-sodium chicken
   broth
1 19-ounce can cannellini beans
   (white kidney beans),* rinsed
   and drained
1 12-ounce package frozen
   white whole kernel corn
   (shoe peg)
1 4- to 4.5-ounce can diced
   green chile peppers,
   undrained
1 teaspoon ground cumin
½ teaspoon salt
½ teaspoon dried oregano,
   crushed
¼ teaspoon black pepper
½ teaspoon finely shredded
   lime peel
1 tablespoon lime juice
¼ cup vegetable oil
2 6-inch corn tortillas,* cut into
   thin strips

1. In a Dutch oven cook sweet pepper, onion, and garlic in the 1 tablespoon oil over medium heat about 5 minutes or until tender. Add chicken; cook for 5 to 7 minutes or until chicken is no longer pink.

2. Stir in broth, beans, corn, chile peppers, cumin, the ½ teaspoon salt, the oregano, and ¼ teaspoon black pepper. Bring to boiling; reduce heat. Simmer, uncovered, for 20 minutes. Stir in lime peel and lime juice. Using a potato masher, coarsely mash beans. Season to taste with additional salt and black pepper.

3. In a large skillet heat the ¼ cup oil over medium heat. Add tortilla strips, half at a time, and cook about 2 minutes or until browned and crisp. Drain on paper towels.

4. Serve chili topped with the tortilla strips.

PER SERVING: 430 cal., 19 g fat (2 g sat. fat), 75 mg chol., 1,003 mg sodium, 45 g carb., 11 g fiber, 32 g pro.

Slow Cooker Directions: Prepare as directed in Step 1. Transfer chicken mixture to a 3½- or 4-quart slow cooker. Stir in broth, beans, corn, chile peppers, cumin, ½ teaspoon salt, oregano, and ¼ teaspoon black pepper. Cover and cook on low-heat setting for 7 to 8 hours or on high-heat setting for 3½ to 4 hours. Stir in lime peel and lime juice. Continue as directed.

*Tip: Check the labels of these products carefully to be sure they do not contain added gluten.

Fresh Corn and Chicken Chowder

START TO FINISH: 30 minutes
MAKES: 4 servings

12 **ounces skinless, boneless chicken breast halves or chicken thighs**
4 **ears fresh sweet corn**
1 **32-ounce container gluten-free, reduced-sodium chicken broth**
½ **cup chopped green sweet pepper**
1¼ **cups instant mashed potato flakes**
1 **cup milk**
Salt and black pepper
Crushed red pepper (optional)

1. In a Dutch oven combine chicken, corn, and broth. Bring to boiling; reduce heat. Simmer, covered, about 12 minutes or until no pink remains in chicken (170°F). Transfer chicken and corn to a cutting board.

2. Add ¼ cup of the sweet pepper to broth in Dutch oven. Stir in potato flakes and milk; set aside.

3. Using two forks, shred chicken. Return chicken to Dutch oven. Using a kitchen towel to hold hot corn, cut kernels from cobs. Add corn to chowder in Dutch oven; heat through. Season to taste with salt and black pepper.

4. Top each serving with 1 tablespoon chopped sweet pepper. If desired, sprinkle with crushed red pepper.

PER SERVING: 269 cal., 3 g fat (1 g sat. fat), 54 mg chol., 721 mg sodium, 33 g carb., 3 g fiber, 29 g pro.

To Make Ahead: Prepare chowder as directed; let cool. Transfer chowder to an airtight container. Cover and store in the refrigerator for up to 3 days. Reheat chowder in Dutch oven over medium heat until heated through.

Thai Chicken-Noodle Soup

START TO FINISH: 35 minutes
MAKES: 6 servings

1 cup canned crushed tomatoes
½ cup gluten-free chunky peanut butter
1 tablespoon sesame oil (not toasted)
1 pound skinless, boneless chicken thighs, cut into 1-inch pieces
4 cloves garlic, minced
2 teaspoons grated fresh ginger
6 cups gluten-free, reduced-sodium chicken broth
2 teaspoons fish sauce
3 ounces dried rice noodles, broken if desired
2 cups shredded green cabbage
1 cup canned bean sprouts, rinsed and drained
¼ cup chopped green onions
  Snipped fresh cilantro (optional)
  Coarsely chopped unsalted peanuts (optional)
  Crushed red pepper (optional)

1. In a small bowl combine tomatoes and peanut butter; set aside. In a 4-quart Dutch oven heat oil over medium-high heat. Add chicken, garlic, and ginger; cook about 5 minutes or until chicken is browned, stirring frequently.

2. Stir in tomato mixture, broth, and fish sauce. Bring to boiling. Stir in noodles; reduce heat. Simmer for 5 minutes. Stir in cabbage. Simmer about 5 minutes more or just until cabbage is tender. Remove from heat. Stir in bean sprouts and green onions.

3. Ladle soup into bowls. If desired, top with cilantro, peanuts, and/or crushed red pepper.

PER SERVING: 334 cal., 16 g fat (3 g sat. fat), 72 mg chol., 1,011 mg sodium, 24 g carb., 4 g fiber, 25 g pro.

Spicy Thai Chicken-Coconut Soup

PREP: 30 minutes   **COOK:** 20 minutes   **MAKES:** 6 servings

2 **tablespoons grated fresh ginger**
2 **tablespoons peanut oil**
1 **teaspoon crushed red pepper**
6 **cups gluten-free, reduced-sodium chicken broth**
½ **cup uncooked jasmine rice**
5 **fresh kaffir lime leaves (optional)**
1 **stalk fresh lemongrass (white part only)**
3 **cups coarsely shredded cooked chicken**
1 **cup unsweetened coconut milk***
1 **cup thinly sliced fresh button mushrooms**
1 **cup red sweet pepper strips**
½ **cup chopped onion**
¼ **cup fish sauce**
2 **tablespoons snipped fresh cilantro**
2 **to 3 tablespoons lime juice**
   Sliced green onions (optional)
   Fresh cilantro sprigs (optional)
   Lime wedges (optional)

1. In a large saucepan combine ginger, oil, and crushed red pepper. Cook and stir over medium heat for 2 minutes. Add broth; bring to boiling. Stir in rice; reduce heat. Simmer, covered, for 15 to 20 minutes or until rice is tender.

2. Tear lime leaves in several places from the edges toward the centers (if using). Cut lemongrass into 1-inch pieces; bruise with the flat side of a knife. Stir lime leaves, lemongrass, chicken, coconut milk, mushrooms, sweet pepper, chopped onion, fish sauce, and snipped cilantro into rice. Bring to boiling; reduce heat. Simmer, uncovered, for 5 minutes.

3. Remove and discard lime leaves and lemongrass. Stir lime juice into soup. If desired, sprinkle servings with green onions and cilantro sprigs and serve with lime wedges.

PER SERVING: 357 cal., 19 g fat (11 g sat. fat), 62 mg chol., 1,566 mg sodium, 20 g carb., 2 g fiber, 26 g pro.

*Tip: Check the label of this product carefully to be sure it does not contain added gluten.

Chicken and Tortilla Soup

PREP: 35 minutes
COOK: 1 hour
MAKES: 6 servings

1 3½-pound whole roasting chicken, cut into 8 pieces
6 cups water
1 cup chopped yellow onion
½ cup chopped carrot
½ cup chopped celery
8 sprigs fresh cilantro
2 bay leaves
1½ teaspoons ground cumin
1 teaspoon chili powder*
½ teaspoon ground ancho chile pepper
½ teaspoon dried oregano, crushed
  Vegetable oil
8 6-inch corn tortillas,* cut into ½-inch-wide strips
  Salt
1 32-ounce container gluten-free, reduced-sodium chicken broth
2 medium carrots, sliced ¼ inch thick (1 cup)
2 cups sugar snap pea pods, halved diagonally
2 small zucchini, sliced ¼ inch thick (2 cups)
1 cup chopped fresh tomatoes
½ of a fresh jalapeño chile pepper, seeded and finely chopped (see tip, page 21)
  Freshly ground black pepper
4 ounces sharp cheddar cheese, shredded (1 cup)
  Fresh cilantro leaves

1. In a 6-quart Dutch oven combine chicken, the water, onion, carrot, celery, cilantro sprigs, bay leaves, cumin, chili powder, ground ancho pepper, and oregano. Bring to boiling; reduce heat. Simmer, covered, for 1 to 1½ hours or until chicken is very tender.

2. Meanwhile, in a large heavy saucepan pour oil to ½-inch depth. Heat oil to 375°F. Add tortilla strips, about one-fourth at a time, and cook for 30 to 60 seconds or until crisp and lightly browned. Using a slotted spoon, remove strips and drain on paper towels. Sprinkle with salt.

3. Remove chicken from cooking liquid. Strain cooking liquid, discarding solids. Return liquid to Dutch oven. Add broth. Bring to simmering over medium heat.

4. Remove chicken from bones; discard skin and bones. Tear chicken into 1-inch pieces; return to Dutch oven. Add sliced carrots; simmer for 3 minutes. Stir in sugar snap peas, zucchini, tomatoes, and jalapeño pepper. Simmer about 3 minutes more or until vegetables are tender. Season to taste with salt and black pepper.

5. Ladle soup into bowls. Sprinkle with cheese and top with tortilla strips and cilantro leaves.

PER SERVING: 375 cal., 14 g fat (2 g sat. fat), 89 mg chol., 618 mg sodium, 29 g carb., 6 g fiber, 34 g pro.

*Tip: Check the labels of these products carefully to be sure they do not contain added gluten.

Wild Rice Chicken Soup

PREP: 10 minutes
COOK: 45 minutes
MAKES: 6 servings

- 2 **cups water**
- ½ **cup uncooked wild rice, rinsed and drained**
- ½ **cup uncooked long grain brown rice**
- 2 **14.5-ounce cans gluten-free reduced-sodium chicken broth**
- 4 **cloves garlic, minced**
- 4 **cups chopped tomatoes or two 14.5-ounce cans diced tomatoes, undrained**
- 2 **cups chopped cooked chicken breast**
- 1 **cup finely chopped zucchini**
- ¼ **teaspoon freshly ground black pepper**
- 1 **tablespoon snipped fresh thyme or 1 teaspoon dried thyme, crushed**
- 1 **tablespoon Madeira or dry sherry (optional)**

1. In a large saucepan bring the water to boiling. Stir in wild rice and brown rice. Return to boiling; reduce heat. Simmer, covered, for 40 to 45 minutes or until rice is tender and most of the liquid is absorbed.

2. Meanwhile, in a 4-quart Dutch oven combine broth and garlic; bring to boiling. Stir in tomatoes, chicken, zucchini, and pepper. Return to boiling; reduce heat. Simmer, covered, for 5 minutes. Stir in cooked rice, thyme, and, if desired, Madeira; heat through.

PER SERVING: 218 cal., 3 g fat (1 g sat. fat), 40 mg chol., 361 mg sodium, 29 g carb., 3 g fiber, 21 g pro.

Curried Chicken Stew

PREP: 20 minutes
SLOW COOK: 8 hours 30 minutes (low) or 4 hours (high) + 15 minutes (high)
MAKES: 4 servings

1¼ pounds skinless, boneless chicken thighs
¾ cup chopped red sweet pepper
¾ cup chopped yellow sweet pepper
1 small onion, sliced
1 fresh jalapeño chile pepper, seeded and finely chopped (see tip, page 21)
2 cloves garlic, minced
1 cup gluten-free, low-sodium chicken broth
½ cup golden raisins
½ cup shredded coconut
3 tablespoons curry powder*
1 teaspoon salt
¼ teaspoon ground cinnamon
¼ teaspoon cayenne pepper (optional)
½ cup unsweetened coconut milk*
1 tablespoon cornstarch*
2 cups hot cooked rice (optional)
¾ cup lightly salted cashews,* coarsely chopped

1. In a 3½- or 4-quart slow cooker combine chicken, sweet peppers, onion, jalapeño pepper, and garlic. Stir in broth, raisins, coconut, curry powder, salt, cinnamon, and, if desired, cayenne pepper.

2. Cover and cook on low-heat setting for 8½ to 9 hours or on high-heat setting for 4 to 4½ hours.

3. If using low-heat setting, turn to high-heat setting. In a small bowl stir coconut milk into cornstarch until smooth; stir into slow cooker. Cover and cook for 15 to 20 minutes more or until slightly thickened.

4. If desired, serve stew over hot cooked rice. Sprinkle with cashews.

PER SERVING: 489 cal., 23 g fat (8 g sat. fat), 118 mg chol., 868 mg sodium, 39 g carb., 6 g fiber, 35 g pro.

*Tip: Check the labels of these products carefully to be sure they do not contain added gluten.

Adobo Black Bean Chili

PREP: 20 minutes
COOK: 20 minutes
MAKES: 4 servings

12 ounces lean ground beef
½ cup chopped onion
¾ cup chopped green sweet pepper
2 cloves garlic, minced
1 15-ounce can no-salt-added black beans,* rinsed and drained, or 1¾ cups cooked black beans
1 14.5-ounce can no-salt-added diced tomatoes, undrained
1 8-ounce can gluten-free, no-salt-added tomato sauce
½ cup frozen whole kernel corn
1 tablespoon gluten-free canned chipotle chile peppers in adobo sauce, finely chopped
2 teaspoons chili powder*
1 teaspoon dried oregano, crushed
1 teaspoon ground cumin
¼ teaspoon black pepper
¼ cup light sour cream*
2 tablespoons shredded reduced-fat cheddar cheese*

1. In a 4-quart Dutch oven cook ground beef, onion, sweet pepper, and garlic until meat is browned and onion is tender, stirring with a wooden spoon to break up meat. Drain off fat. Stir in beans, diced tomatoes, tomato sauce, corn, chile peppers, chili powder, oregano, cumin, and black pepper. Bring to boiling; reduce heat. Simmer, covered, for 20 minutes, stirring occasionally.

2. Top each serving with sour cream and cheddar cheese.

PER SERVING: 317 cal., 7 g fat (3 g sat. fat), 59 mg chol., 184 mg sodium, 35 g carb., 10 g fiber, 28 g pro.

*Tip: Check the labels of these products carefully to be sure they do not contain added gluten.

Texas Beef with Butternut Squash

PREP: 25 minutes   SLOW COOK: 8 hours (low) or 4 hours (high)   MAKES: 8 servings

1½ pounds beef chuck roast
 4 cups cubed, peeled butternut squash (1½-inch cubes)
 2 14.5-ounce cans fire-roasted diced tomatoes, undrained
1½ cups gluten-free, no-salt-added beef broth or water
 ¾ cup chopped onion
 1 4-ounce can diced green chiles, undrained
 1 tablespoon ground ancho chile pepper
 2 teaspoons unsweetened cocoa powder
 1 teaspoon ground cumin
 1 teaspoon dried oregano, crushed
 3 cloves garlic, minced
    Snipped fresh cilantro
    Hot cooked gluten-free polenta or hot cooked rice (optional)

1. Trim fat from beef roast; cut beef into 2-inch pieces. In a 5- to 6-quart slow cooker stir together beef, squash, tomatoes, broth, onion, chiles, ground ancho pepper, cocoa powder, cumin, oregano, and garlic.

2. Cover and cook on low-heat setting for 8 to 10 hours or on high-heat setting for 4 to 5 hours. Sprinkle servings with cilantro. If desired, serve with polenta or hot cooked rice.

PER SERVING: 258 cal., 13 g fat (5 g sat. fat), 75 mg chol., 313 mg sodium, 16 g carb., 4 g fiber, 19 g pro.

Smoky Cauliflower Soup with Crumbled Bacon

PREP: 25 minutes
COOK: 45 minutes
MAKES: 6 servings

1 large onion
3 slices gluten-free, lower-sodium, less-fat bacon
1 teaspoon smoked paprika
6 cups cauliflower florets
3 cloves garlic, minced
4 cups gluten-free, reduced-sodium chicken broth
1 tablespoon snipped fresh tarragon
½ cup half-and-half or light cream
½ teaspoon salt
¼ teaspoon ground white pepper
Snipped fresh tarragon (optional)

1. Peel onion. Cut onion lengthwise into quarters, keeping the root end intact; set aside. In a Dutch oven cook bacon over medium heat until crisp. Remove bacon, reserving 1 tablespoon drippings in pan. Drain bacon on paper towels. Crumble bacon; set aside.

2. Add onion and paprika to the reserved drippings in pan. Cook over medium heat for 3 minutes, stirring paprika constantly and turning onion occasionally. Stir in cauliflower and garlic; add broth. Bring to boiling; reduce heat. Simmer, covered, for 25 minutes. Remove from heat. Stir in 1 tablespoon tarragon.

3. Using tongs, remove and discard all but one quarter of the onion. Using an immersion blender, puree cauliflower mixture. (Or cool slightly. Transfer mixture, in batches, to a food processor or blender. Cover and blend until smooth, removing cap from blender lid and holding a folded kitchen towel over opening in lid. Repeat with remaining soup. Return soup to pan.) Add half-and-half, the 1 teaspoon salt, and the white pepper. Heat through, stirring occasionally. Season to taste with additional salt.

4. If soup is too thick, thin with additional stock or broth. Ladle soup into bowls. Sprinkle with bacon and, if desired, additional tarragon.

PER SERVING: 89 cal., 3 g fat (2 g sat. fat), 9 mg chol., 638 mg sodium, 10 g carb., 3 g fiber, 6 g pro.

Pork and Green Chile Stew

PREP: 25 minutes
SLOW COOK: 7 hours (low) or 4 hours (high)
MAKES: 6 servings

- 2 **pounds boneless pork sirloin roast or shoulder roast**
- 1 **tablespoon vegetable oil**
- ½ **cup chopped onion**
- 4 **cups cubed, peeled potatoes**
- 3 **cups water**
- 1 **15.25- or 15.5-ounce can hominy or whole kernel corn, drained**
- 2 **4-ounce cans diced green chile peppers, undrained**
- 2 **tablespoons quick-cooking tapioca**
- 1 **teaspoon garlic salt**
- ½ **teaspoon ground cumin**
- ½ **teaspoon ground ancho chile pepper**
- ½ **teaspoon black pepper**
- ¼ **teaspoon dried oregano, crushed**
  Snipped fresh cilantro (optional)

1. Trim fat from meat. Cut meat into ½-inch pieces. In a large skillet cook half of the meat in hot oil over medium-high heat until browned. Using a slotted spoon, remove meat from skillet. Cook the remaining meat and onion in the skillet until meat is browned. Drain off fat.

2. Transfer all of the meat and the onion to a 3½- to 4½-quart slow cooker. Stir in potatoes, the water, hominy, green chile peppers, tapioca, garlic salt, cumin, ground ancho pepper, black pepper, and oregano.

3. Cover and cook on low-heat setting for 7 to 8 hours or on high-heat setting for 4 to 5 hours. If desired, sprinkle servings with cilantro.

PER SERVING: 347 cal., 7 g fat (2 g sat. fat), 89 mg chol., 592 mg sodium, 34 g carb., 4 g fiber, 36 g pro.

Pork and Hominy Soup

PREP: 35 minutes   **COOK:** 20 minutes   **MAKES:** 4 servings

12 ounces pork tenderloin, trimmed of fat and cut into bite-size pieces

1 medium poblano or Anaheim pepper, seeded and chopped (see tip, page 21)

1 large onion, cut into thin wedges

3 cloves garlic, minced

2 teaspoons vegetable oil

1 15.5-ounce can golden or white hominy, rinsed and drained

1 14.5-ounce can no-salt-added diced tomatoes, undrained

1 14.5-ounce can gluten-free, reduced-sodium chicken broth

1¾ cups water

1 tablespoon lime juice

2 teaspoons snipped fresh oregano or 1 teaspoon dried oregano, crushed

1 teaspoon ground cumin

1 teaspoon ground pasilla, ancho, or chipotle chile pepper*

¼ teaspoon black pepper

¼ cup sliced radishes, shredded cabbage, and/or sliced green onions

1. In a Dutch oven cook pork, poblano pepper, onion wedges, and garlic in hot oil over medium heat about 5 minutes or until pork is no longer pink and vegetables are tender. Stir in hominy, tomatoes, broth, water, lime juice, oregano, cumin, ground pasilla pepper, and black pepper. Bring to boiling; reduce heat. Simmer, covered, for 15 minutes.

2. Top servings with radishes, cabbage, and/or green onions.

PER SERVING: 258 cal., 6 g fat (1 g sat. fat), 55 mg chol., 569 mg sodium, 29 g carb., 6 g fiber, 23 g pro.

*Tip: For milder flavor, choose pasilla or ancho chile pepper; for spicy smoky flavor, choose chipotle chile pepper.

Caribbean Seafood Stew

START TO FINISH: 30 minutes
MAKES: 4 servings

1 pound fresh or frozen
skinless white-flesh fish
fillets, such as tilapia or cod
8 ounces fresh or frozen peeled
and deveined medium shrimp
2 tablespoons olive oil
1 tablespoon lime juice
¼ teaspoon salt
⅛ teaspoon black pepper
1 cup chopped onion
1 cup chopped green sweet
pepper
6 cloves garlic, minced
1 fresh jalapeño chile pepper,
seeded and finely chopped
(see tip, page 21)
1 14.5-ounce can diced
tomatoes, undrained
½ cup unsweetened coconut
milk *
½ cup snipped fresh cilantro
2 cups hot cooked rice
2 tablespoons snipped fresh
cilantro
Hot pepper sauce* (optional)

1. Thaw fish and shrimp, if frozen. Rinse fish; pat dry with paper towels. Cut fish into 1-inch pieces. In a medium bowl stir together 1 tablespoon of the oil, the lime juice, salt, and black pepper. Add fish and toss gently to coat; set aside. Rinse shrimp; pat dry with paper towels. Set shrimp aside.

2. In a large saucepan heat the remaining 1 tablespoon oil over medium-high heat. Add onion, sweet pepper, garlic, and jalapeño pepper. Cook and stir about 4 minutes or until onion is tender. Stir in tomatoes and coconut milk. Bring to boiling; reduce heat. Simmer, uncovered, for 10 minutes, stirring occasionally. Stir in fish, shrimp, and the ½ cup cilantro. Return to boiling; reduce heat. Simmer, uncovered, about 5 minutes more or until fish flakes when tested with a fork and shrimp are opaque, stirring occasionally.

3. Serve in bowls over hot cooked rice. Sprinkle with the 2 tablespoons cilantro. If desired, serve with hot pepper sauce.

PER SERVING: 400 cal., 15 g fat (7 g sat. fat), 120 mg chol., 716 mg sodium, 34 g carb., 3 g fiber, 33 g pro.

*Tip: Check the labels of these products carefully to be sure they do not contain added gluten.

Smoky Tomato–Salmon Chowder

PREP: 25 minutes
ROAST: 15 minutes at 425°F
STAND: 15 minutes
BAKE: 4 minutes per ½-inch thickness at 425°F
MAKES: 6 servings

3 **6-ounce fresh or frozen skinless salmon fillets**
1 **to 2 teaspoons chili powder***
½ **teaspoon salt**
2 **medium red sweet peppers, halved lengthwise and seeded**
1 **medium sweet onion, cut into ½-inch slices**
1 **jalapeño pepper, halved lengthwise and seeded (see tip, page 21)**
2½ **cups gluten-free, reduced-sodium chicken broth**
1 **14.5-ounce can fire-roasted diced tomatoes, undrained**
1 **cup water**
1 **large tomato, chopped**
2 **tablespoons coarsely chopped fresh Italian parsley**
1 **medium avocado, peeled, seeded, and sliced**
Chili powder*

1. Preheat oven to 425°F. Thaw salmon, if frozen. Rinse salmon; pat dry with paper towels. Sprinkle salmon with 1 to 2 teaspoons chili powder and the salt. Cover and refrigerate while roasting vegetables.

2. Place sweet peppers, onion, and jalapeño pepper, cut sides down, on a foil-lined baking sheet. Roast for 15 to 20 minutes or until charred. Loosely wrap vegetables in foil; let stand 15 minutes.

3. Meanwhile, place salmon in a shallow greased baking pan; fold under thin edges. Bake until fish flakes when tested with a fork. Allow 4 to 6 minutes per ½-inch thickness of fish. Keep warm.

4. Using a sharp knife, peel off and discard skins from peppers. Coarsely chop peppers and onion; transfer to a large saucepan. Add broth, tomatoes, and the water. Bring to boiling, stirring occasionally. Remove from heat. Stir in chopped tomato and parsley.

5. Ladle chowder into shallow bowls. Break salmon into pieces and divide among bowls. Top with avocado slices and sprinkle with chili powder.

PER SERVING: 216 cal., 9 g fat (1 g sat. fat), 47 mg chol., 636 mg sodium, 13 g carb., 3 g fiber, 20 g pro.

*Tip: Check the label of this product carefully to be sure it does not contain added gluten.

Creamy Potato and Asparagus Soup

START TO FINISH: 30 minutes
MAKES: 4 servings

1¼ pounds fresh asparagus spears, trimmed
1¼ pounds potatoes, peeled and chopped (½-inch pieces or smaller)
1¼ cups water
1 12-ounce can evaporated milk
½ teaspoon salt
½ teaspoon black pepper
6 slices gluten-free bacon
1 tablespoon honey
Toppings such as finely shredded lemon peel, snipped fresh Italian parsley, coarse salt, and/or freshly ground black pepper (optional)

1. Set aside about one-third of the asparagus. In a large saucepan combine the remaining asparagus, the potatoes, the water, evaporated milk, ½ teaspoon salt, and ½ teaspoon pepper. Bring to boiling; reduce heat. Simmer, covered, about 10 minutes or until potatoes are tender. Cool slightly.

2. In a blender place half of the soup. Cover and blend until smooth, removing cap from blender lid and holding a folded kitchen towel over opening in lid. Repeat with remaining soup. Return all the soup to Dutch oven; keep warm.

3. Meanwhile, in a skillet cook bacon until crisp. Remove bacon, reserving 1 tablespoon drippings in skillet. Drain bacon on paper towels; set aside. Add reserved asparagus spears to drippings in skillet. Cook for 5 to 6 minutes or until asparagus is crisp-tender, stirring occasionally.

4. Coarsely chop bacon and place in a microwave-safe pie plate. Drizzle bacon with honey; cover with vented plastic wrap. Just before serving, microwave for 30 seconds.

5. Ladle soup into bowls and top with asparagus, bacon, and assorted toppings.

PER SERVING: 356 cal., 15 g fat (7 g sat. fat), 41 mg chol., 673 mg sodium, 43 g carb., 4 g fiber, 15 g pro.

Thai-Style Pumpkin Soup

PREP: 20 minutes
COOK: 30 minutes
MAKES: 6 servings

- 1 15-ounce can pumpkin or 1¾ cups pumpkin puree
- 1 14.5-ounce can gluten-free vegetable broth or stock
- 1½ cups mango or apricot nectar
- 1 tablespoon minced fresh ginger
- 2 cloves garlic, minced
- 1 5-ounce can evaporated milk (⅔ cup) or ⅔ cup unsweetened coconut milk*
- ¼ cup gluten-free creamy peanut butter
- 2 tablespoons rice vinegar
  Hot pepper sauce* or ¼ teaspoon crushed red pepper
- ¼ cup chopped fresh cilantro (optional)
  Sour cream* or plain yogurt* (optional)

1. In a large saucepan combine pumpkin, vegetable broth, nectar, ginger, and garlic. Bring to boiling; reduce heat. Simmer, uncovered, for 30 minutes, stirring occasionally.

2. Whisk in the milk, peanut butter, vinegar, and hot pepper sauce until mixture is smooth. If desired, stir in the cilantro. Ladle into bowls.

3. If desired, top servings with sour cream or yogurt.

PER SERVING: 236 cal., 14 g fat (0 g sat. fat), 7 mg chol., 402 mg sodium, 23 g carb., 4 g fiber, 9 g pro.

*Tip: Check the labels of these products carefully to be sure they do not contain added gluten.

Butternut Squash Soup with Polenta Croutons

PREP: 30 minutes **COOK:** 25 minutes **CHILL:** 8 hours **ROAST:** 1 hour at 350°F
BAKE: 1 hour at 375°F **MAKES:** 6 servings

1 recipe Firm Polenta
1 3-pound butternut squash, seeded, peeled, and cut into 1-inch pieces
1 teaspoon kosher salt
½ teaspoon freshly ground black pepper
3 tablespoons olive oil
1 tablespoon unsalted butter
1 cup chopped onion
5 to 7 cups gluten-free vegetable broth
  Snipped fresh chives (optional)

1. Prepare Firm Polenta.

2. Preheat oven to 350°F. In a large shallow roasting pan combine squash, salt, and pepper. Drizzle with 2 tablespoons of the oil; toss to coat. Spread squash in a single layer. Roast about 1 hour or until tender, stirring once.

3. Increase oven temperature to 375°F. Lightly grease a 3-quart rectangular baking dish; set aside. For polenta croutons, remove polenta from loaf pan and cut into 1-inch cubes. Spread polenta cubes in the prepared baking dish. Brush with the remaining 1 tablespoon oil. Bake about 1 hour or until polenta croutons are lightly browned.

4. Meanwhile, in a 4- to 6-quart Dutch oven melt butter over medium-low heat. Add onion; cook about 20 minutes or until golden, stirring occasionally. Add roasted squash and 5 cups of the broth. Bring to boiling; reduce heat. Simmer, uncovered, for 15 minutes. Cool slightly.

5. Working in batches, transfer soup to a blender. Cover and blend until smooth, removing cap from blender lid and holding a folded kitchen towel over opening in lid. Repeat with remaining soup. Return soup to Dutch oven. Stir in additional broth to desired consistency. Heat through. Top each serving with polenta croutons and, if desired, chives.

Firm Polenta: In a medium saucepan bring 2½ cups water to boiling. Meanwhile, in a medium bowl stir together 1 cup gluten-free coarse-ground yellow cornmeal, 1 cup cold water, and 1 teaspoon salt. Slowly add cornmeal mixture to the boiling water, stirring constantly. Cook and stir until mixture returns to boiling. Reduce heat to medium-low. Cook for 25 to 30 minutes or until mixture is very thick and tender, stirring frequently and adjusting heat as necessary to maintain a slow boil. Pour into an 8×4×2-inch loaf pan, spreading evenly. Cover and chill for at least 8 hours or up to 3 days.

PER SERVING: 272 cal., 9 g fat (2 g sat. fat), 5 mg chol., 859 mg sodium, 46 g carb., 6 g fiber, 4 g pro.

Spicy Moroccan Vegetable Stew

PREP: 25 minutes
COOK: 45 minutes
MAKES: 7 servings

1 tablespoon olive oil
1 small bulb fennel, cored and chopped
1 cup sliced carrots
¾ cup chopped onion
2 cloves garlic, minced
1½ teaspoons grated fresh ginger
½ teaspoon salt
½ teaspoon ground turmeric
¼ teaspoon ground cinnamon
4 cups gluten-free, reduced-sodium vegetable or chicken broth
½ cup apple cider or apple juice
¾ cup dry lentils
1 15-ounce can fire-roasted diced tomatoes, undrained
1 15-ounce can garbanzo beans (chickpeas),* rinsed and drained

1. In a 5- to 6-quart Dutch oven heat oil over medium-high heat. Add fennel and carrots; cook and stir for 5 minutes. Add onion and garlic; cook and stir for 10 to 12 minutes or until tender. Add ginger, salt, turmeric, and cinnamon. Cook and stir for 1 minute.

2. Add vegetable broth, apple cider, and lentils. Bring to boiling; reduce heat. Simmer, covered, for 15 minutes. Add tomatoes; simmer for 5 to 10 minutes more or until lentils are tender. Add garbanzo beans; heat through.

PER SERVING: 186 cal., 3 g fat (0 g sat. fat), 0 mg chol., 474 mg sodium, 32 g carb., 9 g fiber, 9 g pro.

*Tip: Check the label of this product carefully to be sure it does not contain added gluten.

Egg and Rice Noodle Soup

START TO FINISH: 30 minutes
MAKES: 6 servings

- 2 **cups frozen shelled sweet soybeans (edamame), thawed**
- 4 **ounces dried rice noodles or gluten-free soba (buckwheat noodles)**
- 8 **cups gluten-free, reduced-sodium chicken broth**
- 3 **tablespoons cornstarch***
- 3 **sheets nori (seaweed), coarsely crushed**
- 3 **tablespoons gluten-free, reduced-sodium soy sauce or gluten-free tamari**
- 1 **tablespoon grated fresh ginger**
- 3 **eggs**
- 1 **cup sliced green onions**
- 3 **tablespoons rice vinegar**
- 2 **teaspoons sesame oil (not toasted)**
  Sriracha sauce*

1. Cook edamame according to package directions; do not drain. Stir in noodles. Return to boiling; reduce heat. Simmer for 3 minutes; drain well.

2. Meanwhile, in a small bowl stir together ¼ cup of the broth and the cornstarch; set aside. In a Dutch oven combine the remaining broth, the nori, soy sauce, and ginger. Bring to simmering. Stir in cornstarch mixture; cook and stir for 1 minute.

3. In a liquid measuring cup lightly beat eggs with a fork. Gently stir broth clockwise three times, then drizzle beaten eggs into moving broth. Turn off heat and let stand for 2 minutes. Stir in green onions, vinegar, and sesame oil.

4. To serve, divide edamame and noodles among bowls. Ladle soup over noodle mixture. Top with sriracha sauce to taste.

PER SERVING: 242 cal., 7 g fat (1 g sat. fat), 93 mg chol., 1,183 mg sodium, 29 g carb., 4 g fiber, 16 g pro.

*Tip: Check the labels of these products carefully to be sure they do not contain added gluten.

Gingered Carrot–Sweet Potato Soup with Chive Cream

START TO FINISH: 30 minutes   MAKES: 4 servings

1 pound carrots, thinly sliced

1 large sweet potato, peeled and cut into ½-inch pieces

1 teaspoon ground ginger

3 14.5-ounce cans gluten-free, reduced-sodium vegetable broth

½ cup sour cream* or crème fraîche*

2 tablespoons snipped fresh chives or sliced green onion

1 19-ounce can cannellini beans (white kidney beans),* rinsed and drained
Salt and black pepper
Snipped fresh chives and/or ground ginger (optional)

1. In a 4-quart Dutch oven combine carrots, sweet potato, and the 1 teaspoon ginger. Add broth. Bring to boiling; reduce heat. Simmer, covered, for 10 to 12 minutes or until vegetables are tender. Cool slightly.

2. Meanwhile, for chive cream, in a small bowl combine sour cream and the 2 tablespoons snipped chives.

3. In a blender combine one-fourth of the carrot mixture and one-fourth of the beans. Cover and blend until smooth, removing cap from blender lid and holding a folded kitchen towel over opening in lid. Set mixture aside. Blend the remaining carrot mixture and beans, one-fourth at a time. Return the soup to the Dutch oven; heat through. Season to taste with salt and pepper.

4. Top each serving with chive cream. If desired, sprinkle with additional chives and/or ginger.

PER SERVING: 248 cal., 5 g fat (3 g sat. fat), 12 mg chol., 708 mg sodium, 40 g carb., 11 g fiber, 8 g pro.

*Tip: Check the labels of these products carefully to be sure they do not contain added gluten.

Sides

When it comes to side dishes, getting into a rut is easy—even if you're not on a restricted diet. These can-do recipes show how unexpected ingredients and smart cooking techniques elevate in-season veggies and gluten-free grains to new heights.

Skillet White Beans

PREP: 20 minutes   COOK: 25 minutes   MAKES: 12 servings

3 tablespoons butter
1 large sweet onion, such as Vidalia, Maui, or Walla Walla, halved and thinly sliced
½ cup maple syrup
⅓ cup white balsamic vinegar or lemon juice
2 tablespoons packed brown sugar
2 tablespoons snipped fresh sage
2 tablespoons tomato paste
1 teaspoon salt
½ teaspoon freshly ground black pepper
2 15.5- to 16-ounce cans navy beans,* rinsed and drained
2 15.5- to 16-ounce cans butter beans,* rinsed and drained
1 15.5- to 16-ounce can garbanzo beans (chickpeas),* rinsed and drained
   Sour cream* (optional)
   Yellow, red, and/or green tomatoes, chopped (optional)
   Fresh sage leaves (optional)

1. In an extra-large skillet melt butter over medium heat. Add onion; cook about 15 minutes or until very tender and golden, stirring occasionally. Stir in maple syrup, vinegar, brown sugar, snipped sage, tomato paste, salt, and pepper. Add navy beans, butter beans, and garbanzo beans; stir to coat.

2. Cook, covered, over medium heat for 10 to 15 minutes or until heated through, stirring occasionally. Transfer to a serving bowl. If desired, top with sour cream, tomatoes, and sage leaves.

PER SERVING: 246 cal., 7 g fat (4 g sat. fat), 21 mg chol., 570 mg sodium, 43 g carb., 9 g fiber, 10 g pro.

*Tip: Check the labels of these products carefully to be sure they do not contain added gluten.

Quinoa with Roasted Beets and Chive Vinaigrette

PREP: 25 minutes
ROAST: 40 minutes at 400°F
STAND: 15 minutes
COOK: 15 minutes
MAKES: 6 servings

1½ pounds baby beets
4 cloves garlic, peeled
4 tablespoons olive oil
Salt and black pepper
3 cups water
1½ cups quinoa, rinsed and drained
3 tablespoons white balsamic vinegar or white wine vinegar
1 tablespoon snipped fresh chives
1 teaspoon gluten-free Dijon-style mustard
3 ounces ricotta salata or feta cheese, crumbled (¾ cup)
⅓ cup chopped walnuts, toasted
1 shallot, thinly sliced
Snipped fresh chives

1. Preheat oven to 400°F. Cut tops off beets and trim root ends. Halve or quarter beets. Place beets and garlic in a 15×10×1-inch baking pan. Drizzle with 1 tablespoon of the oil and sprinkle with ¼ teaspoon salt and ¼ teaspoon pepper; toss to coat. Cover with foil.

2. Roast for 40 to 45 minutes or until beets are tender. Let stand, covered, for 15 minutes. To remove skins, wrap beets, one at a time, in a paper towel and gently rub to remove skins. (If skins are very tender, you do not need to remove them.) Mash garlic and set aside.

3. Meanwhile, in a medium saucepan combine the water, quinoa, and ¼ teaspoon salt. Bring to boiling; reduce heat. Simmer, covered, about 15 minutes or until liquid is absorbed.

4. For vinaigrette, in a screw-top jar combine the remaining 3 tablespoons oil, the vinegar, the 1 tablespoon chives, and the mustard. Season to taste with salt and pepper.

5. In a medium bowl combine cooked quinoa, the vinaigrette, cheese, walnuts, and shallot. Toss to combine.

6. Divide quinoa mixture among six plates. Top with roasted beets. Sprinkle with additional snipped chives. Serve warm or at room temperature.

PER SERVING: 364 cal., 19 g fat (2 g sat. fat), 13 mg chol., 521 mg sodium, 38 g carb., 6 g fiber, 11 g pro.

Roasted Beet Salad with Shredded Greens, Golden Raisins, and Pine Nuts

PREP: 25 minutes
ROAST: 55 minutes at 450°F
MAKES: 4 servings

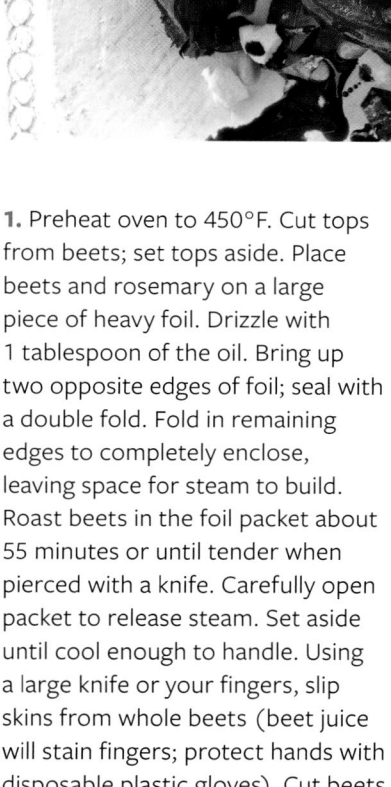

- 2 **pounds fresh beets with tops**
- 2 **sprigs fresh rosemary**
- 3 **tablespoons olive oil**
- ¾ **cup balsamic vinegar**
  Salt and black pepper
- ⅓ **cup golden raisins**
- 2 **tablespoons pine nuts, toasted**
- 4 **ounces ricotta salata or feta cheese, crumbled**

1. Preheat oven to 450°F. Cut tops from beets; set tops aside. Place beets and rosemary on a large piece of heavy foil. Drizzle with 1 tablespoon of the oil. Bring up two opposite edges of foil; seal with a double fold. Fold in remaining edges to completely enclose, leaving space for steam to build. Roast beets in the foil packet about 55 minutes or until tender when pierced with a knife. Carefully open packet to release steam. Set aside until cool enough to handle. Using a large knife or your fingers, slip skins from whole beets (beet juice will stain fingers; protect hands with disposable plastic gloves). Cut beets into wedges. Discard rosemary.

2. Meanwhile, thoroughly wash and dry beet tops. Remove and discard stalks. Thinly slice greens from beet tops.

3. For balsamic vinegar reduction, in a small saucepan bring balsamic vinegar to boiling. Reduce heat to maintain a simmer; simmer about 15 minutes or until reduced to ¼ cup. Let cool. Reduction will thicken as it cools.

4. In a large bowl gently toss together warm beets, sliced beet greens, and the remaining 2 tablespoons oil until greens are slightly wilted. Season to taste with salt and pepper.

5. On a large platter or four salad plates arrange beets and greens. Sprinkle with raisins and pine nuts. Top with cheese. Drizzle with balsamic vinegar reduction to taste.

PER SERVING: 343 cal., 19 g fat (5 g sat. fat), 21 mg chol., 602 mg sodium, 36 g carb., 5 g fiber, 10 g pro.

Skillet-Browned Broccoli with Pan-Toasted Garlic

START TO FINISH: 30 minutes   MAKES: 8 servings

3 **large broccoli heads with stem ends attached**
3 **tablespoons olive oil**
½ **teaspoon salt**
¼ **teaspoon black pepper**
3 **tablespoons thinly sliced garlic cloves**
Sea salt (optional)

1. Slice broccoli heads lengthwise into 1-inch-thick slices, cutting from the bottom of the stems through the crown to preserve the shape of the broccoli (reserve any florets that fall away for another use). Brush both sides of each broccoli slice with some of the olive oil and sprinkle with salt and pepper.

2. Preheat an extra-large cast-iron skillet over medium heat. Place half the broccoli slices in the heated skillet and set a heavy medium skillet on the slices to press them down. Cook over medium heat for 3 to 4 minutes or until well browned. Turn slices and cook second sides for 3 to 4 minutes more or until browned (for more tender broccoli, cook over medium-low heat for 5 to 6 minutes per side). Transfer to a warm platter; cover and keep warm.* Cook remaining broccoli slices.

3. Drizzle the remaining olive oil into the hot skillet; reduce heat to medium-low. Add garlic slices. Cook garlic about 2 minutes or until the slices are lightly browned. If desired, sprinkle with sea salt, stirring gently and constantly. Drain garlic on paper towels.

4. Arrange broccoli on a serving platter. Sprinkle toasted garlic slices over broccoli.

PER SERVING: 79 cal., 5 g fat (1 g sat. fat), 0 mg chol., 174 mg sodium, 7 g carb., 2 g fiber, 3 g pro.

*Tip: Keep cooked broccoli slices warm in a 300°F oven or cover with foil while cooking the remaining broccoli.

Shaved Brussels Sprouts with Green Onion Vinaigrette

START TO FINISH: 45 minutes
MAKES: 16 servings

- 8 **green onions**
- ½ **cup olive oil**
- ½ **cup lemon juice**
- 2 **tablespoons white wine vinegar**
- 2 **tablespoons honey**
- 2 **teaspoons ground coriander**
- 2 **pounds Brussels sprouts**
- 4 **oranges, peeled and sectioned, or 1½ cups mandarin orange segments**
- 1 **cup cashews, toasted**
- 1 **teaspoon kosher salt**

1. For vinaigrette, chop green onions, separating white parts from green tops. In a blender or food processor combine the white parts of the onions, the oil, lemon juice, vinegar, honey, and coriander. Cover and blend or process until smooth; set aside.

2. Trim Brussels sprouts.* Very thinly slice sprouts. In an extra-large bowl combine Brussels sprout slices and the green onion tops. Pour vinaigrette over sprout mixture; toss gently to coat. Add orange sections, cashews, and salt; toss gently to combine.

PER SERVING: 162 cal., 11 g fat (2 g sat. fat), 0 mg chol., 140 mg sodium, 15 g carb., 3 g fiber, 4 g pro.

To Make Ahead: Prepare as directed. Cover and chill up to 4 hours.

*Tip: To trim Brussels sprouts, cut off the stems just at the spot where the leaves are attached. Remove dark green outer leaves until tender, light green leaves are uniformly exposed.

Cabbage and Carrot Salad with Peanut Sauce

START TO FINISH: 25 minutes
MAKES: 4 servings

1   3.75-ounce package bean threads (cellophane noodles)
¼   cup gluten-free chicken broth
3   tablespoons gluten-free creamy peanut butter
2   tablespoons gluten-free tamari or liquid aminos
2   tablespoons honey
1   teaspoon lime juice
½   teaspoon toasted sesame oil
1   clove garlic, minced
3   cups shredded cabbage
1   cup coarsely shredded carrots
½   cup snipped fresh cilantro
¼   cup chopped gluten-free honey-roasted peanuts
    Lime wedges

1. In a large bowl combine bean threads and enough hot water to cover; let stand for 10 minutes. Drain well. If desired, use kitchen scissors to snip bean threads into shorter strands.

2. Meanwhile, in a large bowl combine broth, peanut butter, tamari, honey, lime juice, sesame oil, and garlic. Add cabbage and carrots; toss to coat.

3. Divide bean threads among salad plates. Top with cabbage mixture and sprinkle with cilantro and peanuts. Serve with lime wedges.

PER SERVING: 275 cal., 10 g fat (2 g sat. fat), 0 mg chol., 668 mg sodium, 43 g carb., 4 g fiber, 6 g pro.

Spice-and-Honey Roasted Carrots

PREP: 20 minutes   ROAST: 25 minutes at 425°F   MAKES: 6 servings

1½ **pounds regular or rainbow carrots**
1 **tablespoon olive oil**
½ **cup coarsely chopped hazelnuts (filberts)**
1 **tablespoon coriander seeds (optional)**
1 **tablespoon sesame seeds (optional)**
1½ **teaspoons cumin seeds (optional)**
½ **teaspoon salt**
¼ **teaspoon black pepper**
1 **tablespoon honey**
Lemon wedges

1. Preheat oven to 425°F. Trim carrots, reserving tops if desired. Scrub carrots and, if desired, peel. Halve any large carrots lengthwise.

2. Line a shallow roasting pan with parchment paper or foil. Evenly spread carrots in prepared roasting pan. Drizzle with olive oil. Roast carrots, uncovered, for 20 minutes.

3. Meanwhile, heat a small dry skillet over medium-high heat. Add hazelnuts; cook and stir about 3 minutes or until fragrant and toasted. Transfer to a bowl. Add coriander seeds, sesame seeds, and cumin seeds (if using) to hot skillet. Cook and stir over medium-high heat about 2 minutes or until fragrant and toasted. Remove spices from heat and transfer to another bowl; cool for 10 minutes.

4. Using a spice grinder, coffee grinder, or mortar and pestle, grind or crush toasted spices just until coarsely ground or desired consistency. Add the hazelnuts, salt, and pepper, crushing nuts slightly. Remove carrots from the oven. Drizzle with honey; toss to evenly coat. Sprinkle carrots with half of the hazelnut mixture. Roast for 5 to 10 minutes more or until carrots are tender.

5. Serve roasted carrots with lemon wedges.

PER SERVING: 152 cal., 9 g fat (1 g sat. fat), 0 mg chol., 274 mg sodium, 17 g carb., 5 g fiber, 3 g pro.

Skillet Corn

START TO FINISH: 35 minutes
MAKES: 6 servings

4 slices gluten-free bacon
2 cups fresh or frozen whole kernel corn
1 cup frozen shelled sweet soybeans (edamame)
1 cup grape tomatoes or cherry tomatoes, halved
½ of a medium red onion, thinly sliced
2 tablespoons snipped fresh cilantro
1 small fresh jalapeño chile pepper, seeded and finely chopped (see tip, page 21)
1 tablespoon olive oil
½ teaspoon finely shredded lime peel
1 tablespoon lime juice
2 cloves garlic, minced
¼ teaspoon ground cumin
⅛ teaspoon salt
⅛ teaspoon chili powder*

1. In a large skillet cook bacon over medium heat until crisp. Remove bacon and drain on paper towels, reserving 2 tablespoons drippings in skillet. Crumble bacon; set aside. Add corn and edamame to the reserved drippings. Cook and stir for 3 to 4 minutes or just until vegetables are crisp-tender.

2. In a large bowl combine corn, edamame, tomatoes, red onion, cilantro, and jalapeño pepper.

3. For dressing, in a screw-top jar combine oil, lime peel, lime juice, garlic, cumin, salt, and chili powder. Cover and shake well. Pour dressing over corn mixture; toss gently to coat. Sprinkle with crumbled bacon.

PER SERVING: 182 cal., 11 g fat (3 g sat. fat), 9 mg chol., 160 mg sodium, 17 g carb., 3 g fiber, 7 g pro.

To Make Ahead: Prepare as directed. Cover and chill up to 4 hours before serving.

*Tip: Check the label of this product carefully to be sure it does not contain added gluten.

Sweet Corn Risotto with Basil and Bacon

PREP: 20 minutes
SLOW COOK: 1 hour (high)
MAKES: 6 servings

6 slices gluten-free bacon
4½ cups gluten-free, reduced-sodium chicken broth
½ cup finely chopped Vidalia or other sweet onion
½ cup dry white wine or gluten-free, reduced-sodium chicken broth
2 cups Arborio rice
4 ears fresh sweet corn, kernels cut from cobs (2 cups)
½ teaspoon salt
2 tablespoons butter, softened
½ cup packed fresh basil leaves, cut into thin strips

1. In a large skillet cook bacon until crisp. Drain bacon on paper towels, reserving 2 tablespoons drippings in skillet. Crumble bacon; reserve for topping.

2. Meanwhile, in a medium saucepan bring broth to boiling; reduce heat to maintain simmer.

3. Add onion to reserved drippings in skillet; cook and stir over medium heat about 4 minutes or until tender. Add wine; bring to boiling. Reduce heat; simmer, uncovered, for 2 minutes, stirring to scrape up any browned bits from the bottom of the skillet. Stir in rice.

4. Transfer rice mixture to a 4- to 5-quart slow cooker. Stir in simmering broth, corn, and salt.

5. Cover and cook on high-heat setting for 1 to 1¼ hours or until rice is tender and liquid is absorbed, stirring once. Stir in butter.

6. Top with crumbled bacon and basil. Serve immediately.

PER SERVING: 395 cal., 12 g fat (5 g sat. fat), 23 mg chol., 797 mg sodium, 59 g carb., 2 g fiber, 11 g pro.

Baked Fennel with Parmesan

PREP: 20 minutes
COOK: 5 minutes
BAKE: 15 minutes at 425°F
MAKES: 8 servings

Butter
3 bulbs fennel, cored and cut into thin wedges (reserve fronds for garnish)
1 small sweet onion, such as Vidalia or Maui, cut into thin wedges
4 cloves garlic, thinly sliced
¼ teaspoon salt
¼ teaspoon black pepper
⅛ teaspoon freshly grated nutmeg
½ cup half-and-half or light cream
2 ounces Parmigiano-Reggiano cheese, finely shredded (½ cup)
2 tablespoons butter, cut up
¼ cup chopped walnuts, toasted
Snipped fennel fronds (optional)

1. Preheat oven to 425°F. Butter a 2-quart gratin dish or shallow baking dish; set aside. In a Dutch oven cook fennel and onion in a large amount of boiling salted water about 5 minutes or until softened. Drain well.

2. Spoon drained fennel and onion into the prepared dish. Sprinkle with garlic, salt, pepper, and nutmeg. Drizzle with half-and-half. Sprinkle with Parmigiano-Reggiano cheese. Dot surface with the 2 tablespoons butter.

3. Bake about 15 minutes or until butter is melted and bubbly. Sprinkle with walnuts. If desired, top with snipped fennel fronds.

PER SERVING: 137 cal., 9 g fat (4 g sat. fat), 18 mg chol., 273 mg sodium, 10 g carb., 3 g fiber, 5 g pro.

Roasted Cauliflower Steaks

PREP: 30 minutes
ROAST: 25 minutes at 450°F
MAKES: 4 servings

¼ teaspoon crushed red pepper
2½ tablespoons olive oil
2 medium heads cauliflower
(1½ to 2 pounds)
2 10-ounce zucchini, halved
lengthwise and cut into
½-inch slices (about 5 cups)
2 cups grape tomatoes
1 cup thin wedges red onion
4 cloves garlic, minced
¼ teaspoon kosher salt
¼ teaspoon freshly ground
black pepper
2 tablespoons balsamic vinegar
1 ounce Parmesan cheese,
shredded (¼ cup)

1. Preheat oven to 450°F. In a small bowl stir crushed red pepper into 1½ tablespoons of the oil. Brush about one-third of the oil-red pepper mixture onto the bottom of a 3-quart rectangular baking dish.

2. Remove leaves from the cauliflower. Carefully trim stem ends, leaving cores intact and florets attached. Place cauliflower heads core sides down. Cut two 1-inch-thick slices from the center of each cauliflower head. (Store the remaining cauliflower for another use.) Place the four "steaks" in the prepared baking dish; brush with another third of the oil-red pepper mixture.

3. In a second 3-quart rectangular baking dish toss together zucchini, tomatoes, red onion, garlic, salt, pepper, and the remaining 1 tablespoon oil.

4. Place baking dishes side by side in the oven. Roast for 15 minutes. Remove dishes from the oven; carefully turn cauliflower over. Brush with the remaining oil-red pepper mixture. Roast for 10 to 15 minutes more or until cauliflower is crisp-tender. Meanwhile, drizzle balsamic vinegar over the zucchini mixture; stir. Roast for 5 to 10 minutes more or until vegetables are crisp-tender and lightly browned.

5. To serve, spoon the zucchini mixture over cauliflower steaks. Sprinkle with Parmesan cheese.

PER SERVING: 215 cal., 12 g fat (3 g sat. fat), 5 mg chol., 314 mg sodium, 23 g carb., 7 g fiber, 9 g pro.

Cauliflower "Couscous"

START TO FINISH: 50 minutes
MAKES: 8 servings

¼ cup dried cranberries
¼ cup snipped dried apricots
2 medium heads cauliflower (1½ to 2 pounds each), cored and cut into florets (8 cups)
2 tablespoons butter
1 tablespoon olive oil
1 medium onion, halved and thinly sliced
2 cloves garlic, minced
1 5-ounce package fresh baby spinach, chopped
½ cup toasted walnuts, chopped
½ teaspoon salt
½ cup sliced green onions

1. Place the dried cranberries and apricots in a small bowl. Cover with boiling water and let stand for 10 minutes or until plump; drain well. Set aside.

2. Meanwhile, place the cauliflower, in batches, in a food processor; cover and pulse four to six times or until crumbly and the texture of couscous.

3. In an extra-large skillet heat 1 tablespoon of the butter and the olive oil over medium-high heat. Add the onion; cook and stir about 3 minutes or until tender and just starting to brown. Add garlic; cook and stir for 30 seconds more. Add the cauliflower, spreading in an even layer. Cook about 8 minutes or until cauliflower is evenly golden, stirring occasionally. Spread evenly in skillet.

4. Add the cranberries and apricots, the spinach, walnuts, and salt. Cook and stir until combined. Stir in the remaining 1 tablespoon butter and the green onions. Toss until butter is melted.

PER SERVING: 139 cal., 8 g fat (3 g sat. fat), 8 mg chol., 217 mg sodium, 14 g carb., 4 g fiber, 4 g pro.

To Make Ahead: Prepare as directed through Step 3. Place in an airtight container; cover. Chill up to 24 hours. To serve, reheat the cauliflower mixture in a lightly oiled extra-large skillet. Continue as directed. Or prepare the recipe as directed through Step 4. Cover and let stand at room temperature up to 4 hours. Serve at room temperature.

Eggplant Caprese Salad

PREP: 25 minutes
STAND: 20 minutes
GRILL: 10 minutes
MAKES: 6 servings

1 cup boiling water
¼ cup dried tomatoes (not oil-packed)
1 1-pound eggplant
3 tablespoons olive oil
1 teaspoon salt
½ teaspoon black pepper
⅓ cup coarsely snipped fresh basil
¼ cup olive oil
2 tablespoons balsamic vinegar
2 7- to 8-ounce balls fresh mozzarella cheese, thinly sliced
4 large heirloom tomatoes, such as Brandywine, cored and thinly sliced
Coarse salt and black pepper
Small fresh basil leaves

1. In a small bowl combine boiling water and dried tomatoes. Let stand for 20 minutes. Drain, discarding water; chop tomatoes.

2. Trim stem and blossom ends of eggplant; cut eggplant crosswise into ½-inch slices. Place slices on a baking sheet; brush both sides with the 3 tablespoons oil. Sprinkle with the 1 teaspoon salt and the ½ teaspoon pepper.

3. For a charcoal or gas grill, place eggplant on the grill rack directly over medium heat. Cover and grill for 10 to 12 minutes or until slightly charred and tender, turning once halfway through grilling. Cool to room temperature.

4. For dressing, in a food processor or blender combine dried tomatoes, the snipped basil, the ¼ cup oil, and the vinegar. Cover and process or blend until finely chopped.

5. On a large platter arrange eggplant, mozzarella cheese, and tomatoes, overlapping slices. Sprinkle lightly with coarse salt and pepper. Spoon dried tomato dressing over salad. Sprinkle with basil leaves. Serve at room temperature.

PER SERVING: 376 cal., 30 g fat (12 g sat. fat), 47 mg chol., 710 mg sodium, 11 g carb., 4 g fiber, 14 g pro.

Winter Garden Slow Cooker Polenta

PREP: 15 minutes
SLOW COOK: 3 hours (low) or 1½ hours (high)
MAKES: 4 servings

½ cup oil-pack dried tomatoes
5 cups boiling water
1½ cups gluten-free coarse cornmeal or gluten-free polenta
2 ounces Parmesan cheese, finely shredded (½ cup)
1 teaspoon salt
1 teaspoon dried basil, crushed
¼ teaspoon crushed red pepper
1 8-ounce package sliced fresh mushrooms (3 cups)
4 cups fresh baby spinach
Crumbled Parmesan cheese (optional)
Crushed red pepper (optional)

1. Drain tomatoes, reserving 1 tablespoon of the oil. Snip tomatoes into bite-size pieces.

2. In a 3½- or 4-quart slow cooker combine tomatoes, the boiling water, cornmeal, the ½ cup Parmesan, the salt, basil, and crushed red pepper; stir well to combine. Cover and cook on low-heat setting for 3 hours or on high-heat setting for 1½ hours or until cornmeal is tender.

3. About 15 minutes before serving, in a large skillet heat the reserved oil from the tomatoes. Add mushrooms to hot oil; cook and stir about 5 minutes or until tender. Add spinach; cook and stir just until wilted. Season to taste with salt.

4. Stir polenta; spoon into four bowls. Top with spinach-mushroom mixture. If desired, sprinkle with crumbled Parmesan and/or crushed red pepper.

PER SERVING: 293 cal., 10 g fat (3 g sat. fat), 7 mg chol., 859 mg sodium, 43 g carb., 6 g fiber, 11 g pro.

Shredded Swiss Chard Salad

START TO FINISH: 20 minutes
MAKES: 4 servings

1 **large bunch Swiss chard (12 ounces)**
½ **of a clove garlic**
   Kosher salt
2 **tablespoons olive oil**
1 **tablespoon cider vinegar**
1 **tablespoon finely chopped shallot**
1 **fresh hot chile pepper, stemmed, seeded, and very thinly sliced (see tip, page 21)**
   Black pepper
5 **ounces fresh mozzarella cheese, coarsely torn (about 1½ cups)**

1. Wash and dry the chard leaves. Remove the stems. Stack the leaves, then roll tightly; thinly slice crosswise.

2. For the vinaigrette, in a small bowl mash garlic with a pinch of kosher salt to make a paste. In a large bowl whisk garlic paste with the oil, vinegar, shallot, chile pepper, ½ teaspoon kosher salt, and ¼ teaspoon black pepper.

3. Toss the chard with the vinaigrette. Sprinkle with mozzarella cheese. Season to taste with kosher salt and black pepper.

PER SERVING: 180 cal., 14 g fat (6 g sat. fat), 25 mg chol., 319 mg sodium, 4 g carb., 2 g fiber, 8 g pro.

Tip: Turn this salad into a main-dish by topping it with grilled chicken and/or toasted almonds.

Butter Lettuce and Spring Pea Salad with Mustard Vinaigrette

START TO FINISH: 30 minutes   MAKES: 6 servings

2 cups shelled fresh peas or frozen peas
1 tablespoon snipped fresh dill
1 tablespoon lemon juice
1 tablespoon cider vinegar
2 teaspoons gluten-free Dijon-style mustard
¼ teaspoon salt
¼ teaspoon freshly ground black pepper
3 tablespoons olive oil
2 small heads Belgian endive
1 large head butterhead or Bibb lettuce, separated into leaves
  Freshly ground black pepper
3 tablespoons chopped macadamia nuts, toasted (optional)
  Snipped fresh dill or chives (optional)

1. In a medium saucepan cook peas in enough boiling water to cover for 1 minute, stirring once. Immediately drain in a colander. Rinse well with cold water. Drain peas again and set aside.

2. For mustard vinaigrette, in a medium bowl combine dill, lemon juice, vinegar, mustard, salt, and the ¼ teaspoon pepper. Slowly add the oil in a thin stream, whisking until fully blended. Add peas to vinaigrette; toss to coat.

3. Slice endive in half lengthwise and remove core. Slice endive lengthwise into thin strips. Add endive to pea mixture; lightly toss to mix.

4. Arrange lettuce on a platter; top with pea salad. Sprinkle with additional pepper. If desired, top with nuts and dill.

PER SERVING: 107 cal., 7 g fat (1 g sat. fat), 0 mg chol., 142 mg sodium, 8 g carb., 3 g fiber, 3 g pro.

Stuffed Mushrooms with Lemon-Pea Hummus

PREP: 25 minutes
BAKE: 13 minutes at 425°F
MAKES: 4 servings

12 large fresh mushrooms (1½ to 2 inches in diameter)
Nonstick cooking spray*
1 cup shelled fresh English peas (1 pound in pods)
2 tablespoons olive oil
½ teaspoon finely shredded lemon peel
1 tablespoon lemon juice
1 to 2 teaspoons snipped fresh mint
1 tablespoon chopped fresh spring garlic**
Salt and black pepper
½ ounce Parmigiano-Reggiano or Grana Padano cheese, grated (2 tablespoons)
Fresh pea shoots and/or small fresh mint leaves (optional)

1. Preheat oven to 425°F. Remove stems from mushrooms; discard stems or save for another use. Place mushroom caps, stemmed sides down, in a 15×10×1-inch baking pan. Lightly coat tops of mushroom caps with cooking spray. Bake for 5 minutes. Remove mushrooms and drain, stemmed sides down, on a double thickness of paper towels. Set pan aside.

2. For hummus, in a medium saucepan cook peas in boiling water for 2 to 3 minutes or just until tender; drain. Plunge peas into a bowl of ice water to cool quickly; drain again. Place ¾ cup of the peas in a blender or food processor. Add oil, lemon peel, lemon juice, and snipped mint. Cover and blend or process until nearly smooth. Transfer pea hummus to a medium bowl. Stir in the remaining peas and spring garlic. Season to taste with salt and pepper.

3. Spoon hummus into mushroom caps. Arrange the stuffed mushrooms in the same baking pan. Sprinkle with cheese. Bake about 8 minutes more or until mushrooms are heated through and cheese is melted. Serve warm or at room temperature. If desired, garnish with pea shoots and/or mint leaves.

PER SERVING: 119 cal., 8 g fat (1 g sat. fat), 2 mg chol., 117 mg sodium, 8 g carb., 3 g fiber, 5 g pro.

*Tip: Check the label of this product carefully to be sure it does not contain added gluten.

**Tip: If spring garlic is not available, substitute 1 tablespoon chopped green onions and 1 clove garlic, minced.

Caramelized Balsamic Onions

PREP: 20 minutes
BAKE: 50 minutes at 425°F
MAKES: 8 servings

2 tablespoons butter, melted
1 tablespoon olive oil
⅓ cup balsamic vinegar
2 tablespoons dry white wine; gluten-free reduced-sodium chicken broth; or water
1 tablespoon sugar
¼ teaspoon salt
⅛ teaspoon freshly ground black pepper
4 medium yellow onions (about 1½ pounds total)
Fresh thyme leaves (optional)

1. Preheat oven to 425°F. In 3-quart rectangular baking dish combine butter and olive oil. Whisk in vinegar, wine, sugar, salt, and pepper. Set aside.

2. Peel off papery outer layers of onions but do not cut off either end. Cut onions in half from stem through root end. Place onions in dish, cut sides up. Cover loosely with foil and bake for 30 minutes.

3. Remove foil. Using tongs, carefully turn onions over to cut sides down. Bake, uncovered, for 20 to 25 minutes more or until onions are tender and vinegar mixture is thickened and caramelized. Serve onions cut sides up. If desired, sprinkle with fresh thyme leaves.

PER SERVING: 81 cal., 5 g fat (2 g sat. fat), 8 mg chol., 103 mg sodium, 9 g carb., 1 g fiber, 1 g pro.

Parsnip–Potato Mash with Leeks and Hazelnut Browned Butter

PREP: 20 minutes
COOK: 20 minutes
MAKES: 8 servings

1 pound Yukon gold potatoes, peeled and coarsely chopped
1¼ pounds parsnips, peeled and sliced
6 tablespoons butter
3 to 4 tablespoons whole milk
⅔ cup sliced leeks (white part only)
½ teaspoon salt
¼ teaspoon black pepper
2 tablespoons snipped fresh parsley
¼ cup finely chopped hazelnuts (filberts), toasted

1. In a Dutch oven cook the potatoes, covered, in a small amount of boiling salted water about 5 minutes. Add the parsnips; cook about 15 minutes more or until the potatoes and parsnips are tender. Drain well. Return potatoes and parsnips to the Dutch oven; add 2 tablespoons of the butter. Mash with a potato masher or fork, adding whole milk as needed to moisten; keep warm.

2. Meanwhile, in a small saucepan cook leeks in 2 tablespoons of the butter about 7 minutes or until tender and just beginning to brown. Add salt and pepper. Stir leek mixture and parsley into the parsnip-potato mash.

3. For hazelnut browned butter, in the same saucepan melt the remaining 2 tablespoons butter over low heat. Continue heating until butter turns a light golden brown. Remove from heat; add the hazelnuts.

4. Gently heat and stir parsnip-potato mash over medium heat until heated through. Season to taste with additional salt and pepper. Transfer to a serving bowl. Top with hazelnut browned butter.

PER SERVING: 186 cal., 11 g fat (6 g sat. fat), 23 mg chol., 452 mg sodium, 20 g carb., 4 g fiber, 3 g pro.

To Prep Ahead: Peel and chop potatoes; place in a bowl of water to cover. Cover and chill up to 24 hours. Peel and slice parsnips and leeks. Place in an airtight container; cover. Chill up to 24 hours. Drain potatoes well. Prepare as directed.

Pumpkin-Parmesan Risotto

PREP: 20 minutes
COOK: 45 minutes
MAKES: 4 servings

3 tablespoons unsalted butter
1 cup finely chopped onion
1 clove garlic, minced
2 cups uncooked Arborio rice
1 cup dry white wine
1½ tablespoons snipped fresh sage
2 to 2½ cups water
1¾ cups gluten-free chicken broth
1 cup canned pumpkin
2 ounces Parmigiano-Reggiano cheese, finely shredded (½ cup)
Parmigiano-Reggiano cheese, shaved (optional)
Fresh sage leaves (optional)

1. In a heavy 4-quart saucepan melt butter over medium heat. Add onion and garlic; cook about 3 minutes or until tender, stirring occasionally. Add rice; cook and stir for 2 minutes. Carefully add wine; cook and stir until liquid is absorbed. Stir in snipped sage.

2. Meanwhile, in a large saucepan bring the water and the broth to boiling; reduce heat and simmer. Slowly add 1 cup of the broth mixture to rice mixture, stirring constantly. Continue to cook and stir over medium heat until most of the liquid is absorbed. Add another 1 cup of the broth mixture, stirring constantly. Continue to cook and stir until most of the liquid is absorbed. Add enough of the remaining broth mixture, about 1 cup at a time, cooking and stirring just until rice is tender but firm and risotto is creamy.

3. Stir in pumpkin and the ½ cup shredded cheese. Cook about 1 minute or until heated through, stirring occasionally. If desired, top with shaved cheese and sage leaves.

PER SERVING: 385 cal., 12 g fat (7 g sat. fat), 26 mg chol., 547 mg sodium, 61 g carb., 6 g fiber, 10 g pro.

Red Quinoa Salad with Raspberries and Beets

PREP: 30 minutes   COOK: 15 minutes   STAND: 5 minutes   MAKES: 6 servings

1½ cups water
 1 cup red or white quinoa, rinsed and drained
1⅓ cups fresh raspberries
 1 small red Fresno chile pepper or red jalapeño pepper, halved and seeded (see tip, page 21)
 2 tablespoons chopped shallot
 1 tablespoon sugar
 ½ teaspoon salt
 ¼ cup white wine vinegar
 ¼ cup olive oil
 4 cups torn red leaf lettuce
 4 small beets, cooked* and sliced (about 1 pound)
 4 large red radishes, sliced
 ⅓ cup roasted pistachio nuts, coarsely chopped
 ½ cup small fresh cilantro sprigs

1. In a small saucepan bring the water to boiling. Add quinoa; return to boiling. Reduce heat to low. Simmer, covered, about 15 minutes or until liquid is absorbed. Remove from heat. Let stand, covered, for 5 minutes. Transfer to a large bowl; cool to room temperature.

2. For dressing, in a food processor combine ⅓ cup of the raspberries, the chile pepper, shallot, sugar, and salt. Cover and process until pureed. Scrape down sides. Add vinegar; process until combined. With food processor running, slowly add oil in a thin steady stream (dressing will thicken as oil is added).

3. In a large bowl gently combine quinoa, lettuce, beets, and radishes. Drizzle dressing over salad; toss gently to mix. Transfer salad to a serving bowl. Top with pistachios, cilantro, and the remaining 1 cup raspberries.

PER SERVING: 303 cal., 14 g fat (2 g sat. fat), 0 mg chol., 263 mg sodium, 38 g carb., 9 g fiber, 7 g pro.

To Make Ahead: Cook quinoa as directed in Step 1; cool. Transfer to an airtight container. Store in the refrigerator up to 24 hours.

*Tip: To cook beets, place unpeeled beets in a large saucepan. Add enough water to cover. Bring to boiling; reduce heat. Cook, covered, for 30 to 35 minutes or until tender. Drain and cool. Slip skins off beets.

Basil Quinoa Salad

START TO FINISH: 30 minutes
MAKES: 6 servings

1 cup fresh basil leaves
2 tablespoons grated Parmesan cheese*
2 tablespoons lemon juice
2 tablespoons olive oil
4 cloves garlic, minced
¼ teaspoon salt
¼ teaspoon black pepper
2 cups cooked quinoa**
1 15-ounce can no-salt-added red kidney beans,* rinsed and drained or 1¾ cups cooked red kidney beans
1 cup chopped yellow sweet pepper
½ cup chopped, seeded tomato
½ cup sliced green onions
4 cups baby spinach or arugula

1. For dressing, place basil in a food processor. Add Parmesan cheese, lemon juice, olive oil, garlic, salt, and black pepper. Cover and process until nearly smooth, stopping to scrape down sides as needed; set aside.

2. In a medium bowl stir together cooked quinoa, beans, sweet pepper, tomato, and green onions. Add dressing; stir to coat. Serve over baby spinach.

PER SERVING: 177 cal., 6 g fat (1 g sat. fat), 1 mg chol., 235 mg sodium, 24 g carb., 8 g fiber, 8 g pro.

*Tip: Check the labels of these products carefully to be sure they do not contain added gluten.

**Tip: For 2 cups cooked quinoa, place ½ cup quinoa in a fine-mesh strainer and rinse under cold running water; drain. In a small saucepan combine the quinoa, 1¼ cups water, and ¼ teaspoon salt. Bring to boiling; reduce heat. Simmer, covered, for 15 minutes. Let stand to cool slightly. Drain off any remaining liquid.

Wild Rice-Stuffed Acorn Squash with Cranberries, Pecans, and Pancetta

PREP: 30 minutes
BAKE: 1 hour 10 minutes at 400°F
MAKES: 6 servings

- 3 1½-pound acorn squash, halved lengthwise and seeds removed
- ¼ cup butter, melted
- ¼ cup packed brown sugar
- ½ teaspoon salt
- ¼ teaspoon freshly ground black pepper
- 4 ounces gluten-free pancetta, chopped
- ½ cup chopped onion
- 2 cups lightly packed baby spinach
- 1 tablespoon snipped fresh sage
- 2 cups cooked brown and/or wild rice
- ⅔ cup pecans, toasted and chopped
- ½ cup dried cranberries

1. Preheat oven to 400°F. Add water to a depth of ½ inch in a large roasting pan. Arrange the squash halves, cut sides down, in the roasting pan. Bake, uncovered, for 30 minutes. Turn squash halves cut sides up. Brush cut sides of squash with 2 tablespoons of the melted butter. Sprinkle with brown sugar, salt, and pepper. Bake, uncovered, for 20 to 25 minutes more or just until tender.

2. Meanwhile, in a large skillet cook and stir pancetta over medium heat for 5 to 6 minutes or until crisp. Using a slotted spoon, remove pancetta from skillet. Drain on paper towels.

3. For filling, add onion to drippings in skillet; cook and stir for 4 to 5 minutes or until onion is tender. Add spinach, sage, and the crisped pancetta. Cook and stir for 2 minutes or until spinach is wilted. Remove skillet from heat. Stir in the cooked rice, pecans, and cranberries. Mix well.

4. Divide filling among squash halves, about ⅔ cup each. Drizzle with the remaining 2 tablespoons melted butter. Bake, uncovered, for 20 to 25 minutes more or until filling is heated through.

PER SERVING: 462 cal., 23 g fat (8 g sat. fat), 27 mg chol., 391 mg sodium, 63 g carb., 7 g fiber, 9 g pro.

DIY Pantry

Gluten is a hidden ingredient in many foods—especially salad dressings, sauces, condiments, and seasoning blends. Stock your pantry with homemade versions of these staples so you'll know exactly what goes into them. The added bonus? They're much tastier than their store-bought counterparts.

Homemade Pesto

START TO FINISH: 15 minutes   MAKES: 10 servings

- 3 cups firmly packed fresh basil leaves (3 ounces)
- ⅔ cup walnuts or almonds
- ⅔ cup grated Parmesan or Romano cheese*
- ½ cup olive oil
- 4 cloves garlic, quartered
- ½ teaspoon salt
- ¼ teaspoon black pepper

1. In a food processor or blender combine basil, nuts, cheese, oil, garlic, salt, and pepper. Cover and process or blend until nearly smooth, stopping to scrape sides as necessary.

2. Place 2 tablespoons of the pesto in each slot of a standard ice cube tray; cover tightly with foil. Freeze for up to 3 months.**

PER SERVING: 173 cal., 17 g fat (3 g sat. fat), 5 mg chol., 199 mg sodium, 2 g carb., 1 g fiber, 4 g pro.

Serving Suggestion: Use 2 tablespoons pesto to coat 1 cup hot cooked gluten-free pasta.

*Tip: Check the label of this product carefully to be sure it does not contain added gluten.

**Tip: If you prefer, transfer pesto to an airtight storage container. Cover surface of pesto with plastic wrap; cover container. Store in the refrigerator for up to 2 days.

Puttanesca Sauce

PREP: 25 minutes
COOK: 12 minutes
MAKES: 4 servings

½ cup chopped onion
2 cloves garlic, minced
1 tablespoon olive oil
1 14.5-ounce can diced tomatoes, undrained
¼ cup dry red wine or gluten-free, reduced-sodium chicken broth
2 tablespoons tomato paste
¼ teaspoon crushed red pepper
12 pitted small Kalamata olives, sliced
3 canned anchovy fillets, cut into ½-inch pieces (optional)
3 tablespoons snipped fresh Italian parsley
2 tablespoons drained capers

1. In a large skillet cook onion and garlic in hot oil over medium heat until tender. Add tomatoes, wine, tomato paste, and crushed red pepper. Bring to boiling; reduce heat. Simmer, uncovered, for 12 to 15 minutes or until sauce is desired consistency, stirring occasionally.

2. Stir in olives, anchovies (if desired), parsley, and capers; heat through.

PER SERVING: 109 cal., 5 g fat (0 g sat. fat), 0 mg chol., 454 mg sodium, 11 g carb., 2 g fiber, 1 g pro.

All-Purpose Pizza Sauce

START TO FINISH: 10 minutes
MAKES: 6 servings

- 1 **28-ounce can crushed tomatoes, undrained**
- 1½ **teaspoons red wine vinegar**
- ½ **teaspoon granulated garlic**
- ½ **teaspoon dried basil**
- ¼ **teaspoon dried oregano**
- ¼ **teaspoon dried thyme**
- ¼ **teaspoon black pepper**
- ¼ **to ½ cup water**
- ¼ **to ½ teaspoon salt**

1. In a medium bowl whisk together tomatoes, vinegar, garlic, basil, oregano, thyme, and pepper. Whisk in ¼ cup of the water and enough of the salt to taste. If necessary, add more of the water to thin. (If the sauce is thick at this stage, it will be pasty on the pizza. It should easily spread over the dough.) Add remaining salt to taste.

2. For an 8- to 10-inch pizza, use ¼ cup of the sauce.

PER ¼ CUP SAUCE:: 22 cal., 0 g fat, 0 mg chol., 136 mg sodium, 5 g carb., 1 g fiber, 1 g pro.

Tomato-Basil Pesto Sauce: Prepare All-Purpose Pizza Sauce as directed, except whisk ½ cup Homemade Pesto (recipe, page 282) or purchased gluten-free basil pesto into the pizza sauce. Taste and, if desired, add more pesto.

Alfredo Sauce

START TO FINISH: 30 minutes
MAKES: 4 servings

2 cloves garlic, minced
2 tablespoons butter
1 cup whipping cream
½ teaspoon salt
⅛ teaspoon black pepper
2 ounces Parmesan cheese, grated (½ cup)

1. In a large saucepan cook garlic in hot butter over medium-high heat for 1 minute. Add cream, salt, and pepper. Bring to boiling; reduce heat. Boil gently, uncovered, for 3 minutes or until sauce begins to thicken. Remove from heat and stir in ½ cup Parmesan cheese.

PER SERVING: 302 cal., 31 g fat (19 g sat. fat), 106 mg chol., 540 mg sodium, 4 g carb., 0 g fiber, 4 g pro.

Lemony Fettuccine Alfredo with Shrimp and Peas: Prepare sauce as directed, except add 6 ounces cooked peeled and deveined shrimp, 1 cup thawed frozen peas, 1 tablespoon lemon juice, and 1 teaspoon finely shredded lemon peel to sauce after it begins to thicken. Heat through before removing from heat then stir in the ½ cup Parmesan cheese. Stir in cooked fettuccine pasta. Sprinkle with freshly ground black pepper.

20-Minute Marinara Sauce

START TO FINISH: 20 minutes
MAKES: 20 servings

- 2 28-ounce cans whole tomatoes, undrained
- 6 tablespoons snipped fresh basil
- 2 tablespoons olive oil
- 2 cloves garlic, minced
- 1 teaspoon crushed red pepper
- ½ teaspoon salt
- ½ teaspoon black pepper

1. Place tomatoes in a food processor or blender. Cover and process or blend until nearly smooth. Stir in basil; set aside.

2. In a large skillet heat oil over medium heat. Add garlic; cook and stir until garlic is lightly browned. Stir in pureed tomato mixture, crushed red pepper, salt, and black pepper. Bring to boiling; reduce heat. Simmer, uncovered, for 10 minutes.

PER SERVING: 26 cal., 1 g fat (0 g sat. fat), 0 mg chol., 172 mg sodium, 3 g carb., 1 g fiber, 1 g pro.

Fire-Roasted Tomato Salsa

PREP: 30 minutes
GRILL: 6 minutes
MAKES: 32 servings

3 cloves garlic, peeled
1 teaspoon olive oil
10 roma tomatoes (about 2 pounds), cored
3 jalapeño chile peppers
1 medium yellow onion, peeled and halved
3 tablespoons snipped fresh cilantro
¼ cup fresh lime juice
1 teaspoon kosher salt

1. Place the garlic cloves on a 6-inch square of heavy foil. Drizzle with oil. Bring up edges of foil around the garlic cloves to enclose. For a charcoal or gas grill, place eight of the tomatoes, the jalapeños, and one onion half on the rack of a covered grill directly over medium-high heat. Grill for 6 minutes or until tomatoes and peppers are blackened and blistered and onion is charred, turning all once halfway through grilling. Add foil packet with garlic cloves to the grill rack for the last 3 minutes of grilling. Remove all ingredients and let cool. Stem and, if desired, seed the jalapeños (see tip, page 21).

2. Meanwhile, finely chop the remaining onion half and chop the remaining 2 tomatoes. Set aside.

3. In a blender place the grilled tomatoes, grilled onion, jalapeños, and garlic with oil. Cover and blend until nearly smooth. Transfer to a medium bowl; add the chopped tomatoes, finely chopped onion, cilantro, lime juice, and salt; stir to combine. Season to taste with additional lime juice and salt.

PER SERVING: 17 cal., 0 g fat, 0 mg chol., 126 mg sodium, 3 g carb., 1 g fiber, 1 g pro.

Salsa Verde

PREP: 20 minutes
BROIL: 7 minutes
STAND: 10 minutes
MAKES: 24 servings

12 ounces fresh tomatillos, husks removed, rinsed, and drained
1 fresh poblano chile pepper
1 fresh serrano chile pepper
2 cloves garlic, minced
½ teaspoon salt
¼ teaspoon sugar
2 tablespoons chopped onion
2 tablespoons snipped fresh cilantro

1. Preheat broiler. Arrange tomatillos and chile peppers on a foil-lined broiler pan. Broil 4 to 5 inches from the heat for 7 to 8 minutes or until charred, turning tomatillos and chile peppers once or twice during broiling. Bring foil up around tomatillos and chile peppers and fold edges together to enclose. Let stand for 10 minutes. Using a sharp knife, loosen edges of the skins on chile peppers; gently pull off skins in strips and discard (see tip, page 21).

2. In a food processor combine tomatillos, chile peppers, garlic, salt, and sugar. Cover and pulse with several on/off turns until chopped. Stir in chopped onion and cilantro. For a thinner salsa, stir in water, 1 tablespoon at a time, to make desired consistency.

PER SERVING: 7 cal., 0 g fat, 0 mg chol., 49 mg sodium, 1 g carb., 0 g fiber, 0 g pro.

Kansas City Barbecue Sauce

PREP: 15 minutes
COOK: 30 minutes
MAKES: 10 servings

½ cup finely chopped onion
2 cloves garlic, minced
1 tablespoon olive oil or vegetable oil
¾ cup apple juice
½ of a 6-ounce can (⅓ cup) tomato paste
¼ cup cider vinegar
2 tablespoons packed brown sugar
2 tablespoons molasses
1 tablespoon paprika
1 tablespoon gluten-free prepared horseradish
1 tablespoon gluten-free Worcestershire sauce
1 teaspoon salt
½ teaspoon black pepper

1. In a medium saucepan cook onion and garlic in hot oil over medium heat until onion is tender, stirring occasionally. Stir in apple juice, tomato paste, vinegar, brown sugar, molasses, paprika, horseradish, Worcestershire sauce, salt, and pepper. Bring to boiling; reduce heat. Simmer, uncovered, about 30 minutes or until sauce reaches desired consistency, stirring occasionally.

2. Brush sauce over beef, pork, and poultry during the last 10 minutes of grilling. If desired, reheat and serve additional sauce on the side.

PER SERVING: 59 cal., 2 g fat (0 g sat. fat), 1 mg chol., 263 mg sodium, 10 g carb., 1 g fiber, 1 g pro.

Teriyaki Sauce

START TO FINISH: 15 minutes
MAKES: 4 servings

¼ cup granulated sugar
2 tablespoons packed brown sugar
1 tablespoon cornstarch*
½ cup gluten-free tamari or liquid aminos
⅓ cup water
2 tablespoons rice vinegar
2 teaspoons grated fresh ginger
2 cloves garlic, minced
1 teaspoon finely shredded lemon peel or orange peel
¼ to ½ teaspoon crushed red pepper (optional)

1. In a medium saucepan stir together granulated sugar, brown sugar, and cornstarch. Stir in tamari, the water, vinegar, ginger, garlic, lemon peel, and, if desired, crushed red pepper.

2. Cook and stir over medium heat until thickened and bubbly. Store in the refrigerator for up to 1 week.

PER SERVING: 21 cal., 0 g fat, 0 mg chol., 374 mg sodium, 5 g carb., 0 g fiber, 1 g pro.

Serving Suggestions: Brush this sauce onto fish, chicken, beef, or tofu during the last few minutes of cooking. It also tastes delicious tossed with roasted, sauteed, and steamed veggies.

*Tip: Check the label of this product carefully to be sure it does not contain added gluten.

Blue Cheese Dressing

START TO FINISH: 10 minutes **MAKES:** 20 servings

- ½ **cup plain yogurt or sour cream***
- ¼ **cup cottage cheese***
- ¼ **cup mayonnaise***
- 3 **to 4 ounces blue cheese, crumbled (¾ to 1 cup)**
- ¼ **teaspoon salt**
- ¼ **teaspoon coarsely ground black pepper**
- 1 **to 2 tablespoons milk (optional)**

1. In a blender or food processor combine yogurt, cottage cheese, mayonnaise, ¼ cup of the crumbled blue cheese, the salt, and pepper. Cover and blend or process until smooth. Stir in remaining blue cheese. If necessary, stir in milk to make the dressing desired consistency. Serve immediately or cover and store in the refrigerator up to 2 weeks. Stir or shake well before using.

PER SERVING: 44 cal., 4 g fat (2 g sat. fat), 6 mg chol., 127 mg sodium, 1 g carb., 0 g fiber, 2 g pro.

***Tip:** Check the labels of these products carefully to be sure they do not contain added gluten.

Honey–Mustard Dressing

START TO FINISH: 10 minutes
MAKES: 16 servings

¼ cup gluten-free stone-ground mustard
¼ cup olive oil or vegetable oil
¼ cup lemon juice
¼ cup honey
2 cloves garlic, minced

1. In a screw-top jar combine mustard, oil, lemon juice, honey, and garlic. Cover and shake well. Serve immediately or cover and store in refrigerator for up to 1 week. Stir or shake well before using.

PER SERVING: 51 cal., 4 g fat (0 g sat. fat), 0 mg chol., 51 mg sodium, 5 g carb., 0 g fiber, 0 g pro.

Red Pepper–Tomato Dressing

PREP: 10 minutes
MAKES: 8 servings

- 1 12-ounce jar roasted red sweet peppers, drained
- 2 ripe large tomatoes, quartered
- ⅓ cup olive oil
- 2 to 3 tablespoons sherry vinegar or white wine vinegar
- 1 clove garlic, minced
- 1 teaspoon smoked paprika
   Salt and black pepper

1. In a blender combine roasted peppers, tomatoes, oil, 2 tablespoons of the vinegar, the garlic, and paprika. Cover and blend until very smooth. If desired, stir in the remaining 1 tablespoon vinegar. Season to taste with salt and black pepper.

2. Serve immediately or pour dressing into an airtight container. Cover and chill for up to 4 days. Stir before serving.

PER SERVING: 27 cal., 3 g fat (0 g sat. fat), 0 mg chol., 22 mg sodium, 1 g carb., 0 g fiber, 0 g pro.

Warm Bacon Salad Dressing

START TO FINISH: 15 minutes
MAKES: 4 servings

2 slices gluten-free bacon
½ cup thinly sliced green onions
2 cloves garlic, minced
¼ cup red wine vinegar
2 teaspoons sugar
1 teaspoon gluten-free coarse-grain mustard
¼ teaspoon black pepper

1. In a medium skillet cook bacon over medium heat until crisp. Using a slotted spoon, remove bacon from skillet, reserving 2 tablespoons of the drippings in skillet (discard the remaining drippings or add olive oil, if necessary, to measure 2 tablespoons). Drain bacon on paper towels. Crumble bacon; set aside.

2. Add green onions and garlic to the reserved drippings in skillet; cook and stir until green onions are tender. Stir in vinegar, sugar, mustard, and pepper. Stir in crumbled bacon; heat through. Serve warm over salad greens.

PER SERVING: 94 cal., 8 g fat (3 g sat. fat), 10 mg chol., 116 mg sodium, 4 g carb., 0 g fiber, 1 g pro.

Thousand Island Dressing

START TO FINISH: 15 minutes
MAKES: 24 servings

- 1 **cup mayonnaise***
- ¼ **cup bottled chili sauce***
- 2 **tablespoons sweet pickle relish***
- 2 **tablespoons finely chopped sweet pepper**
- 2 **tablespoons finely chopped onion**
- 1 **teaspoon gluten-free Worcestershire sauce**
- 1 **to 2 tablespoons milk (optional)**

1. In a small bowl combine mayonnaise and chili sauce. Stir in relish, sweet pepper, onion, and Worcestershire sauce.

2. Serve immediately or cover and store in the refrigerator for up to 1 week. Before serving, if necessary, stir in milk until dressing reaches desired consistency.

PER SERVING: 71 cal., 7 g fat (1 g sat. fat), 3 mg chol., 93 mg sodium, 1 g carb., 0 g fiber, 0 g pro.

*Tip: Check the labels of these products carefully to be sure they do not contain added gluten.

Creamy Garlic Dressing

START TO FINISH: 10 minutes
MAKES: 8 servings

¾ cup mayonnaise*
¼ cup sour cream*
2 teaspoons white wine vinegar
3 cloves garlic, minced
½ teaspoon Italian seasoning,* crushed
¼ teaspoon dry mustard
⅛ teaspoon salt
1 to 2 tablespoons milk (optional)

1. In a small bowl stir together mayonnaise, sour cream, vinegar, garlic, Italian seasoning, mustard, and salt.

2. To store, cover and chill for up to 1 week. Before serving, if necessary, stir in enough of the milk to make dressing desired consistency.

PER SERVING: 82 cal., 9 g fat (2 g sat. fat), 5 mg chol., 77 mg sodium, 0 g carb., 0 g fiber, 0 g pro.

*Tip: Check the labels of these products carefully to be sure they do not contain added gluten.

Buttermilk Pesto Dressing

PREP: 10 minutes
CHILL: 2 hours
MAKES: 8 servings

½ cup buttermilk
¼ cup fat-free plain Greek yogurt*
¼ cup light mayonnaise*
4 teaspoons Homemade Pesto (recipe, page 282) or purchased gluten-free basil pesto
½ teaspoon black pepper

1. In a medium bowl whisk together all ingredients. Cover and chill for at least 2 hours or up to 24 hours.

PER SERVING: 47 cal., 4 g fat (1 g sat. fat), 4 mg chol., 92 mg sodium, 2 g carb., 0 g fiber, 2 g pro.

*Tip: Check the labels of these products carefully to be sure they do not contain added gluten.

Fresh Herb Vinaigrette

START TO FINISH: 10 minutes   MAKES: 14 servings

1   cup olive oil
⅓   cup red wine vinegar
¼   cup finely chopped shallots
2   tablespoons snipped fresh oregano basil, thyme, and/or parsley
1   tablespoon gluten-free Dijon-style mustard
2   to 3 teaspoons sugar
2   cloves garlic, minced
    Salt and black pepper

1. In a screw-top jar combine oil, vinegar, shallots, oregano, mustard, sugar, and garlic. Cover and shake well. Season to taste with salt and pepper. Serve immediately or cover and store in the refrigerator for up to 3 days. (Olive oil will solidify when chilled; let vinaigrette stand at room temperature for 1 hour before using.) Stir or shake well before using.

PER SERVING: 143 cal., 15 g fat (2 g sat. fat), 0 mg chol., 47 mg sodium, 1 g carb., 0 g fiber, 0 g pro.

Green Onion Vinaigrette: Prepare as directed, except substitute ½ cup lemon juice and 2 tablespoons white wine vinegar for red wine vinegar; omit shallots, oregano, and garlic; and substitute 2 tablespoons honey for the sugar. Chop the white and light green portions of 16 green onions (3 ounces). In a blender combine green onions, olive oil, lemon juice, white wine vinegar, and honey. Add 2 teaspoons ground coriander. Cover and blend until smooth. Season to taste with salt and pepper. Transfer to a screw-top jar. Store as directed.

Dill Vinaigrette: Prepare as directed, except substitute ½ cup canola oil for ½ cup of the olive oil, tarragon vinegar or white wine vinegar for red wine vinegar, and snipped fresh dill for oregano. In a blender combine canola oil, olive oil, tarragon vinegar, shallots, dill, mustard, sugar, and garlic. Add ¼ to ½ teaspoon hot pepper sauce.* Cover and blend until smooth. Season to taste with salt and pepper. Transfer to a screw-top jar. Store as directed.

Asian-Ginger Vinaigrette: Prepare as directed, except substitute canola oil for olive oil and ¼ cup white wine vinegar for red wine vinegar; omit shallots, oregano, and mustard. In a screw-top jar combine canola oil, white wine vinegar, sugar, and garlic. Add ¼ cup gluten-free soy sauce; 1 small fresh jalapeño pepper, seeded and finely chopped (see tip, page 21); 1 tablespoon finely chopped pickled ginger; 1 tablespoon liquid from the jar of pickled ginger; 1 tablespoon lime juice; and 1 tablespoon toasted sesame oil. Cover tightly and shake well. Season to taste with salt and pepper. Store as directed.

*__Tip:__ Check the label of this product carefully to be sure it does not contain added gluten.

ASIAN-GINGER
VINAIGRETTE

DILL
VINAIGRETTE

FRESH HERB
VINAIGRETTE

GREEN
ONION
VINAIGRETTE

SPICY
BARBECUE
RUB

JAMAICAN
JERK RUB

ITALIAN
SEASONING
BLEND

TACO
SEASONING
MIX

Jamaican Jerk Rub

MAKES: about ½ cup

- 2 tablespoons sugar
- 4½ teaspoons onion powder
- 4½ teaspoons dried thyme, crushed
- 1 tablespoon ground allspice
- 1 tablespoon black pepper
- 1½ to 3 teaspoons cayenne pepper or paprika
- 1½ teaspoons salt
- ¾ teaspoon ground nutmeg
- ¼ teaspoon ground cloves

1. In a small bowl stir together all ingredients.

2. Store in an airtight container at room temperature for up to 6 months.

Spicy Barbecue Rub

MAKES: about ⅓ cup

- ¼ cup paprika
- 1 tablespoon salt
- 1 tablespoon ground cumin
- 1 tablespoon packed brown sugar
- 1 tablespoon gluten-free chili powder
- 1 tablespoon black pepper
- 1½ teaspoons cayenne pepper
- ¼ teaspoon ground cloves

1. In a small bowl combine all of the ingredients.

2. Store in an airtight container at room temperature for up to 6 months.

Italian Spice Blend

MAKES: about ¾ cup

- 1 ounce Parmesan cheese, grated (¼ cup)
- 2 tablespoons black pepper
- 2 tablespoons fennel seeds, crushed or ground
- 2 tablespoons dried oregano, crushed
- 2 teaspoons garlic powder
- ½ teaspoon salt

1. In a small bowl stir together all ingredients. If desired, make mixture into a powder by grinding the mixture in a coffee grinder.

2. Store in an airtight container in the refrigerator for up to 6 months.

Taco Seasoning Mix

MAKES: about ¾ cup

- 3 to 4 tablespoons gluten-free chili powder
- 2 tablespoons sugar
- 2 tablespoons ground cumin
- 3 to 4 teaspoons garlic powder
- 1 tablespoon gluten-free cornstarch
- 1 tablespoon salt
- 1 to 2 teaspoons black pepper
- 1 teaspoon dried oregano, crushed
- ½ to 1 teaspoon crushed red pepper

1. In a small bowl stir together all ingredients.

2. Store in an airtight container at room temperature for up to 6 months.

Sweets

End the meal at your gluten-free table on a sweet note by serving one of these tempting treats. From rich, chocolaty brownies to peanut butter cookies to elegant cream puffs, no one will ever guess these amazing desserts are gluten-free.

Fudgy Brownies

PREP: 20 minutes   BAKE: 30 minutes at 350°F   MAKES: 16 servings

½ cup butter
3 ounces unsweetened chocolate, coarsely chopped
1 cup sugar
2 eggs
1 teaspoon vanilla extract*
⅔ cup Gluten-Free Flour Mix (recipe, page 312) or purchased gluten-free all-purpose flour
¼ teaspoon baking soda
½ cup chopped nuts (optional)
1 recipe Chocolate-Cream Cheese Frosting (optional)

1. In a medium saucepan heat and stir butter and unsweetened chocolate over low heat until melted and smooth. Remove from heat; cool. Meanwhile, preheat oven to 350°F. Line an 8×8×2-inch baking pan with foil, extending foil over edges of pan. Grease foil; set aside.

2. Stir sugar into cooled chocolate mixture. Add eggs, one at a time, beating with a wooden spoon just until combined. Stir in vanilla. In a small bowl stir together Gluten-Free Flour Mix and baking soda. Add flour mixture to chocolate mixture, stirring just until combined. If desired, stir in nuts. Pour batter into the prepared baking pan, spreading evenly.

3. Bake for 30 minutes. Cool in pan on a wire rack. If desired, spread Chocolate-Cream Cheese Frosting over cooled brownies. Using the edges of the foil, lift uncut brownies out of pan. Cut into brownies.

PER SERVING: 157 cal., 10 g fat (6 g sat. fat), 43 mg chol., 90 mg sodium, 18 g carb., 1 g fiber, 2 g pro.

Chocolate-Cream Cheese Frosting: In a small saucepan cook and stir 1 cup semisweet chocolate pieces over low heat until melted and smooth. In a medium bowl stir together 6 ounces softened cream cheese* and ½ cup powdered sugar. Stir in melted chocolate until smooth.

To Store: Place brownies in a single layer in an airtight container; cover. Store in the refrigerator up to 3 days.

*Tip: Check the labels of these products carefully to be sure they do not contain added gluten.

Blondies

PREP: 20 minutes
BAKE: 15 minutes at 350°F
MAKES: 36 servings

2 cups packed brown sugar
⅔ cup butter, cut up
2 eggs
2 teaspoons vanilla extract*
2 cups Gluten-Free Flour Mix (recipe, page 312) or purchased gluten-free all-purpose flour
1 teaspoon gluten-free baking powder
¼ teaspoon baking soda
1 cup gluten-free butterscotch-flavor pieces or semisweet chocolate pieces

1. Preheat oven to 350°F. Grease a 13×9×2-inch baking pan; set aside. In a medium saucepan cook and stir brown sugar and butter over medium heat until butter is melted and mixture is smooth. Remove from heat; cool slightly. Add eggs, one at a time, beating with a wooden spoon just until combined. Stir in vanilla.

2. In a medium bowl stir together Gluten-Free Flour Mix, baking powder, and baking soda. Add flour mixture to egg mixture, stirring just until combined. Stir in butterscotch pieces. Pour batter into the prepared baking pan, spreading evenly to the edges.

3. Bake for 15 to 18 minutes or until a wooden toothpick inserted near the center comes out clean. Cool slightly in pan on a wire rack. Cut into bars while warm.

PER SERVING: 149 cal., 6 g fat (4 g sat. fat), 19 mg chol., 67 mg sodium, 24 g carb., 0 g fiber, 1 g pro.

***Tip:** Check the label of this product carefully to be sure it does not contain added gluten.

Chocolate Cake with Sour Cream Glaze

PREP: 30 minutes
STAND: 30 minutes
BAKE: 20 minutes at 350°F
MAKES: 8 servings

- 2 **egg whites**
- ½ **cup milk**
- 2 **tablespoons unsweetened cocoa powder**
- 1 **tablespoon butter**
- 2 **ounces sweet baking chocolate, chopped Brown rice flour**
- ⅔ **cup brown rice flour**
- ¼ **cup sugar**
- ½ **teaspoon gluten-free baking powder**
- ⅛ **teaspoon baking soda**
- ⅛ **teaspoon salt**
- ¼ **cup sugar**
- 1 **recipe Sour Cream Glaze Cocoa powder**

1. In a medium mixing bowl allow egg whites to stand at room temperature for 30 minutes. Meanwhile, in a small saucepan combine milk, cocoa powder, and butter. Heat over medium heat just until boiling, whisking constantly. Remove from heat. Add baking chocolate, whisking until smooth. Cool to room temperature.

2. Preheat oven to 350°F. Grease an 8×1½- or 9×1½-inch round baking pan. Line the bottom of the pan with parchment paper or waxed paper; grease paper. Flour pan using brown rice flour; set aside. In a medium bowl stir together the ⅔ cup brown rice flour, ¼ cup sugar, the baking powder, baking soda, and salt. Add cooled chocolate mixture to flour mixture, stirring until well mixed (batter will be thick). Set aside.

3. Beat egg whites with an electric mixer on medium speed until soft peaks form (tips curl). Gradually add ¼ cup sugar, about 1 tablespoon at a time, beating on high speed until stiff peaks form (tips stand straight). Gently fold one-third of the beaten egg whites into the chocolate batter. Fold in the remaining beaten egg whites just until combined. Spread batter evenly in prepared baking pan.

4. Bake for 20 to 25 minutes or until top springs back when lightly touched. Cool in pan on wire rack for 10 minutes. Remove cake from pan. Remove and discard parchment paper. Cool completely. Top with Sour Cream Glaze. Sprinkle with cocoa powder.

Sour Cream Glaze: In a small bowl stir together ½ cup sour cream,* ¼ cup powdered sugar, and ½ teaspoon vanilla extract* until smooth.

PER SERVING: 237 cal., 8 g fat (4 g sat. fat), 28 mg chol., 153 mg sodium, 39 g carb., 3 g fiber, 4 g pro.

*Tip: Check the labels of these products carefully to be sure they do not contain added gluten.

Cheesecake with Tequila Banana Sauce

PREP: 30 minutes   BAKE: 40 minutes at 325°F   STAND: 30 minutes   COOL: 45 minutes   CHILL: 4 hours   MAKES: 16 servings

- 3 **8-ounce packages reduced-fat cream cheese (Neufchâtel),* softened**
- ½ **cup agave nectar**
- 2 **tablespoons fat-free milk**
- 2 **teaspoons vanilla extract***
- 2 **eggs**
- 1 **recipe Tequila Banana Sauce Toasted coconut (optional)**

1. Preheat oven to 325°F. Grease an 8-inch springform pan. Place pan on a double layer of 18×12-inch heavy foil. Bring edges of foil up and mold around sides of pan to form a watertight seal; set aside.

2. In a large mixing bowl beat cream cheese with an electric mixer on medium speed until smooth. Beat in agave nectar, milk, and vanilla until well combined. Add eggs. Beat on low speed just until combined (do not overbeat).

3. Pour filling into prepared pan. Place pan in a roasting pan. Pour enough boiling water into roasting pan to reach halfway up sides of the springform pan. Bake about 40 minutes or until center appears nearly set when shaken gently. Turn oven off; allow cheesecake to stand in oven for 30 minutes (cheesecake will continue to set up). Carefully remove springform pan from water bath. Remove foil from pan.

4. Cool in the pan on a wire rack for 15 minutes. Using a small sharp knife, loosen the cheesecake from the sides of the pan; cool for 30 minutes more. Remove sides of pan; cool cheesecake completely on rack. Cover and chill at least 4 hours before serving.

5. To serve, cut cheesecake into 16 wedges; divide among plates. Spoon warm Tequila Banana Sauce evenly over each serving. If desired, top with toasted coconut.

Tequila Banana Sauce: In a large nonstick skillet melt 2 tablespoons butter over medium heat. Add 4 medium bananas, cut crosswise into ½-inch slices; cook for 3 to 5 minutes or until softened and browned, turning once. Remove skillet from heat; transfer banana slices to a large plate. Add ¼ cup tequila to skillet. Cook over medium heat for 2 to 3 minutes or until most of the liquid is evaporated, scraping up any banana bits from the bottom of the skillet. Add ¼ cup agave nectar. In a small bowl stir together ½ cup water and ½ teaspoon cornstarch* until smooth. Add to skillet. Cook and stir over medium heat until bubbly and slightly thickened. Return banana slices to skillet. Cook about 2 minutes more or until thickened and bubbly, stirring gently.

PER SERVING: 214 cal., 12 g fat (7 g sat. fat), 59 mg chol., 166 mg sodium, 20 g carb., 1 g fiber, 5 g pro.

*Tip: Check the labels of these products carefully to be sure they do not contain added gluten.

Chocolate Chip Cookies

PREP: 40 minutes
BAKE: 7 minutes per batch at 375°F
COOL: 2 minutes per batch
MAKES: 48 servings

¾ **cup shortening**
¼ **cup butter, softened**
1 **cup packed brown sugar**
½ **cup granulated sugar**
½ **teaspoon baking soda**
½ **teaspoon salt**
2 **eggs**
1 **teaspoon vanilla extract***
2¾ **cups Gluten-Free Flour Mix or purchased gluten-free all-purpose flour**
1 **12-ounce package (2 cups) semisweet chocolate pieces**
1½ **cups chopped walnuts, pecans, or hazelnuts (filberts), toasted if desired (optional)**

1. Preheat oven to 375°F. In a large mixing bowl beat shortening and butter with an electric mixer on medium to high speed for 30 seconds. Add brown sugar, granulated sugar, baking soda, and salt. Beat about 2 minutes or until light and fluffy, scraping sides of bowl occasionally. Beat in eggs and vanilla until combined. Beat in as much of the Gluten-Free Flour Mix as you can with the mixer. Using a wooden spoon, stir in any remaining flour mix, the chocolate pieces, and, if desired, nuts.

2. Drop dough by rounded teaspoons 2 inches apart onto an ungreased cookie sheet. Bake for 7 to 8 minutes or until evenly browned. Cool on cookie sheet for 2 minutes. Transfer to a wire rack; cool.

PER SERVING: 132 cal., 7 g fat (3 g sat. fat), 10 mg chol., 54 mg sodium, 19 g carb., 1 g fiber, 1 g pro.

Gluten-Free Flour Mix: In a large airtight container whisk together 3 cups white rice flour, 3 cups potato starch, 2 cups sorghum flour, and 4 teaspoons xanthan gum. Cover and store at room temperature for up to 3 months. Makes 8 cups.

***Tip:** Check the label of this product carefully to be sure it does not contain added gluten.

Easy Peanut Butter Cookies

PREP: 15 minutes
BAKE: 10 minutes per batch at 350°F
MAKES: 24 servings

- 1 **egg**
- 1 **cup gluten-free crunchy peanut butter**
- ½ **cup sugar**
- 1 **teaspoon gluten-free baking powder**
- ½ **teaspoon vanilla extract***
- ¼ **teaspoon salt**
- ¼ **cup semisweet chocolate pieces (optional)**
  Sugar

1. Preheat oven to 350°F. Line a cookie sheet with parchment paper; set aside. In a small bowl stir together egg and peanut butter; stir in the ½ cup sugar, the baking powder, vanilla, and salt. If desired, stir in chocolate pieces. Roll dough by teaspoonfuls into balls; roll in additional sugar and arrange on prepared cookie sheet. (Or drop by rounded teaspoonfuls onto prepared cookie sheet.) Flatten with a fork.

2. Bake for 10 to 13 minutes or just until set in center. Transfer to a wire rack; cool.

PER SERVING: 86 cal., 6 g fat (1 g sat. fat), 8 mg chol., 99 mg sodium, 8 g carb., 1 g fiber, 3 g pro.

***Tip:** Check the label of this product carefully to be sure it does not contain added gluten.

No-Bake Peanut Butter-Oat Bites

PREP: 20 minutes
CHILL: 1 hour
MAKES: 30 servings

- ½ **cup gluten-free peanut butter**
- ⅓ **cup honey**
- 1 **teaspoon vanilla extract***
- 1¼ **cups shredded unsweetened coconut**
- 1 **cup gluten-free rolled oats**
- ¼ **cup semisweet chocolate pieces**
- ¼ **cup snipped dried cherries, dried apricots, and/or raisins**

1. In a medium bowl stir together peanut butter, honey, and vanilla until well mixed. Stir in ½ cup of the coconut, the oats, chocolate pieces, and dried fruit. Cover and chill for 30 minutes.

2. Place the remaining ¾ cup coconut in a food processor. Cover and process with several on/off turns until chopped. Shape peanut butter mixture into 30 balls, each about 1 inch in diameter. Roll balls in chopped coconut to coat, pressing slightly to adhere. Cover and chill for 30 minutes before serving.

PER SERVING: 111 cal., 7 g fat (5 g sat. fat), 0 mg chol., 23 mg sodium, 11 g carb., 2 g fiber, 3 g pro.

To Store: Place in a single layer in an airtight container. Cover and store in the refrigerator up to 1 week.

***Tip:** Check the label of this product carefully to be sure it does not contain added gluten.

Cashew Truffles

PREP: 45 minutes
FREEZE: 2 hours
BAKE: 8 minutes at 350°F
STAND: 30 minutes
MAKES: 20 servings

8 **ounces bittersweet chocolate, chopped**
½ **cup fat-free half-and-half***
1 **tablespoon pure maple syrup**
¾ **cup whole cashews**
¼ **teaspoon coarse salt**

1. Place chocolate in a medium bowl; set aside. In a small saucepan bring half-and-half just to boiling; pour over chocolate. Stir until chocolate is melted. Stir in maple syrup. Cover; freeze about 2 hours or until firm.

2. Meanwhile, preheat oven to 350°F. Place cashews in a shallow baking pan. Bake for 8 to 10 minutes or until golden, stirring once. Set aside 40 whole cashews. In a food processor combine the remaining cashews and the salt. Cover and process with several on/off turns until nuts are finely chopped. Transfer finely chopped nuts to a small bowl; set aside.

3. Divide chocolate mixture into 40 portions. One at a time, place a whole cashew in the center of each portion; shape into a ball. Roll ball in the chopped cashew mixture. Place on a baking sheet. Repeat to make 40 truffles total. Cover and chill until serving time. Let stand at room temperature for 30 minutes before serving. If desired, serve in small paper candy cups.

PER SERVING: 93 cal., 7 g fat (3 g sat. fat), 1 mg chol., 62 mg sodium, 9 g carb., 1 g fiber, 2 g pro.

*Tip: Check the label of this product carefully to be sure it does not contain added gluten.

Pumpkin-Spiced Gingersnap Truffles

PREP: 20 minutes   **CHILL:** 2 hours 30 minutes   **MAKES:** 20 servings

1¼ cups semisweet chocolate pieces
¼ teaspoon pumpkin pie spice*
¼ teaspoon vanilla extract*
½ cup whipping cream
¾ cup chopped gluten-free gingersnaps (about 10 cookies)
⅓ cup finely crushed gluten-free gingersnaps (about 7 cookies) and/or ¼ cup unsweetened cocoa powder

1. In a medium bowl combine chocolate pieces, pumpkin pie spice, and vanilla.

2. In a medium microwave-safe bowl microwave cream about 70 seconds or just until boiling. (Or in a saucepan heat cream just to boiling.) Pour cream over chocolate mixture; let stand for 5 minutes. Whisk until smooth. Stir in chopped gingersnaps. Cover and chill for 1½ to 2 hours or until firm but soft enough to form into balls.

3. Place crushed gingersnaps and/or cocoa powder in separate small bowls. Using a small spoon, scoop 1-tablespoon portions of chocolate mixture and shape into balls. Roll balls in crushed gingersnaps or cocoa powder to coat. Cover and chill about 1 hour or until firm. Store in an airtight container in the refrigerator for up to 3 days.

PER SERVING: 97 cal., 6 g fat (3 g sat. fat), 8 mg chol., 42 mg sodium, 12 g carb., 1 g fiber, 1 g pro.

To Store: Place truffles in a single layer in an airtight container. Cover and store in the refrigerator up to 3 days.

***Tip:** Check the labels of these products carefully to be sure they do not contain added gluten.

Coconut Cream-and Pineapple-Filled Cream Puffs

PREP: 35 minutes
CHILL: 2 hours
BAKE: 25 minutes at 400°F
COOL: 5 minutes
MAKES: 10 servings

3 tablespoons sugar
2 tablespoons cornstarch*
1¼ cups unsweetened light coconut milk*
1 egg yolk
1 teaspoon vanilla extract*
½ cup water
¼ cup butter
⅛ teaspoon salt
⅔ cup brown rice flour
2 eggs
⅔ cup chopped grilled fresh pineapple**
¼ cup flaked coconut, toasted if desired

1. For coconut cream, in a small saucepan combine sugar and cornstarch. Stir in coconut milk. Cook and stir over medium heat until thickened and bubbly; reduce heat. Cook and stir for 2 minutes more. Remove from heat.

2. Gradually whisk about ½ cup of the hot coconut milk mixture into egg yolk. Add egg yolk mixture to the coconut milk mixture in saucepan. Bring to a gentle boil; reduce heat. Cook and stir for 2 minutes more. Remove from heat. Stir in vanilla. Place saucepan in an extra-large bowl half-filled with ice water. Stir constantly for 2 minutes to cool quickly. Transfer to a medium bowl. Cover with plastic wrap. Chill for 2 to 24 hours.

3. For cream puffs, preheat oven to 400°F. Lightly grease a baking sheet or line with parchment paper. In a small saucepan combine the water, the butter, and salt. Bring to boiling. Add brown rice flour all at once, stirring vigorously. Cook and stir until mixture forms a ball. Remove from heat. Cool for 10 minutes. Add eggs, one at a time, beating well after each addition.

4. Drop dough into 10 mounds on prepared baking sheet. Bake for 25 to 30 minutes or until golden brown and firm. Transfer to a wire rack; cool for 5 minutes. When just cool enough to handle, cut off tops of puffs and set aside. Scoop out and discard any excess soft dough from the centers. Cool completely.

5. To serve, divide coconut cream among bottoms of puffs. Sprinkle with pineapple and, if desired, flaked coconut. Top with puff tops.

PER SERVING: 153 cal., 9 g fat (5 g sat. fat), 68 mg chol., 92 mg sodium, 16 g carb., 1 g fiber, 3 g pro.

*Tip: Check the labels of these products carefully to be sure they do not contain added gluten.

**Tip: To grill fresh pineapple, heat a lightly greased grill pan over medium heat. Place two ¾-inch slices fresh pineapple on hot grill pan; grill for 8 to 10 minutes or until golden brown, turning once. When cool enough to handle, core slices and chop pineapple.

Honey-Berry Compote

PREP: 15 minutes
CHILL: 2 hours
MAKES: 8 servings

2 teaspoons finely shredded orange peel
½ cup orange juice
¼ cup honey
1 tablespoon snipped fresh mint (optional)
2 cups halved green or red seedless grapes
2 cups fresh blueberries
2 cups halved fresh strawberries
2 cups fresh raspberries and/or blackberries
Small fresh mint leaves (optional)

1. For dressing, in a medium bowl whisk together orange peel, orange juice, honey, and, if desired, the 1 tablespoon snipped mint.

2. In a large bowl combine grapes, blueberries, and strawberries. Gently stir in the dressing. Cover and chill for 2 to 24 hours.

3. Just before serving, stir in raspberries and/or blackberries. If desired, garnish with fresh mint leaves.

PER SERVING: 103 cal., 1 g fat (0 g sat. fat), 0 mg chol., 2 mg sodium, 26 g carb., 4 g fiber, 1 g pro.

Apple-Pistachio Crisp

PREP: 25 minutes **BAKE:** 30 minutes at 375°F **MAKES:** 6 servings

6 **cups sliced, peeled cooking apples**

3 **to 4 tablespoons granulated sugar**

½ **cup gluten-free regular rolled oats**

½ **cup packed brown sugar**

¼ **cup Gluten-Free Flour Mix (recipe, page 312) or purchased gluten-free all-purpose flour**

¼ **teaspoon ground cinnamon**

¼ **cup butter**

¼ **cup roasted salted pistachio nuts,* chopped**

1. Preheat oven to 375°F. Grease a shallow 2-quart baking dish. In a large bowl combine apples and granulated sugar; spoon into the prepared baking dish. Set aside.

2. For topping, in a medium bowl combine oats, brown sugar, Gluten-Free Flour Mix, and cinnamon. Using a pastry blender, cut in butter until mixture resembles coarse crumbs. Stir in nuts. Sprinkle topping over apple mixture.

3. Bake about 30 minutes or until apples are tender and topping is golden brown. (If necessary, cover with foil for the last 10 minutes of baking to prevent overbrowning.) Serve warm.

PER SERVING: 291 cal., 11 g fat (5 g sat. fat), 20 mg chol., 97 mg sodium, 49 g carb., 4 g fiber, 3 g pro.

Peach or Cherry Pistachio Crisp: Prepare as directed, except substitute 6 cups sliced, peeled ripe peaches or pitted fresh tart red cherries (or two 16-ounce packages frozen unsweetened peach slices or frozen pitted tart red cherries) for the apples. For the filling, increase granulated sugar to ½ cup and add 3 tablespoons Gluten-Free Flour Mix (recipe, page 312) or purchased gluten-free all-purpose flour. If using frozen fruit, bake for 50 to 60 minutes or until filling is bubbly across entire surface. (If necessary, cover with foil for the last 10 minutes of baking to prevent overbrowning.)

***Tip:** Check the label of this product carefully to be sure it does not contain added gluten.

Sweet Ricotta and Strawberry Parfaits

PREP: 20 minutes
STAND: 15 minutes
MAKES: 6 servings

1 **pound fresh strawberries, hulled and halved or quartered**
1 **tablespoon snipped fresh mint**
1 **teaspoon sugar**
1 **15-ounce carton part-skim ricotta cheese***
3 **tablespoons agave nectar or honey**
½ **teaspoon vanilla extract***
¼ **teaspoon finely shredded lemon peel**
Fresh mint

1. In a medium bowl gently stir together strawberries, the 1 tablespoon snipped mint, and the sugar. Let stand about 15 minutes or until berries are softened and starting to release their juices.

2. In a medium mixing bowl combine ricotta cheese, agave nectar, vanilla, and lemon peel. Beat with an electric mixer on medium speed for 2 minutes.

3. Scoop 2 tablespoons of the ricotta mixture into each of six parfait glasses. Top each with a large spoonful of strawberry mixture. Repeat layers. Garnish with additional fresh mint. Serve immediately or cover and chill up to 4 hours.

PER SERVING: 159 cal., 6 g fat (4 g sat. fat), 22 mg chol., 90 mg sodium, 18 g carb., 2 g fiber, 9 g pro.

***Tip:** Check the labels of these products carefully to be sure they do not contain added gluten.

Cinnamon and Brown Sugar Custards

PREP: 20 minutes
COOK: 20 minutes
BAKE: 30 minutes at 350°F
MAKES: 4 servings

1½ cups diced carrots
2 eggs, lightly beaten
⅓ to ½ cup packed brown sugar
¼ cup milk
½ teaspoon ground cinnamon
   Whipped cream (optional)

1. Preheat oven to 350°F. Lightly grease four 6- to 8-ounce ramekins or custard cups; place in a 13×9×2-inch baking pan. Set aside.

2. Meanwhile, place diced carrots in a medium saucepan; cover with 2 inches of water. Bring to boiling; reduce heat. Simmer, covered, for 20 to 25 minutes or until very tender. Drain; rinse with cold water and drain again.

3. Place carrots in a food processor. Cover and process about 20 seconds or until smooth. Add eggs, brown sugar, milk, and cinnamon; cover and process until smooth.

4. Divide carrot custard among prepared ramekins. Place baking pan on oven rack. Pour enough hot water into the baking pan to reach halfway up sides of ramekins. Bake for 30 to 35 minutes or until a knife inserted off-center comes out clean. Cool on a wire rack. If desired, serve with whipped cream. Chill within 2 hours.

PER SERVING: 130 cal., 3 g fat (1 g sat. fat), 93 mg chol., 79 mg sodium, 24 g carb., 1 g fiber, 4 g pro.

Creamy Rice Pudding

PREP: 20 minutes   COOK: 25 minutes   COOL: 30 minutes   MAKES: 6 servings

  1 **cup water**
  ¾ **cup milk**
  ¼ **teaspoon salt**
  ½ **cup Arborio rice or long grain rice**
  1 **teaspoon butter**
  1 **cup half-and-half or light cream**
  ½ **of a vanilla bean, halved lengthwise**
  2 **egg yolks**
  ⅓ **cup sugar**
     Half-and-half or light cream (optional)
     Strawberry, cherry, or raspberry jam* (optional)
     Ground cinnamon (optional)

1. In a medium saucepan heat the water, milk, and salt over medium heat until nearly boiling. Stir in the uncooked rice and butter. Bring to boiling; immediately reduce heat to very low. Simmer, covered, for 25 to 30 minutes or until thick and nearly all the liquid is absorbed, stirring every 5 minutes toward the end of cooking. Transfer rice to a medium bowl.

2. Meanwhile, for sauce, place the 1 cup half-and-half in a small saucepan. Using a paring knife, scrape seeds from the vanilla bean; add seeds to the half-and-half in saucepan. Heat just until boiling. In a medium bowl whisk together egg yolks and sugar. Gradually whisk in hot half-and-half; return all to the saucepan. Cook and stir over medium-low heat for 3 to 5 minutes or until sauce thickens and coats the back of a metal spoon.

3. Stir sauce into rice in bowl; cool for 30 minutes. Serve warm. (Or cover and chill for several hours or overnight. If desired, just before serving, stir in additional half-and-half, 1 tablespoon at a time, until desired consistency.) If desired, top with jam and dust with cinnamon.

PER SERVING: 189 cal., 7 g fat (4 g sat. fat), 89 mg chol., 134 mg sodium, 27 g carb., 0 g fiber, 4 g pro.

*Tip: Check the label of this product carefully to be sure it does not contain added gluten.

Blackberry Floating Island

PREP: 30 minutes
STAND: 30 minutes
CHILL: 2 hours
BAKE: 15 minutes at 300°F
MAKES: 6 servings

5   eggs, separated
1   cup sugar
¼   teaspoon salt
2   cups half-and-half or light cream
1   teaspoon vanilla extract*
½   teaspoon finely shredded lemon peel
½   teaspoon ground ginger
2   cups fresh blackberries, raspberries, and/or blueberries
3   tablespoons sliced almonds, toasted

1. Let egg yolks stand at room temperature for 30 minutes (cover and chill egg whites until needed).

2. For the custard, in a medium bowl whisk together egg yolks, ½ cup of the sugar, and the salt. In a heavy medium saucepan heat the half-and-half just until tiny bubbles begin to break at the edge of the pan. Gradually whisk about 1 cup of the warm half-and-half into the yolk mixture. Gradually whisk yolk mixture back into the remaining half-and-half in saucepan. Cook, stirring constantly, until custard thickens enough to coat the back of a spoon, about 5 minutes. Remove the custard from the heat and strain through a sieve into a bowl. Stir in vanilla and lemon peel. Place the bowl in a larger bowl filled with ice water; stir about 5 minutes or until cool. Cover surface with plastic wrap; chill for 2 to 24 hours.

3. For the meringues, let egg whites stand at room temperature for 30 minutes. Preheat oven to 300°F. Position a rack in the middle of the oven. Line a baking sheet with parchment paper; set aside. In a medium bowl stir together the remaining ½ cup sugar and the ginger. In a large mixing bowl beat egg whites with an electric mixer on medium speed about 2 minutes or until soft peaks form (tips curl).

Gradually add sugar mixture, about 2 tablespoons at a time, beating on high speed until stiff, glossy peaks form (tips stand straight) and sugar is dissolved. Divide meringue into six mounds on the prepared baking sheet. Shape mounds by pulling up some of the peaks of meringue with the back of a spoon. Bake meringues about 15 minutes or until set and very lightly browned.

4. To serve, spoon the custard into six shallow bowls. Scatter berries over custards. Using a large spatula, carefully transfer a meringue to each bowl. Sprinkle with almonds. Serve immediately or chill, uncovered, for up to 1 hour.

PER SERVING: 336 cal., 15 g fat (7 g sat. fat), 206 mg chol., 188 mg sodium, 44 g carb., 2 g fiber, 9 g pro.

***Tip:** Check the label of this product carefully to be sure it does not contain added gluten.

Strawberry Zabaglione Loaf

PREP: 30 minutes
COOK: 15 minutes
FREEZE: 12 hours
MAKES: 12 servings

    Nonstick cooking spray*
4 **cups chopped fresh strawberries**
1 **cup sugar**
½ **teaspoon finely shredded orange peel**
4 **egg yolks**
2 **eggs**
¾ **cup champagne or white grape juice**
1 **cup whipping cream**
1 **teaspoon vanilla extract***
    Halved fresh strawberries (optional)
1 **recipe Sweetened Whipped Cream (optional)**
    Ground cinnamon (optional)

1. Lightly coat a 9×5×3-inch loaf pan with cooking spray. Line pan with plastic wrap; set aside.

2. In a food processor process the 4 cups chopped strawberries until smooth. Transfer to a small bowl; stir in ¼ cup of the sugar and the orange peel; set aside.

3. In a double boiler set over simmering water combine egg yolks, whole eggs, and the remaining ¾ cup sugar. Stir in champagne. Cook and stir until mixture thickens and reaches 160°F on an instant-read thermometer, about 15 minutes.

4. Remove double boiler insert from the saucepan and place in a bowl of ice water. Whisk mixture about 5 minutes or until cool. Stir strawberry puree into egg mixture.

5. In a chilled medium bowl beat whipping cream and vanilla with an electric mixer on medium speed until soft peaks form (tips curl). Fold whipped cream into custard. Spoon into prepared pan. Cover and freeze for 12 to 24 hours.

6. To serve, briefly dip the loaf pan into warm water. Invert onto a serving plate. Remove plastic wrap. Cut into slices. If desired, serve topped with halved strawberries, Sweetened Whipped Cream, and/or cinnamon.

PER SERVING: 232 cal., 14 g fat (8 g sat. fat), 146 mg chol., 26 mg sodium, 24 g carb., 1 g fiber, 3 g pro.

Sweetened Whipped Cream: In a small chilled mixing bowl combine 1 cup whipping cream, 2 tablespoons sugar, and ½ teaspoon vanilla or almond extract.* Beat with the chilled beaters of an electric mixer on medium to high speed just until stiff peaks form (tips stand straight). Do not overbeat.

***Tip:** Check the labels of these products carefully to be sure they do not contain added gluten.

Index

Metric Information

The charts on this page provide a guide for converting measurements from the U.S. customary system, which is used throughout this book, to the metric system.

Product Differences

Most of the ingredients called for in the recipes in this book are available in most countries. However, some are known by different names. Here are some common American ingredients and their possible counterparts:

- Sugar (white) is granulated, fine granulated, or castor sugar.
- Powdered sugar is icing sugar.
- All-purpose flour is enriched bleached or unbleached white household flour. When self-rising flour is used in place of all-purpose flour in a recipe that calls for leavening, omit the leavening agent (baking soda or baking powder) and salt.
- Light-color corn syrup is golden syrup.
- Cornstarch is cornflour.
- Baking soda is bicarbonate of soda.
- Vanilla or vanilla extract is vanilla essence.
- Green, red, or yellow sweet peppers are capsicums or bell peppers.
- Golden raisins are sultanas.

Volume and Weight

The United States traditionally uses cup measures for liquid and solid ingredients. The chart below shows the approximate imperial and metric equivalents. If you are accustomed to weighing solid ingredients, the following approximate equivalents will be helpful.

- 1 cup butter, castor sugar, or rice = 8 ounces = ½ pound = 250 grams
- 1 cup flour = 4 ounces = ¼ pound = 125 grams
- 1 cup icing sugar = 5 ounces = 150 grams

Canadian and U.S. volume for a cup measure is 8 fluid ounces (237 ml), but the standard metric equivalent is 250 ml.

1 British imperial cup is 10 fluid ounces.

In Australia, 1 tablespoon equals 20 ml, and there are 4 teaspoons in the Australian tablespoon.

Spoon measures are used for smaller amounts of ingredients. Although the size of the tablespoon varies slightly in different countries, for practical purposes and for recipes in this book, a straight substitution is all that's necessary. Measurements made using cups or spoons always should be level unless stated otherwise.

Common Weight Range Replacements

IMPERIAL / U.S.	METRIC
½ ounce	15 g
1 ounce	25 g or 30 g
4 ounces (¼ pound)	115 g or 125 g
8 ounces (½ pound)	225 g or 250 g
16 ounces (1 pound)	450 g or 500 g
1¼ pounds	625 g
1½ pounds	750 g
2 pounds or 2¼ pounds	1,000 g or 1 Kg

Oven Temperature Equivalents

FAHRENHEIT SETTING	CELSIUS SETTING*	GAS SETTING
300°F	150°C	Gas Mark 2 (very low)
325°F	160°C	Gas Mark 3 (low)
350°F	180°C	Gas Mark 4 (moderate)
375°F	190°C	Gas Mark 5 (moderate)
400°F	200°C	Gas Mark 6 (hot)
425°F	220°C	Gas Mark 7 (hot)
450°F	230°C	Gas Mark 8 (very hot)
475°F	240°C	Gas Mark 9 (very hot)
500°F	260°C	Gas Mark 10 (extremely hot)
Broil	Broil	Grill

*Electric and gas ovens may be calibrated using Celsius. However, for an electric oven, increase Celsius setting 10 to 20 degrees when cooking above 160°C. For convection or forced air ovens (gas or electric), lower the temperature setting 25°F/10°C when cooking at all heat levels.

Baking Pan Sizes

IMPERIAL / U.S.	METRIC
9×1½-inch round cake pan	22- or 23×4-cm (1.5 L)
9×1½-inch pie plate	22- or 23×4-cm (1 L)
8×8×2-inch square cake pan	20×5-cm (2 L)
9×9×2-inch square cake pan	22- or 23×4.5-cm (2.5 L)
11×7×1½-inch baking pan	28×17×4-cm (2 L)
2-quart rectangular baking pan	30×19×4.5-cm (3 L)
13×9×2-inch baking pan	34×22×4.5-cm (3.5 L)
15×10×1-inch jelly roll pan	40×25×2-cm
9×5×3-inch loaf pan	23×13×8-cm (2 L)
2-quart casserole	2 L

U.S. / Standard Metric Equivalents

⅛ teaspoon = 0.5 ml	
¼ teaspoon = 1 ml	
½ teaspoon = 2 ml	
1 teaspoon = 5 ml	
1 tablespoon = 15 ml	
2 tablespoons = 25 ml	
¼ cup = 2 fluid ounces = 50 ml	
⅓ cup = 3 fluid ounces = 75 ml	
½ cup = 4 fluid ounces = 125 ml	
⅔ cup = 5 fluid ounces = 150 ml	
¾ cup = 6 fluid ounces = 175 ml	
1 cup = 8 fluid ounces = 250 ml	
2 cups = 1 pint = 500 ml	
1 quart = 1 litre	